S0-ACJ-117

SPIRITUAL DIRECTION

AND THE

CARE OF SOULS

A GUIDE TO CHRISTIAN APPROACHES AND PRACTICES

EDITED BY

GARY W. MOON

AND

DAVID G. BENNER

InterVarsity Press
Downers Grove, Illinois

BV
8053
S68
2004

InterVarsity Press
P.O. Box 1400, Downers Grove, IL 60515-1426
World Wide Web: www.ivpress.com
E-mail: mail@ivpress.com

©2004 by Gary W. Moon and David G. Benner

All rights reserved. No part of this book may be reproduced in any form without written permission from InterVarsity Press.

InterVarsity Press® is the book-publishing division of InterVarsity Christian Fellowship/USA®, a student movement active on campus at hundreds of universities, colleges and schools of nursing in the United States of America, and a member movement of the International Fellowship of Evangelical Students. For information about local and regional activities, write Public Relations Dept., InterVarsity Christian Fellowship/USA, 6400 Schroeder Rd., P.O. Box 7895, Madison, WI 53707-7895, or visit the IVCF website at <www.intervarsity.org>.

All Scripture quotations, unless otherwise indicated, are taken from the Holy Bible, New International Version®. NIV®. *Copyright ©1973, 1978, 1984 by International Bible Society. Used by permission of Zondervan Publishing House. All rights reserved.*

Chapter two uses the New King James Version, published by Thomas Nelson Inc.

Chapter three uses the New American Bible, copyright © 1991, 1986, 1970 Confraternity of Christian Doctrine, Inc., Washington, D.C.

Design: Cindy Kiple

Images: Rosemary Clavert/Getty Images

ISBN 0-8308-2777-3

Printed in the United States of America ∞

Library of Congress Cataloging-in-Publication Data

Spiritual direction and the care of souls: a guide to Christian
approaches and practices / edited by Gary W. Moon and David G. Benner.
      p. cm.
Includes bibliographical references and index.
ISBN 0-8308-2777-3 (alk. paper)
1. Spiritual direction. 2. Pastoral counseling. I. Moon, Gary W.,
1956- II. Benner, David G.
BV5053.S68 2004
253.5'3—dc22

2003027944

P	20	19	18	17	16	15	14	13	12	11	10	9	8	7	6	5	4	3	2	1
Y	17	16	15	14	13	12	11	10	09	08	07	06	05	04						

CONTENTS

PREFACE

The number of recent publications on spiritual direction bears witness to a widely noted but nonetheless remarkable rise of interest in spirituality. Clergy, Christian educators, youth ministry specialists, counselors (both mental health and pastoral) and large numbers of Christians without any formal ministry involvement in soul care are all reading books on spiritual direction and attending conferences and retreats on spiritual formation. In large sectors of the church, few would have ever even heard of the concepts of spiritual formation or direction until recently. Yet the seminaries and colleges of many of those traditions are now busy refashioning departments of Christian education into programs in spiritual formation, while clergy and laity alike seek opportunities to learn about spiritual direction.

The parallel development of interest in spirituality among mental health professionals has also been remarkable. For a century counselors and psychotherapists have held their privileged positions in soul care with remarkable lack of awareness of the spiritual guidance tradition out of which their roles developed. Even Christian therapists have, by and large, practiced their calling with little attention to spirituality. Theories of the divine (theology) have seemed of more interest than experience of the divine (spirituality) as Christian mental health professionals focused on the integration of psychology and theology. How easily we missed the fact that the most essential integration is the synthesis that occurs within the individual—something that occurs optimally when it is grounded in an ever-deepening experience of the divine.

Miriam E. and Todd W. Hall (1997) have summarized the important milestones along the road to incorporating spiritual beliefs and practices into the process of psychotherapy that are already in the rearview mirror. Specifically, they noted (1) "the inclusion of religion as an element of human diversity in the American Psychological Association's . . . (1992) code of ethics," (2) "the inclusion of spiritual problems as a V-code in the DSM-IV" (American Psychiatric Association 1994), and (3) "a number of important publications dedicated to religious therapy" (see Worthington, Kurusu, McCullough and Sandage 1996 for a review of these).

Lowering the microscope to focus on the predominantly evangelical movement known as "the integration of psychology and theology" reveals a growing shift in attention to Christian spirituality and its potential role in clinical practice. *Psychotherapy and the Spiritual Quest* (Benner 1988) was a permission-giving volume for those who desired to venture across the chasm that had been dug between professional psychology and spiritual longing. In 1995 the Christian Association of Psychological Studies held its international conference under the banner "Our Heritage of Soul Care." According to Thomas Oden (1995), this was the first gathering of either mental health professionals or pastoral counselors that had adopted a theme from Christian spirituality. A special issue of the *Journal of Psychology and Christianity* followed that was devoted to "Christian spirituality and mental health" (Moon 1995). In 1997 Gary W. Moon's *Homesick for Eden* discussed the explicit integration of spiritual direction practices into psychotherapy. A few years later the *Journal of Psychology and Theology* gave two volumes of attention to "Christian Spirituality: Theoretical and Empirical Perspectives" (McMinn and Hall 2000; 2001).

Interest in spiritual direction on the part of pastoral counselors has also been developing. Israel Galindo (1997) offered a landmark comparison of the ways pastoral counseling and spiritual direction address spiritual needs and issues, and J. J. Shea (1997) presented an important discussion of the way in which each contribute to faith development. David Benner has recently addressed pastoral counseling from the perspective of spiritual direction (2002) and vice versa (2003).

Unfortunately, however, the picture of spiritual direction presented in this developing literature has often been quite one-dimensional, failing to reflect the rich diversity of Christian spiritual formation and direction. Typically speaking from within the perspective of a single denominational framework or theological tradition, each represents only an extremely small part of the remarkably rich whole that has yet to be presented.

The present volume addresses this omission by presenting articles on spiritual formation and direction from representatives of seven major traditions of the Christian church. Borrowing from Richard Foster's (1998) classification, at the heart of the book will be the voices of seven different pastors, priests or theologians who will describe the history and process of spiritual direction and understanding of spiritual formation from within their tradition—these including Orthodox, Roman Catholic, Episcopal, Reformed, holiness, social justice and charismatic Christianity.

For ease of reading and comparison, the seven contributors have agreed to use the topics as section headings:

- definition of spiritual direction
- practice of spiritual direction
- process of authentic transformation

- role of the spiritual director
- indirect indicators of mature spirituality
- relationship of spiritual direction, psychotherapy and pastoral counseling
- referrals to other soul care professionals
- bibliographic suggestions

Recognizing that spiritual direction is a form of soul care that is of keen interest to pastoral and other Christian counselors, we then address this interface with four chapters that compare and contrast spiritual direction, pastoral counseling and psychotherapy. The focus of these chapters is not merely academic distinctions but practical contributions each expression of soul care can make to the others.

The majority of the chapters in this book are adapted from articles first presented in two special issues of the *Journal of Psychology and Theology* in 2003, focusing on spiritual direction and mental health. All were refocused for the present book, with additional chapters being written to anchor spiritual direction in relation to Christian soul care, not simply psychotherapy.

This book has been compiled with the hope that it will aid in the rediscovery of spiritual direction throughout the Christian community. While it is important that our understandings of spiritual formation and transformation be anchored in the richness of historic Christian spirituality in all its diversity, it is also essential that we realistically face the challenge of reintegrating streams of soul care that have been separated for nearly a century. To do this we need respectful interdisciplinary dialogue and ecumenical openness. It is hoped that this volume will contribute to this climate and thereby help all who seek to understand or facilitate the process of soul care.

REFERENCES

American Psychological Association. 1992. Ethical principles of psychologists and code of conduct. *American Psychologist* 47:1597-1611.

———. 1994. *Diagnostic and statistical manual of mental disorders.* 4th ed. Washington, D.C.: Author.

Benner, David G. 1988. *Psychotherapy and the spiritual quest.* Grand Rapids, Mich.: Baker.

———. 2002. *Sacred companions: The gift of spiritual friendship and direction.* Downers Grove, Ill.: InterVarsity Press.

———. 2003. *Strategic pastoral counseling.* 2nd ed. Grand Rapids, Mich.: Baker.

Eck, B. E. 2002. An exploration of the therapeutic use of spiritual disciplines in clinical practice. *Journal of Psychology and Christianity* 21 (fall): 266-80.

Foster, Richard J. 1998. *Streams of living water: Celebrating the great traditions of christian faith.* San Francisco: HarperSanFrancisco.

Galindo, Israel. 1997. Spiritual direction and pastoral counseling: addressing the needs of the spirit. *Journal of Pastoral Care* 51, no. 4:395-402.

Hall, M. E. L., and T. W. Hall. 1997. Integration in the therapy room: An overview of the literature. *Journal of Psychology and Theology* 25:86-101.

Moon, Gary W., guest ed. 1995. *Christian spirituality and mental health.* Special issue of *Journal of Psychology and Christianity* 14:291-373.

———. 1997. *Homesick for Eden.* Ann Arbor, Mich.: Servant.

McMinn, Mark R., and T. W. Hall, guest eds. 2000. *Christian spirituality: Theoretical and empirical perspectives.* Special issue of *Journal of Psychology and Theology* 28:251-320.

———, guest eds. 2001. *Christian spirituality: Theoretical and empirical perspectives,* pt. 2. Special issue of *Journal of Psychology and Theology* 29:3-79.

Oden, Thomas C. 1995. Our heritage of soul care. Paper presented at Christian Association of Psychological Studies (CAPS) international conference, Our Heritage of Soul Care: Nurturing the Soul in the Clinic, Community, Family and Academy, Virginia Beach, Va.

Shea, J. J. 1997. Adult faith, pastoral counseling and spiritual direction. *Journal of Pastoral Care* 51, no. 3:259-70.

Worthington, Everett L., Jr., T. A. Kurusu, Michael E. McCullough and Stephen J. Sandage. 1996. Empirical research on religion and psychotherapeutic processes and outcomes: A ten-year review and research prospectus. *Psychological Bulletin* 119:448-87.

1

SPIRITUAL DIRECTION
AND CHRISTIAN SOUL CARE

Gary W. Moon and David G. Benner

Although the language of "spiritual direction" may sound modern, possibly even faddish, its practice has a long and honored place in Christian soul care. That history will become much clearer in the subsequent seven chapters, each of which explores the understanding and practice of spiritual direction within one faith tradition. But before getting to that, this chapter seeks to introduce some of the issues that will be examined. To do so, it is important to place spiritual direction in not simply a historical context but also a conceptual one.

The species of which spiritual direction is one important representation is soul care. The English phrase "care of souls" has its origins in the Latin *cura animarum*. While *cura* is most commonly translated "care," it actually contains the idea of both care and cure. *Care* refers to actions designed to support the well-being of something or someone. *Cure* refers to actions designed to restore well-being that has been lost. The Christian church has historically embraced both meanings of *cura* and has understood soul care to involve nurture and support as well as healing and restoration.

While Christian soul care has taken many forms over the course of church history, William A. Clebsch and C. R. Jaekle (1964) note that it has always involved four primary elements—healing, sustaining, reconciling and guiding. *Healing* involves efforts to help others overcome some impairment and move toward wholeness. These curative efforts can involve physical healing as well as spiritual healing, but the focus is always the total person, whole and holy. *Sustaining* refers to acts of caring designed to help a hurting person endure and transcend a circumstance in which restoration or recuperation is either impossible or improbable. *Reconciling* refers to efforts to reestablish broken relationships; the presence of this component of care demonstrates the communal, not simply individual, nature of Christian soul care. Finally, *guiding* refers to helping people make wise choices and thereby grow in spiritual maturity.

David G. Benner (1998) has classified contemporary forms of soul care in terms of their relative emphasis on care versus cure. Thus, for example, we could identify Christian friendship as high on an emphasis of care and low on an emphasis of cure, while psychotherapy would have an opposite balance. Within such a scheme, Benner suggests that spiritual direction is high on both, as spiritual transformation necessarily contains elements of both nurture and healing.

An understanding of the relationship between spiritual direction and other forms of soul care helps us identify its unique contributions to this spectrum of Christian care and cure activities. Spiritual direction cannot carry total responsibility for the nurture of spiritual development. Despite the pleas of advocates, it is extremely unlikely that all Christians will be in relationships of formal spiritual direction. But all should be in relationships of spiritual friendship, most will be in relationships of general pastoral care, and some will be in relationships of pastoral counseling or clinical psychotherapy. This is why subsequent chapters explore the relationship of spiritual direction to these other forms of soul care. And because the boundaries between spiritual direction, pastoral counseling and psychotherapy are the least clear, it is here that these explorations will focus.

MEANING AND PURPOSE OF SPIRITUAL DIRECTION

Carolyn Gratton uses the following story to introduce her book *The Art of Spiritual Guidance*. It's about a wise fish.

> It seems that there once were some fish who spent their days swimming around in search of water. Anxiously looking for their destination, they shared their worries and confusion with each other as they swam. One day they met a wise fish and asked him the question that had preoccupied them for so long: "Where is the sea?" The wise fish answered: "If you stop swimming so busily and struggling so anxiously, you would discover that you are already in the sea. You need look no further than where you already are." (Gratton 2000:5)

For Gratton, the wise fish represents a spiritual director. The search is for life in God's kingdom; hurry is the devil.

Cultivating an awareness of God's transforming presence as foundational for spiritual direction is a common theme in the literature of devotional theology. In the words of Richard Rohr, "My starting point [for prayer as part of spiritual guidance] is that we're already there. We cannot attain the presence of God. We're already totally in the presence of God. What's absent is awareness" (Rohr 1999:28).

These images provided by Gratton and Rohr bring to mind the mission of the ultimate spiritual director, Jesus, and his advice to all who would listen: Slow down, be at peace, listen to my words, and you will become aware that the NO SWIMMING sign has been removed from the "springs of living water" (see Mt 6:25-34; Jn 4:14; 10:10; 14:27).

The profundity of the simple notion of learning how to experience the presence of God was recently highlighted for one of us (GM) while participating in a round-table discussion of Christian spiritual formation. Each person present had two things in common: a long history of involvement in the evangelical world and a recent, personal captivation by the process of spiritual formation.

The juxtaposition of these two common factors should not be missed. These were long-term, card-carrying members of evangelicalism who had spent their lifetimes in Christian study and service. But only recently, it seemed, had each enrolled in Christianity 101: ongoing enjoyment of the love and presence of God.

Toward the end of our time together, one of the group members uttered words that seem an appropriate summary to that discussion and an introduction to this one: "Could it be that it [the process of spiritual formation] is simply becoming aware that God is everywhere and then learning how to be with him—in the presence of divine love?"

Several heads nodded yes. No one disagreed.

We are not picking on evangelicals; Catholic or Orthodox Christians could have just as easily encircled the table. The point is this: it seems that many in the Christian world have recently reawakened to the truth that wearing the label "Christian" is not synonymous with experiencing the intimate, moment-by-moment relationship with God that souls were designed to enjoy, and these many have begun to place hope in the practice of spiritual direction as a path toward more abundant living. Across denominational barriers, there seems to be a tidal wave of interest in learning how to experience intimate friendship with God and a chorus line singing the praises of "wise fish" (spiritual friends, guides and directors) who are pointing out what has been easily missed.

To understand the process of Christian spiritual formation does not seem difficult, at least not on a broad-brush level. Concisely put, it involves an experiential awareness of God's presence that leads to conversation, communion and ultimately authentic transformation of the entire person by an internal yielding to his will. What is difficult to grasp, however, is why it is so easy to miss experiencing the ocean of divine love for all the water.

Thomas Merton provides indirect hope by reminding us that it has not always been this way. Spiritual direction aimed at authentic transformation through interaction with God was originally basic and normal to church life. "The individual member of the community was 'formed' or 'guided' by his participation in the life of the community, and such instruction as was needed was given first of all by the bishop and presbyters, and then through informal admonitions by one's parents, spouse, friends, and fellow Christians" (Merton 1960:12).

If authentic transformation—becoming like Jesus—was once part of normal Christian living, what happened? If "holiness" for John Wesley meant being consumed by—and transformed into—the love of God, how did that term ever come to connote staying away from beer and chew and dates who do? Why do the words of Dallas Willard ring true for so many? "The current gospel then becomes a 'gospel of sin management.' Transformation of life and character is *no* part of the redemptive message. Moment-to-moment human reality in its depths is not the arena of faith and eternal living" (Willard 1998:41).

At the heart of spiritual formation is becoming aware that God is everywhere and learning to practice his presence and yield to his transforming grace. Yet the actualization of this discovery often is elusive. Perhaps this is, at least in some measure, because the resistance of self-sufficiency stains the fabric of the fallen soul. Three avenues of resistance to authentic spiritual transformation are proposed below as off-ramps from the process of authentic transformation. We will examine each as we simultaneously work toward understanding the meaning and purpose of spiritual direction.

IT IS EASY TO FORGET WHO WE ARE

According to Gratton (2000), ever since the Fall, we human beings have shown a striking tendency to forget who we really are. We were designed to live in a place, Eden, whose name literally means "pleasure" or "delight." We were created to thrive in loving relationship with God and each other. Life was meant to be full and abundant, interactions authentic, and the fruit of God's Spirit the fabric of our character. The only requirement for keeping the party going is to trust that God has our best interests at heart. To allow him to be God and us not God.

But since the Fall human beings seem to have suffered profound memory loss regarding how life was supposed to be lived and instead have developed a "false self," a counterfeit of the deeply buried image of God (of Christ-form). It is the false self that typically sits at the control panel of a person's life, preferring the management of religion to the mystery of spirituality. As Merton (1961) suggests, the core of this false way of living is always a sinful refusal to surrender to God's will. The "true self, and its desire to live in transforming friendship with God, remains buried in the depths of our souls" (Gratton 2000:67).

Yielding to authentic transformation is difficult because it is easy to make the same choice as Adam and Eve, to choose to be God and consequently to live out of a false identity. Once we have let go of God, false attachments—what we *have*, *do* and *control*—become seductive, and the illusion of our divinity becomes strong. In the words of Leo Tolstoy, "All men of the modern world exist in a continual and flagrant antagonism between their consciences and their way of life" (Tolstoy 1936:136).

Christian spiritual formation involves awaking from the dream that we are God and remembering our true identity, our "beloved-of-God-in-Christ" identity, and then saying yes to the pain associated with the mortification of our false self. Dethroning the false self is a pillar of spiritual direction—and a primary cause for the busyness and anxious "swimming" that distract us from enjoying the "water."

UNION WITH GOD IS A SCARY PROPOSAL

Arguably, the most quoted modern definition of spiritual direction is provided by William A. Barry and William J. Connolly.

> We define Christian spiritual direction as help given by one Christian to another which enables that person to pay attention to God's personal communication to him or her, to respond to this personally communicating God, to grow in intimacy with this God, and to live out the consequences of the relationship. The *focus* of this type of spiritual direction is on experience, not ideas, and specifically on religious experience, i.e., any experience of the mysterious Other whom we call God. (Barry and Connolly 1982:8)

This definition is important because of both its simplicity and its breadth. Spiritual direction here is grounded in experiences associated with the development of an intimate relationship with God—conversing with an invisible Friend, if you will, until we become just like him.

As with any "romantic" involvement, developing a relationship with God requires lots of time—for conversation, communion and union. Barry and Connolly place relationship at the heart of their definition of spiritual direction. By "relationship with God" they mean something that is "established by the creation of the human person and exists even when the person is unaware of its existence" (Barry and Connolly 1982:32). They expand on this theme by casting spiritual direction as "an interpersonal process in which two people work together toward the goal of a deeper, more explicitly intimate and mutual relationship with God" (1982:155).

To be alive is to be in relationship with God and in the process of spiritual formation. Each is unavoidable, given breath and consciousness. But all formation is not good formation, and all relationships do not lead to transforming friendship.

The possibility of the directee's walking the path of experiential relationship with God is always before the mind of a discerning director. As Merton reminds us, in its root meaning spiritual direction is a "continuous process of formation and guidance, in which a Christian is led and encouraged *in his special vocation,* so that by faithful correspondence to the graces of the Holy Spirit he may attain to the particular end of his vocation and to union with God" (Merton 1960:13).

For some Protestants this notion of developing intimacy with God that crescendos in union may be unsettling. But it is at the heart of spiritual direction. Again in the words of Merton: "This union with God signifies not only the vision of God in heaven but, as Cassian specifies, that perfect purity of heart which, even on earth, constitutes sanctity and attains to an obscure experience of heavenly things" (1960:13). It also goes to the heart of the words of Jesus in his commencement address to his disciples, when he prayed for them "that all of them may be one, Father, just as you are in me and I am in you. May they also be in us, so that the world may believe that you have sent me" (Jn 17:21).

Dallas Willard has these words to say about the development of this type of intimate relationship with God.

> So our union with God—his presence with us, in which our aloneness is banished and the meaning and full purpose of human existence is realized—consists chiefly in a conversational relationship with God while each is consistently and deeply engaged as his friend and co-laborer in the affairs of the kingdom of the heavens. The process of having a personal relationship with God becomes a concrete and common sense reality rather than a nervous whistling in the dark. (Willard 1999:56)

The pursuit of union with God is a major on-ramp to the process of spiritual direction. But it can also be a crowded exit. Union with the almighty, all-seeing God is a death threat to the autonomous life. It constitutes both the ultimate goal of spiritual formation and much of the reason for its resistance.

A HOUSE DIVIDED

We have stated that spiritual direction involves remembering who we are and then choosing to enter into a relationship with God that leads to union of our entire being with his being. But another factor is important for understanding spiritual formation and the avoidance of this process. Many schools of both psychology and theology have focused their attention on one or more of the component parts of the person and have consequently lost a vision for a holistic understanding. This is more than unfortunate, as authentic transformation involves the whole person.

As Barry and Connolly observe, "Inviting God to communicate with us in prayer and trying to respond to him in prayer tend to involve *all* of our selves. Feeling, mood, thought, desire, hope, will, bodily gestures and attitudes, activity, and direction of life" (1982:41). Spiritual direction must involve the whole person.

In *Renovation of the Heart: Putting on the Character of Christ,* Dallas Willard analyzes various components of human beings and how Christian spiritual formation takes place within all these dimensions. As figure 1.1 shows, Willard posits six basic and inseparable aspects of human life: thought (images, concepts, judgments), feeling (sensation, emotion), choice (will, decision, character), body (action), social context (relations to God and others) and soul (the factor that integrates all the dimensions to form one life). Christian spiritual formation, he says, involves allowing the Word and Spirit of Christ to enter into one's depths and begin to transform each component of the human being to Christlikeness—under the direction of a regenerate will and with constant overtures of grace from God (Willard 2002:42). Willard acknowledges that such transformation is not the result of mere human effort and cannot be accomplished by direct effort. It is a matter of cooperating with grace and desiring to have Jesus live his life through me.

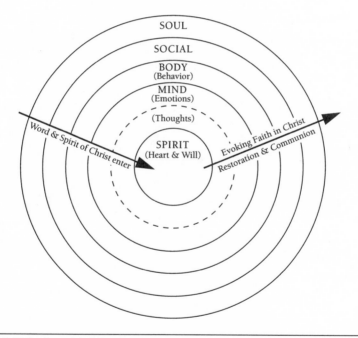

Figure 1.1. Willard's model of the person

Willard's model of the person may remind some readers of how the history of psychology was until it recently became more focused on specific components of the person than on the entirety. The ancient parable of six blind men encountering an elephant quickly comes to mind. In the field of psychology, the past several decades have witnessed a jockeying for preeminence among various psychologies, each devoted to one of Willard's dimensions of the person (behavior, cognition, relationship, etc.), each attempting to explain changes in emotion. Too often attempts have been made to understand the complexities of humans by examining a singular dimension. And while some schools have posited deeper levels of explanation for actions and reactions, the absence of the concept of a unifying soul has left the field of psychology very compartmentalized.

Spiritual direction with its soul talk and holistic view of the person is seen by many as a refreshing alternative to the compartmentalization of modern psychology. As Merton expresses it, "You don't go to a spiritual director to take care of your spirit the way you go to a dentist to have him take care of your teeth. The spiritual director is concerned with the whole person" (1960:14).

The history of psychology reflects the difficulty a person may find in raising the microscope high enough to get the big picture—which, according to Willard, is necessary if we are to view the person in her or his interactive entirety. Authentic transformation, it follows, must involve the whole person, or it will be something other than authentic and less than transforming.

THE PROCESS OF SPIRITUAL DIRECTION

Kallistos Ware tells of a fourth-century desert father, St. Sarapion the Sindonite, who traveled on a pilgrimage to Rome. Once there he was told of a respected recluse who spent all her time in a small room. Sarapion was skeptical of her way of life because of its contrast to his own, which involved much travel. He called on her and asked, "Why are you sitting here?" To this she replied, "I'm not sitting, I am on a journey" (Ware 1993:7).

To be a Christian is to be on a journey from the pigpen of self-rule to the outstretched arms of a loving Father. Not surprisingly, one of the most ancient names for Christianity is simply "the Way" (see Ware 1993:7; Acts 19:23). It is possible that some Protestants have become fascinated with spiritual direction because the richness and texture of viewing Christian transformation as a journey have been diminished in their traditions. Even though Reformers such as Calvin discussed three broad stages of the journey—conversion, sanctification and glorification—in practice it seems that many modern Protestants are more likely to expect a microwave instead of a Crockpot approach to transformation.

As Gregory Rogers observes in this volume, one of the most striking differences between ancient and modern Christianity concerns the view of salvation. "At the risk of oversimplification," he states, "Protestants generally define salvation in legal, juridical or forensic terms. Christ's death pays the just penalty for human sin. We receive salvation (forgiveness of sins) by virtue of our faith in his meritorious sacrifice on our behalf." While not denying the sacrificial aspect of salvation in ancient Christianity, Rogers suggests that it is better to view salvation as a process of transformation and the fulfillment of the image of God in humankind.

Perhaps it should not be surprising to hear Christians described as "forgiven sinners" instead of as beloved children of God on a transformational journey that will lead to restoration of the *imago Dei* and spiritual union. Nor is it startling that someone whose identity has been simply "absolved reprobate" might dance for joy upon being offered a personal invitation to live in union with God.

The journey motif for spiritual formation was adopted by both Roman Catholic and Eastern Orthodox Christians and is conceived of as including three stages: purgation, illumination and union.

Purgation. Purgation is the process by which one's character is purified through confession of sin and a growing detachment from worldly values. Using the imagery of Dallas Willard's model of the person (see figure 1.1), foundational to purgation is a *metanoia,* a radical reorientation of all the dimensions of the person (thoughts, emotions, will, behavior, social interactions, life of the soul) toward God. Here the seeker battles, upheld by the grace of God, against the passions and habits of sin that corrupt human nature. In the imagery of the parable of the prodigal son, purgation is the stage of thinking things through, coming to one's senses—and leaving the pigs to begin the journey back home.

Illumination. Illumination is a deepening experience of the love, joy and peace of God along with a growing desire to surrender the will to God. It is a time of becoming dispassionate regarding all things not God and passionately attached to God and his kingdom. During this stage conversations with God increase and begin to deepen into communion and movement toward unceasing prayer from the heart.

With reference to figure 1.1, illumination can be visualized as an increasing surrender to the presence and passion of the indwelling Spirit of Christ within each dimension of the person until the person's character becomes a better mirror of Christ's. For the prodigal, illumination is the time of gazing into the eyes of the father, realizing the extent of his boundless love and then becoming lost in his embrace.

Union. The final stage of spiritual formation is union with God. This stage will not reach ultimate fruition until heaven. It involves complete interior surrender to the presence and will of God. As this stage is approached, there is nothing to distinguish the character of the believer from that of Christ. The mystery of "Christ-in-me" is realized as an interior surrender of all components of the person—thought, emotion, will, behavior, relationships and soul functioning—is made to the transforming presence of Christ. For the prodigal son, union would mean a full reentry into the family and taking on the mind of the father with such a deep appreciation for his love that the onetime prodigal has become pig-proofed for life.

Willard describes the process of spiritual transformation as the renovation of the heart. He believes that "spiritual formation for the Christian basically refers to the Spirit-driven process of forming the inner world of the human self in such a way that it becomes like the inner being of Christ himself" (2002:22). It also involves a progressive union with God, which takes the form of a conversational relationship that is personal, concrete and ongoing (Willard 1999:56).

As the process of Christian spiritual formation reaches fruition, several things become evident.

1. The directee begins to awaken to her true identity and, with God's grace, dethrones the false self.

2. Conversation and communion with God increase and deepen into a sense of spiritual union.

3. The various dimensions of the person become united by the presence and love of the indwelling Christ.

The truly important thing, the common thread of spiritual formation, according to Thomas Merton (1960), is the journey of surrender to the will of God and his love.

THE ROLE OF THE SPIRITUAL DIRECTOR

It should not be surprising that much disparity exists among descriptions of the role of a spiritual director. This seems in many ways analogous to the range of descriptions of a psychotherapist's role and tasks that can be found in the literature of the field. It appears, however, that it is desirable for both capable counselors and spiritual directors to possess a cluster of personal qualities that transcend both techniques and theoretical orientation, while they do maintain the skill to employ sound technique when warranted.

To sort out the descriptions of an ideal spiritual director, it may be helpful to consider two axes: level of authority and orientation.[1] A spiritual director who assumes a low level of authority may be described as a "trusted friend, or "God's usher," who walks with directees as they attempt to find God's path (Merton 1960). The gift these "spiritual friends" give is their self—hospitality, presence and dialogue (Benner 2002). Those who emphasize a low-authority position may shy away from the term *director* because of the high-authority implication and either redefine the "director" title or instead use a term such as *spiritual friend* or *guide*.

Others such as Rogers (this volume), while emphasizing the need for compassion and relationship skills, emphasize that the director is also in the role of priest, ultimately a position of high authority. High-authority descriptions are sensitive to

---

[1]These categories are suggested by Marty Goehring. For more information see Goehring 1985.

the roles the director may sometimes be called upon to perform such as confessor or soul physician.

The role played by a particular spiritual director will also be influenced by *orientation*. As in the practice of psychotherapy, when considering the role of a spiritual director it may be helpful to consider broad orientation categories such as support (accompaniment and friendship), teaching (instructive, focused on classic devotion practices) or reconstructive (explicit focus on the process of transformation). But even these three orientations, when combined with a continuum of different levels of assumed authority, present a broad spectrum of possible roles a director may assume. Kallistos Ware (1990), for example, discusses five such roles that are common in the practice of spiritual direction: doctor, counselor, intercessor, mediator and sponsor.

While the specific role a spiritual director adopts in working with a directee will certainly vary with the factors we have discussed—assumed level of authority and specific orientation—other parameters such as personality variables, relationship stage and level of training contribute to the nature and rich variety of roles a spiritual director may assume in working with a directee.

As a rule of thumb, spiritual directors are (1) committed to the journey of transformation, including their own pilgrimage (Benner 2002), (2) good and kind listeners (Barry and Connolly 1982), (3) dedicated to helping another to recognize and follow the inspiration of grace in his or her life (Merton 1960), (4) moved by the mystery of God's transforming love (Gratton 2000) and (5) discovered by the community of believers—rather than self-proclaimed—because of the unworldly manner in which they lead their life (Barry and Connolly 1982).

Spiritual Direction, Psychotherapy and Pastoral Counseling

But let us return to the question of the relationship between spiritual direction and its closest soul care relatives, psychotherapy and pastoral counseling. Just how different are these from each other? If we were assembling appropriate images for each, we would end up with three distinctively different film shorts.

A representation of spiritual direction might start with a long, tree-lined entrance to a monastery, trod only by the occasional monk lost in prayer. As you enter the church, the silence and smell of candles make you keenly aware of God's engulfing presence. Later, sitting with a monk, you notice that you can say anything but sense that his interest is focused on how you experience God. Your time ends whenever you finish talking, which sometimes is after ten minutes, sometimes after more than an hour. The monk seems confident that God will finish what he has begun in your life.

Professional psychotherapy brings to mind a contrasting palette of images—

an office building, receptionist, waiting room, warmth with distance, forms, a large desk, comfortable chairs, a prominent clock, a detailed history, lots of questions, techniques and conversation that flow seamlessly together, health insurance and fees.

And pastoral counseling has its own set of associations—a church, a book-lined office, a cross on the wall, a Bible on a small table, warmth balanced by professionalism, obvious concern for your spiritual well-being, a focus on loss or bereavement, sometimes a comforting touch, and engagement with someone who clearly has a religious and spiritual orientation.

But do these images depict necessary differences or merely clusters of personal associations? Are spiritual direction, psychotherapy and pastoral counseling inherently different by virtue of their goals and essential processes, or do the differences reflect only custom? Pastoral counseling and spiritual direction share a concern for spiritual well-being and formation. What if, as C. Stephen Evans (1992) proposes, the ultimate goal of Christian psychotherapy is building Christian character? As Mark McMinn and Barrett McRay have stated, "For the Christian psychotherapist, mental health cannot be defined in a neutral or value-free way because the Christian faith implies a definite view of what mental health is" (1997:103). You don't have to wade in very far here before the water becomes cloudy and the images of psychotherapy, pastoral counseling and spiritual direction begin to bleed into each other.

The normal curve. Figure 1.2 displays two normal curves. The curve labeled "world" is presented to call to mind the typical task of a psychotherapist. By and large, individuals seek a psychotherapist when some aspect of their lives has become abnormal, departing from the mean. Experiences such as depression, anxiety, anger, relationship problems or substance abuse are typically present at abnormal levels of depth or duration. The task of the psychotherapist is to employ generally accepted practices from applied psychology to help the person journey toward the center of the normal curve. Psychotherapy is about *normal making.*

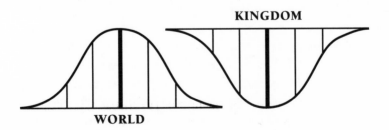

Figure 1.2. The normal curve

Spiritual direction, however, is about *abnormal making*. For the most part, spiritual directors work with individuals who are already living close to the middle of the normal curve but desire to become abnormal—abnormally loving, peaceful, joyful, abnormally aware of God and his loving presence. In spiritual direction the goal is accompany directees on a journey toward normal kingdom living—far from the center of the world's normal curve.

Pastoral counseling takes many different forms but might be thought to usually occupy a place on both curves. Like the psychotherapist, the pastoral counselor takes seriously the problems in living that are presented as the reason for the encounter. The goal is not merely spiritual growth and transformation (as in spiritual direction) but also finding help with the problems that are of concern. So the pastoral counselor in some way has the most difficult job, straddling these two curves as she or he works with the one seeking help to live with less distress and more satisfaction (normal making) while accompanying them on a journey toward spiritual transformation (abnormal making).

Similarities. But we must be careful to not put too much distance between these three forms of soul care, nor to fall into simplistic distinctions. Those experiencing abnormal levels of depression, anxiety, anger and so on are not automatically excluded from entering into the process of spiritual direction, and it is becoming increasingly common for psychotherapy to emphasize wellness or the "positive side" of the normal curve.

All three focus on the same domain of personhood, what Benner (1998) has called the whole person, with particular attention to the inner self. It should not be surprising, therefore, that they employ many common tools. Spiritual directors, psychotherapists and pastoral counselors all offer presence and attentiveness. Practitioners of each seek to be emotionally aware and accessible. They think about what they are hearing and make responses that are designed to help. They all may employ techniques such as guided meditation, reframing of the way one views an experience, exploration of feelings, prayer, discussion of dreams or silence. They all frequently hear about common human problems and experiences. All attend to aspects of experience that are not fully conscious. And all deal with the influence of one's history on one's inner life and outer behavior.

All soul care practitioners should therefore be literate in both the psychological and the spiritual domains of inner life. Even more important, all should be on a personal journey toward health and maturity that integrates these domains of existence. Put another way, we could say that all should be committed to the lifelong journey toward wholeness.

Differences. Differences between psychotherapy and spiritual direction are easier to identify than between pastoral counseling and either psychotherapy or spiritual direction. Subsequent chapters will explore both in much more detail. Let us at this point simply identify some of the most important differences between psychotherapy and spiritual direction.

Psychotherapists approach the inner world with empathy. Their focus is that inner world. Spiritual directors, on the other hand, attend as much to the Spirit as they do to the person with whom they meet. An empathic focus on the inner world of the other must always be balanced by an equal focus on the activity of the Spirit of God in the other, in the interaction and in oneself in the moment (Benner 2002). Gene Barrette (this volume) suggests that spiritual direction shares the focus on the *here and now* of psychotherapy but never settles for it; it also seeks to never lose sight of the *then and always*. This represents quite a different focus.

Psychotherapists seek to understand the inner world and relieve impediments to further growth in those they seek to help. This constitutes what we could describe at the clinical or therapeutic focus of psychotherapists. Spiritual directors, in contrast, are not invested in solving problems. We understand their primary job to be to help the directee attend and respond to God. Seeking God in all things, even the midst of their present experience, the person then finds what John A. Veltri calls "healing of meaning." He describes this as having to do with "learning to tell one's own life stories and re-establish them in the light of the gospel, thus opening oneself for the acceptance of mystery into one's life through the influence and companionship of God's Spirit" (Veltri 1998:520). Thus the focus of spiritual direction should never be simply one's self and one's conflicts. The focus should always be on one's experience of God and one's relationships with God, others and the world as well as oneself.

Gray Temple (this volume) cites Kenneth Leech as suggesting that psychotherapy is the meeting between two humans in the presence of God to pursue a human goal of growth, while spiritual direction is a meeting between a person and God in the presence of another person for the goal of relationship with the divine. Barrette adds that spiritual direction seeks to bring the person in contact with ultimate reality—that is, the Paschal Mystery of Jesus. This is "Good Friday-transformed-into-Easter Sunday" (Barrette, this volume), Christian hope that makes all the difference in facing the vagaries of life. It is this reality to which the spiritual director attends and seeks to introduce the one seeking his or her assistance.

According to Barry and Connolly, "spiritual direction differs from moral guidance, psychological counseling, and the practice of confessional, preaching, or healing ministries (though having affinities with them) in that it directly assists individuals in developing and cultivating their personal relationship with God" (1982:ix). But what they do not address is the notion that developing an experiential relationship with God may be the best way to achieve certain goals of professional counseling, given an appropriate alignment of client/counselor factors (McMinn and McCray 1997).

Len Sperry (2001) provides a helpful distinction between spiritual direction and secular psychotherapy while pointing to the need for an intermediate category he calls "spiritually-attuned psychotherapy and counseling." He contrasts these disciplines across four variables: clientele, goals, relationship with the therapist or director, and intervention methods.

Whereas, according to Sperry, traditional psychotherapists are likely to employ "various psychotherapeutic interventions" (intervention) in their work with "disordered clients or patients with symptoms" (clientele) toward the end of "reducing symptoms and/or impairment, personality change and/or fulfillment" (goals), spiritual directors are more likely to use "listening, instruction in prayer and other spiritual practices" (intervention) as they work with "relatively healthy spiritual seekers" (clientele) in achieving "spiritual growth" (goals). In Sperry's model, spiritually attuned psychotherapists are afforded much freedom and flexibility in the employment of therapeutic goals and techniques.

Perhaps we could suggest that whereas counseling is problem centered, spiritual direction is Spirit centered, and pastoral counseling shares both foci. The goal in spiritual direction is growth in one's relationship to God, not merely resolution of problems. But God must be experienced in the midst of life, and for that reason problems in living are appropriately shared in spiritual direction and are even an essential part of the process of discerning God's presence. Spiritual direction thus shares psychotherapy's focus on problems of living as well as pastoral counseling's focus on spiritual growth and transformation.

CRITICAL ISSUES

Dialogue versus hostile takeover. The present level of dialogue in the Christian community among practitioners of psychotherapy, pastoral counseling and spiritual direction is exciting. Each discipline brings ideas and methodologies that can inform and strengthen the others. Hopefully the dialogue will continue, growing in breadth and depth and crescendoing into mutual enrichment. There is much each can add to the understanding of the dynamics of the soul, including both the process of psychospiritual transformation and the nature of psychospiritual deformation. But caution should be exercised to avoid importing into one's practice rich resources that are only nominally understood and could be incorrectly used. All three forms of soul care are legitimate, and efforts to learn from each other should not become imperialistic attempts to undermine the legitimacy or practice of the other.

Need for more training. The above comment is not intended to imply that Christian psychotherapists or pastoral counselors should stay out of the arena of spiritual direction. For the dialogue between psychotherapy, pastoral counseling and spiritual direction to deepen and center on issues of trilingual praxis will require dramatically increased training opportunities. It is noteworthy, however, that while Christian psychotherapists frequently use spiritual practices with their clients (Moon, Willis, Bailey and Kwasny 1993), training in the use of spiritual practices is conspicuously absent from graduate clinical programs (Moon, Bailey, Kwasny and Willis 1991). Training in both spiritual direction and pastoral counseling may in this regard do a better job, since both more often include some grounding in relevant aspects of psychology. However, both the amount of that exposure and the quality and nature of the training that exists for both pastoral counselors and spiritual directors differ dramatically.

Training programs in all three forms of soul care need to help those who offer soul care with both their personal journey to psychospiritual wholeness and ways to facilitate the journey of others. Helping spiritual directors, pastoral counselors and psychotherapists become literate in both the psychological and the spiritual domains of inner life will add years—not just courses—to current training models.

Ethical guidelines. Finally, much more work needs to be done on ethical guidelines for the integration of forms of practice associated with pastoral counseling, psychotherapy and spiritual direction. As Siang-Yang Tan (this volume) observes, since Christian counseling or psychotherapy often aims at the ultimate goal of facilitating spiritual growth—not just alleviation of symptoms or problem resolution—the use of spiritual direction and other religious resources is often seen as an integral part of such religiously oriented counseling. He goes on to survey the literature and summarize lists of ethical guidelines for the application of spiritual practices in psychotherapy. Broad themes, which echo those of P. Scott Richards and Allen E. Bergin (1997), include the necessity of avoiding dual relationships, displacing religious authority, not imposing religious values on clients, not violating work-setting boundaries and not practicing outside the boundaries of competence.

Brian Eck (2002) has also given helpful thought to ethical considerations for the use of spiritual disciplines in clinical practice. Among other recommendations, he suggests that therapists should employ the disciplines in a way that is consistent with and respectful for their religious intention, be sensitive to issues of spiritual discernment, and work toward better integration of spiritual disciplines into existing treatment models.

Growing commitment to guidelines for ethical practice is crucial if Christian psychotherapists are to practice with integrity and professionalism. Similar guidelines must also be developed for both pastoral counselors and spiritual directors who seek to adapt techniques from each other or from psychotherapy.

SUMMARY

It is our hope that this overview of the context, meaning and scope of spiritual direction and the way it relates to psychotherapy and pastoral counseling will inspire you to both understand and experience more of the journey of authentic transformation. We also hope it sets the stage for increased interdisciplinary dialogue that will bring mutually beneficial clarity to the process of soul formation.

As you read what follows, particularly the chapters devoted to the seven major traditions of Christian spirituality, you will notice significant differences in approaches and practices of spiritual direction. With regard to the level of authority assumed by a spiritual director, some traditions will emphasize a higher level of power (e.g., Orthodox) than others (e.g., social justice). You will also see subtle differences among the various traditions concerning the orientation (supportive vs. didactic vs. reconstructive) taken by the director. And if you look closely, you may observe that certain traditions seem more attentive to one or more of the aspects of the person (thinking, feeling, choosing, behaving, socializing).

The similarities, however, are more striking than the differences. Each tradition stresses the need for accompaniment on the journey of transformation; each acknowledges that the true director is the Holy Spirit; and each defines the goal of Christian spiritual formation as taking on more and more of the life and character of Christ.

Spiritual direction has a unique and important role to play in Christian spiritual formation. But it is a role that is best filled if it is complemented by other forms of soul care. First, then, we shall examine its place and understanding within seven major traditions of Christianity. This will be followed by a more detailed examination of its relationship to the two most closely related forms of soul care: pastoral counseling and psychotherapy.

REFERENCES

Barry, William A., and William J. Connolly. 1982. *The practice of spiritual direction*. New York: Seabury.

Benner, David G. 1998. *Care of souls*. Grand Rapids, Mich.: Baker.

———. 2002. *Sacred companions: The gift of spiritual friendship and direction*. Downers Grove, Ill.: InterVarsity Press.

Clebsch, William A., and C. R. Jaekle. 1964. *Pastoral care in historical perspective*. New York: Aronson.

Eck, Brian. 2002. An exploration of the therapeutic use of spiritual disciplines in clinical practice. *Journal of Psychology and Christianity* 21:266-80.

Evans, C. Stephen. 1992. Christian counseling as character formation. Paper presented at the 2nd International Congress on Christian Counseling, Atlanta.

Goehring, Marty. 1985. Analysis of a model for assessing client therapeutic role preferences.

Ph.D. diss., Fuller Theological Seminary.

Gratton, Carolyn. 2000. *The art of spiritual guidance.* New York: Crossroad.

McMinn, Mark R., and Barrett W. McRay. 1997. Spiritual disciplines and the practice of integration: Possibilities and challenges for christian psychologists. *Journal of Psychology and Theology* 25:102-10.

Merton, Thomas. 1960. *Spiritual direction and meditation.* Collegeville, Minn.: Liturgical.

————. 1961. *New seeds of contemplation.* New York: New Directions.

Moon, Gary W., Judy Bailey, John Kwasny and Dale Willis. 1991. Training in the use of Christian disciplines as counseling techniques within explicitly christian graduate training programs. *Journal of Psychology and Christianity* 10, no. 2:154-65.

Moon, Gary W., Dale Willis, Judy Bailey and John Kwasny. 1993. Self-reported use of Christian guidance techniques by Christian psychotherapists, pastoral counselors and spiritual directors. *Journal of Psychology and Christianity* 12, no. 1:24-37.

Richards, P. Scott, and Allen E. Bergin, eds. 2000. *Handbook of psychotherapy and religious diversity.* Washington, D.C.: American Psychological Association.

Rohr, Richard. 1999. *Everything belongs: The gift of contemplative prayer.* New York: Crossroad.

Sperry, Len. 2001. *Spirituality in clinical practice: Incorporating the spiritual dimension in psychotherapy and counseling.* Philadelphia: Brunner-Rutledge.

Tolstoy, Leo. 1936. *The kingdom of God is within you.* Trans. Aylmer Maude. London: Oxford University Press.

Tan, Siang-Yang. 1996. Practicing the presence of God: The work of Richard J. Foster and its application to psychotherapeutic practice. *Journal of Psychology and Christianity* 15:17-18.

Veltri, John., S.J. 1998. *Orientations, vol. 2: For those who accompany others on the inward journey.* Guelph, Ontario: Guelph Centre for Spirituality.

Ware, Kallistos. 1979. *The orthodox way.* Crestwood, N.Y.: St. Vladimir's Seminary Press.

Willard, Dallas. 1988. *The spirit of the disciplines: Understanding how God changes lives.* San Francisco: Harper & Row.

————. 1998. *The divine conspiracy: Rediscovering our hidden life in God.* San Francisco: HarperSanFrancisco.

————. 1999. *Hearing God: Developing a conversational relationship with God.* Downers Grove, Ill.: InterVarsity Press.

————. 2002. *Renovation of the heart: Putting on the character of Christ.* Colorado Springs, Colo.: NavPress.

PART ONE

THE SEVEN
MAJOR TRADITIONS
OF CHRISTIAN
SPIRITUALITY

2

SPIRITUAL DIRECTION IN THE
ORTHODOX TRADITION

F. Gregory Rogers

Prayer is the test of everything; prayer is also the source of everything; prayer is the driving force of everything; prayer is also the director of everything. If prayer is right, everything is right. For prayer will not allow anything to go wrong" (Theophan the Recluse, quoted in Chariton, 1966:51).

The center of the Orthodox Christian life is communion with God, and the essential characteristic of a life lived with God is prayer. But how do we learn to pray? Jesus' disciples came to him asking that question and received instruction in the form of what is now called the Lord's Prayer. Through the centuries Christians have sought God. And they have learned to find him by turning to those who themselves have drawn near to the "consuming fire" (Heb 12:29).

This essay will look at the practice of spiritual direction, the leading of a disciple to God, in the Orthodox Christian tradition. The history, theology and practice of Orthodox spiritual direction will be examined in detail. In addition, I will briefly consider the relationship of modern psychotherapeutic methods with the traditional conception of spiritual direction in the Orthodox tradition, noting especially circumstances under which the Orthodox spiritual director would consider referring a seeker to a mental health professional. Finally, I will recommend two books for further study.

DEFINITION OF SPIRITUAL DIRECTION

The spirituality of the Orthodox Church centers on the healing of the soul, the restoration and fulfillment of the image and likeness of God in the human person. In the process the person grows into a relationship with God which is ultimately so intimate that it can only be described as *union*. Spiritual direction in the Orthodox tradition, then, involves leading a person through the process of healing the heart and into an ever-deepening relationship with God. This process occurs in a sacramental and corporate context as well as in a personal one-on-one relationship with a spiritual guide.

In the modern world it is easy to think of spirituality as purely an individual concern. A practice is said to be spiritual if it brings one into some consciousness of a transcendent reality, a higher level of ethical awareness and practice, or a New Age mystical experience expanding the boundaries of love and brotherhood. It is even defined in terms of an individual's psychological adjustment, whether to the traumas of her own background or to the environment in which she lives.

In the Orthodox tradition, the individual experience of God, while certainly to be sought, is grounded in the sacramental and corporate life of the church. Orthodoxy takes seriously the mystical union of Christians in the body of Christ and sees the sacraments as the foundation of the spiritual life. Thus in the Orthodox tradition the spiritual development of a person begins with baptism, continues in the experience of Eucharistic communion, is advanced and renewed by the sacrament of confession, and then is further developed by specific guidance from an experienced spiritual director. It is fostered and nurtured by the corporate liturgical experience, shaped by the seasons of fasting and feasting in the liturgical calendar and built by the common ascetical disciplines of traditional Orthodox piety. The first spiritual director is the priest who brings the sacraments and the teaching of the church into the experience of the Orthodox Christian.

The priest also is the first personal director for the Orthodox Christian, most notably in the sacrament of confession. Confession is seen as an indispensable means for making new the grace of forgiveness, providing an opportunity for the penitent to find direction in order to overcome the passions and sins that easily beset the believer. The emphasis is not on the legal aspects of sin but on the healing of the heart that has been damaged by sin. St. James says, "Confess your trespasses to one another, and pray for one another, that you may be healed" (Jas 5:16). The priest who hears confession aids in the healing of the soul.

Spiritual direction, however, goes beyond the confines of the sacrament and may be given by laity. The key is that the director be among those who have been illumined by the Spirit of God. The one who has come to know God, who has wrestled with the passions and put on virtue, is the one from whom direction may be profitably received.

In the Orthodox tradition the director has been seen as *father*, one who gives birth to the life of the Spirit in his spiritual child. For the monk or the nun, this means obedience and submission to one who has traveled the road on which one wants to journey. It means revealing to someone what is transpiring in the depths of one's heart and accepting correction and discipline from him for the sake of the salvation of one's soul. For the layperson, the principle is the same. All are called to prayer and to transformation into the likeness of Christ, to "acquire the Holy Spirit," in the words of St. Seraphim of Sarov (Fedotov 1948:267). So the Orthodox Christian is encouraged to find a confessor, an experienced teacher, to show her the path. The relationship is personal and will reflect the uniqueness of the two individuals involved and the stage of the spiritual development of each.

Unlike the approaches of some other Christian traditions, there is not really an egalitarian quality to traditional Orthodox spiritual direction. While the spiritual father may indeed be a "friend," most of the time direction involves an elder giving counsel, advice, correction and teaching to a spiritual disciple. The exception would be where no experienced guide is available. In that case brothers (or sisters) may submit themselves to each other, cut off self-will, give themselves to prayer, steep themselves in the Scriptures, enter fully into the liturgical tradition of the church, and study diligently the spiritual writings of the fathers of the church. In that case, God himself becomes their director.

One final note: the use of the term *father* does not exclude women from being spiritual directors. There are several notable *ammas* (mothers) among the desert fathers. The primary qualification to be a spiritual director is simply the knowledge of God.

HISTORY OF THE PRACTICE

The early history of the practice of spiritual direction is evidenced in the New Testament. St. John the Baptist has often been the model for those who would later enter the monastic life. His withdrawal to the desert, his ascetic discipline, his call to repentance, his instruction about how to live a godly life, his humility and his pointing to Christ as the One who brings the presence of God to the world all show elements of Christian spiritual direction. The one who would give spiritual direction must first have experienced the path down which he is leading others.

John the Baptist spent years in prayer and ascetic self-discipline, giving an authenticity to the message he proclaimed. His humility in recognizing that he was simply the servant of God who pointed the way, willing to fade into the background when the true Master came, is the same virtue needed by the spiritual guide whose goal is to lead those who come to him to God. Those who came to John the Baptist confessed their sins, being baptized to demonstrate the repentance of their hearts (Mt 3:6; Mk 1:5). In Luke's account, when those who came to John asked for specific instruction for living in accordance with the repentance they were professing, he gave specific instructions to each depending on their station in life, whether soldiers, tax collectors or ordinary people (Lk 3:10-14).

St. Paul also points to the unique relationship between a spiritual guide (father) and his spiritual children. "For though you might have ten thousand instructors in Christ, yet you do not have many fathers; for in Christ Jesus I have begotten you through the gospel. Therefore I urge you, imitate me" (1 Cor 4:15-16). Here the relationship involves more than just the teaching of the gospel. It includes the imitation of the life and character of the spiritual father.

St. Paul amplifies this later: "Imitate me, just as I also imitate Christ. Now I praise you, brethren, that you remember me in all things and keep the traditions just as I delivered them to you" (1 Cor 11:1-2). The spiritual father is to know Christ and follow him; the disciple (or spiritual child) can know Christ by following the example and teaching of the spiritual father. The author of the epistle to the Hebrews echoes this theme, calling on the believers to remember the conduct of their leaders and obey them, knowing they will give an account to God for their souls (Heb 13:7,17). St. Peter exhorts spiritual elders to lead by being a willing example to the flock, knowing that they are accountable to the "Chief Shepherd" (1 Pet 5:2-4).

In the postapostolic era, spiritual direction most frequently came in the context of confession or penance. Often this was formal, done in a public context. Sin was seen to separate the individual from communion with the church; restoration was a readmission to the Eucharistic community, a reconciliation with God and with the church. Some early teachers, including the Shepherd of Hermas and Tertullian, indicate that this formal reconciliation is like a second baptism which cannot be repeated (Sparks 1978:187-88; Jurgens 1970:130-31). Presumably such a public confession and the restriction to a single repentance were applied to serious sins, those for which excommunication was an appropriate response. Tertullian indicates that public contrition included prostrations, fasting, prayer, tears, sackcloth and ashes, confession and asking forgiveness in public. In time, the act of confession was made to a priest who represented the community and not to the community as a whole. The priest would prescribe suitable penance, and the formal reconciliation with the church would be done publicly by the bishop.

In the first three centuries of Christianity, the serious possibility of martyrdom and persecution, along with the potential severity of the discipline of the church, kept the moral standards of the community at a relatively high level. Following the Edict of Toleration issued by Constantine in 313, the church experienced an influx of members and a position in the empire that resulted in a perceived laxity of standards. The desire to make the ultimate sacrifice of martyrdom now gave way to the "giving of one's blood" in asceticism and self-discipline. Many serious Christian seekers withdrew to the desert to seek God and to endeavor to become holy. It was in this monastic context that the flowering of the method of Orthodox spiritual direction and the deepening of the Orthodox understanding of the nature of spiritual growth and development took place.

Spiritual direction in the desert was charismatic. A person who was seeking holiness would go into the desert to find an experienced spiritual guide to lead her on the path to God. The seeker established a personal relationship with an *abba* or an *amma* (a spiritual father or mother) and would submit to their instruction and direction. The paragon of the eremitic (solitary) monastic director is St. Anthony the Great (d. 356 A.D.). In the *Sayings of the Desert Fathers* Anthony explains that spiritual direction is essential for the health of the soul:

> He also said, "Nine monks fell away after many labors and were obsessed with spiritual pride, for they put their trust in their own works and being deceived they did not give due heed to the commandment that says, Ask your father and he will tell you." (Deut. 32:7)
>
> And he said this, "If he is able to, a monk ought to tell his elders confidently how many steps he takes and how many drops of water he drinks in his cell, in case he is in error about it." (*Sayings of the Desert Fathers,* 8-9)

Obedience to a spiritual father kept the monk from pride and self-will, keeping his steps (almost literally) ordered to the Lord.

Often the spiritual disciple would initiate the direction by asking for a word of guidance. The word received would be sparing, incisive and to be applied personally. The monks believed these words to be life-giving, directions that came from God. They were not dialogues or opportunities for debate. Should they be heeded, they would bring about the desired result of holiness of life and communion with God. The topics included the cultivation of virtue, the defeat of the passions and the building of a life of prayer.

The pattern of communication varied depending on the relationship of the spiritual father and disciple. Sometimes the exchanges would be frequent, sometimes infrequent, even scattered across many years. The goal always, though, was the transformation of the monk, to enable him to participate in the energies of God.

> Abba Lot went to see Abba Joseph and said to him, "Abba, as far as I can I say my little office, I fast a little, I pray and meditate, I live in peace and as far as I can, I purify my thoughts. What else can I do?" Then the old man stood up and stretched his hands towards heaven. His fingers became like ten lamps of fire and he said to him, "If you will, you can become all flame." (*Sayings of the Desert Fathers,* 103)

Another type of monastic experience was *cenobitic.* This was for monks who were called to live the ascetic life in a community setting with other monks. The belief was that the challenge of daily life with others helped cut off the self-will of the monk and would teach them to love others, not judge others, and to gain con-

trol of the passions. The head of the monastery, the abbot or *hegumen,* would act
as spiritual director for the monks. In some monasteries the abbot would set aside
time each day, sometimes during the services, when the monks would approach
him and reveal their thoughts, temptations and struggles. He would then give
them direction according to their spiritual need.

In the context of cenobitic monasticism, the classic work on spiritual direction
is St. John of the Ladder's essay *To the Shepherd,* sometimes published as Step 31
of the *Ladder of Divine Ascent* (Climacus 1991). John of the Ladder (known in the
West as John Climacus) lived in the monastery on Mt. Sinai during the seventh
century. St. John notes that the spiritual guide must be one who has experienced
the reality of God and has been transformed himself by the Holy Spirit.

> A genuine teacher is he who has received from God the tablet of spiritual knowledge,
> inscribed by His Divine finger, that is by the in working of illumination, and who has
> no need of other books. It is as unseemly for teachers to give instruction from notes
> taken from other men's writings, as it is for painters to take inspiration from other
> men's compositions. (Climacus 1991:231)

The experienced guide, second, must know the ability, state of advancement
and need of each of his charges. One medicine does not work for all. St. John portrays the good abbot in the midst of the church directing his flock according to
their individual need.

> After the completion of the evening prayers, one could behold that great man sitting
> upon his throne (fashioned outwardly of woven boughs and inwardly of spiritual
> gifts) like some king whom his good synodia and company encircled like wise bees,
> attending to his words and commands as though they were God's. One man he
> would order to recite fifty psalms by heart before sleep, another thirty, another one
> hundred, and another man he would have make so many prostrations. He would or-
> der one to sleep in a sitting position, another to read a certain period of time, and
> yet another to stand for a given period of prayer. . . . Moreover, the great one also
> assigned to each a particular rule of eating, for the diet was not the same, or similar
> for all. With a view to the state of each, he selected what was suitable. . . . And the
> wonder was that his command was carried out without murmuring, as though it
> came from the mouth of God. (Climacus 1991:245-46)

Thus far we have been looking at spiritual direction in the monastic context.
Spiritual growth and experience was not limited to that state of life, though it was
believed that as a monk one could transcend the limitations and temptations that
are part of life in the world. The goal for nonmonastic spiritual direction was the
same as in the monastic context, to bring people to virtue and to the knowledge
of God. The priest functioned as did the spiritual father in the monastery, but without the intensity of the relationship. The layperson was not asked to make vows

of poverty, chastity and obedience, nor to devote all her time and effort to prayer and ascetic labor. But the expectation was that every Christian should make progress according to her ability and station in life. The role of the priest was to facilitate that healing process.

One of the chief means for applying the principles of spiritual growth to the layperson was the sacrament of confession. Sometimes the penitent would go to a monastery to make confession to a spiritual father, sometimes to the parish priest. By the tenth century the text of an order of confession to be used in the churches was published. Included in this order were prayers of preparation, the reading of Psalm 51 (50 in the Septuagint), an examination of conscience and the opportunity for the priest to ask specific questions of the penitent. The questions were personal and specific, according to the leading of the Spirit and the knowledge and experience of the priest. The emphasis in the sacrament was not on the legal aspect, the forgiveness of sins alone or the merits of a penance, but on the healing of the soul through the prayers of the priest and the grace of the Holy Spirit. By going inward and seeing his sins, the penitent was led upward to God. The priest was not a judge but a fellow sinner, coming to God in solidarity with his spiritual child.

Throughout the next few centuries, the monasteries remained a fruitful source of spiritual wisdom. The spiritual literature developed with the writings of St. Gregory Palamas (fourteenth century), which focused on the doctrine of deification and the hesychastic method of prayer—the tradition surrounding the use of the Jesus Prayer. Palamas's teaching forms the foundation of modern Orthodox spirituality. During the Byzantine period there are also some records of correspondence between laypersons and monks, but not any that are greatly detailed.

One of the most important literary events in the history of Orthodox spirituality was the publication in 1782 of *The Philokalia,* a five-volume collection of writings from patristic sources on the spiritual life. Compiled by St. Nikodimos of the Holy Mountain and St. Makarios of Corinth and published originally in Greek, they were translated into Slavonic and then into Russian by St. Paisius Velichkovsky. (Four volumes of these works are now available in English.) These books became a fruitful source of spiritual enrichment for both laypersons and monks in the Orthodox world. They are mentioned specifically in *The Way of a Pilgrim,* an anonymous book describing the spiritual journey of a Russian peasant in the mid-nineteenth century.

The eighteenth and nineteenth centuries saw a flowering of Russian Orthodox monastic spirituality. St. Tikhon of Zadonsk (1724-1783) was the first great Russian *staretz* (elder), and his legacy has been influential for centuries through the elders of Optina monastery. *Staretz* does not denote an official position but a spiritual authority that arises from the experience of the elder himself. It can be recognized, it cannot be given. Those who come to the elder believe they will see God through him. One great staretz, St. Seraphim of Sarov (1759-1833), spent thirty years praying in solitude in the Russian forest, then returned to the monastery to make himself available for spiritual direction to all who would come. In a conversation with Nicholas Motovilov, Seraphim explained the goal of Christian life. "Prayer, fasting, watching, and all other Christian acts, however good they may be, do not alone constitute the aim of our Christian life, although they serve as the indispensable means of reaching this aim. The true aim of our Christian life is to acquire the Holy Spirit of God" (quoted in Fedotov 1948:267). Toward the end of the conversation, as Motovilov was struggling to understand fully what Seraphim meant by acquiring the Holy Spirit, he found himself unable to look at Seraphim.

> Then Father Seraphim took me very firmly by the shoulders and said: "We are both together, son, in the Spirit of God! Why do you not look on me?" I replied: "I cannot look, father, because lightning flashes from your eyes. Your face is brighter than the sun and my eyes ache in pain!" Father Seraphim said: "Fear not, my son; you too have become as bright as I. You too are now in the fullness of God's Spirit; otherwise you would not be able to look on me as I am." (Fedotov 1948:274)

The great hermit and ascetic was illumined, and so was the spiritual son, the layman.

Seeking this Spirit, many Orthodox believers in the past two centuries have sought a spiritual guide. There are extant some important and inspiring letters of direction from St. Theophan the Recluse (1815-1894) to spiritual seekers, illustrating this search (Theophan the Recluse 1995). Some seekers have entered monasteries, but many more have looked for someone like St. Seraphim to teach them the way to a transfigured life. Perhaps the expectation cannot be fulfilled; there are not many like him. But the Spirit of God still rests on his people, his voice still speaks though his humble servants, and God himself leads them.

THE PROCESS OF SPIRITUAL TRANSFORMATION

One of the most striking differences between Orthodoxy and most of Western Christianity concerns their respective views of salvation. At the risk of oversimplification, Protestants generally define salvation in legal, juridical or forensic terms. Christ's death pays the just penalty for humankind's sin. We receive salvation (forgiveness of sins) by virtue of our faith in his meritorious sacrifice on our behalf. While not denying the sacrificial aspect of salvation, Orthodoxy sees salvation as transformation, the fulfillment of the image of God in humankind. The word used by the fathers of the church to denote this process was *theosis,* or deification.

The Scriptures affirm that in the beginning humankind was made in the image and likeness of God (Gen 1:26-27). With the fall of Adam and Eve, the original communion between God and human beings was broken. For Orthodox, the Fall resulted not merely in a legal penalty of death for breaking a law or rule but in true spiritual death, because human beings' union with the Source of Life was broken. The *nous* or "heart" of human beings was darkened. *Nous* means more than simply "mind." It is the central organizing faculty of the human personality, beyond both the discursive reason and the affective (emotional) nature. The central core of the human being was separated from its original union with God, thus made unable to fulfill the purpose for which it was created.

If humankind is to be what God intended in the creation, there must be a restoration of communion with God and the transformation of fallen humanity again into fullness of the image and likeness of God. The incarnation of the Word of God was the supreme act of restoration of the image of God in humankind. St. Irenaeus of Lyons encourages his readers to "follow the only true and reliable Teacher, the Word of God, Jesus Christ our Lord, who, on account of His great love, became what we are, so that He might bring us to be what He Himself is" (quoted in Jurgens 1970:248). St. Athanasius boldly puts it like this: "He became man so that we might be made God" (quoted in Jurgens 1970:342). In Christ we see God as he is (Jn 14:9; Col 1:15) and humanity as it was intended to be. Christ's death and resurrection bring further restoration to human nature, overcoming the final enemy, death itself. In Christ, human nature is restored to permanent communion with God.

Orthodox Christians believe this transformation of human nature is something in which the believer in Christ participates, beginning in baptism. Those who have been baptized into Christ have "put on Christ" (Gal 3:27 NKJV), have been united with him in the likeness of his death and resurrection (Rom 6:3-6) and have been "born again" in the water and the Spirit (Jn 3:5). Through baptism we are brought sacramentally into an ontological union with Christ. As the incarnate Son of God draws life from the Father, so those in union with him participate in his life-giving energies (Jn 15:1-8).

This union is especially nourished through the sacrament of the Eucharist. Jesus says, "He who eats my flesh and drinks my blood abides in me, and I in him" (Jn 6:56). Orthodox Christians believe that in the mystery of the Eucharist we are feeding on the glorified human nature of Christ. Thus we who eat are also transfigured and transformed.

This transformation, however, is not immediate in its effects, nor does it occur without continuing effort on our part. We must be renewed day by day, putting off the sins that so easily beset us and putting on virtues befitting the calling to which we have been called. Most important, we must drink of the Holy Spirit, allowing ourselves to be "transformed by the renewing of [our] mind," being made to conform to the image of God (Rom 12:2; 2 Cor 3:18).

Orthodox teachers have identified three stages in the process of transformation. Different theologians use different names for the three stages, but there is a general consistency of understanding regarding what happens in each of these stages of spiritual development (Vlachos 1994b). In this essay I will use the terms *purification, illumination* and *union* for these stages.

Two things should be noted here. First, even though I use the term *stages,* they are not to be thought of as chronological in the sense that we complete one and move to another, never to repeat the earlier one. We go through these stages and back again, accomplishing a level of virtue and communion with God, then falling into sin or forgetfulness, then advancing further in virtue. The wrestling goes on even to our last breath. The process might be imagined as an ascending spiral, generally moving one "from glory to glory," going over the same ground at a higher level (2 Cor 3:18).

Second, none of this is accomplished by human effort alone. Everything is done by the grace of God. Indeed the goal of the whole process is to be utterly transformed by the grace of God, to become, in Gregory Palamas's memorable phrase, by grace what he is by nature (Meyendorff 1974:175). As Longinus, one of the desert fathers said, "Give blood, and receive the Holy Spirit" (*Sayings of the Desert Fathers,* 123).

Purification. The first stage, purification, begins with *metanoia* (repentance). Repentance is much more than remorse for one's sins. It is a change of mind, a radical reorientation of the whole life toward God. The seeker battles, with the grace of God, against the passions, the patterns of sin within the body and soul that corrupt human nature.

Some writers, notably Evagrius and most Greeks, consider the passions a "disease" in the soul, a disordered impulse, such as anger, jealousy or lust. Others, such as John of the Ladder and Gregory Palamas, consider the passions to be impulses or instincts originally created by God that have been misused. For the former, the passions are to be mortified, combated until the believer has reached a state of dispassion (*apatheia,* in the phrase of Evagrius). For the latter, the passions are to be transformed, to be focused in the service of God. The seeker is to use ascetic discipline to cooperate with the grace of God in gaining control of the passions. These ascetic disciplines include fasting, prayer, obedience to a spiritual guide and almsgiving. Dispassion is not thought of as a mere negative state, the absence of feeling. It is "the replacing of our sinful desires by a new and better energy from God. It is a state of reintegration and spiritual freedom" (Ware 1989:398). Being freed from passions such as lust, we are free to love, to express the fullness of the energies of God.

Another aspect of the purification of the heart is the struggle against the thoughts (*logismoi*) that ultimately develop into passions. This struggle should begin when such thoughts first emerge in the consciousness, before they issue forth in outward actions and take root as passions. The pattern to be aware of is as follows:

- a sinful thought (a momentary disturbance of the intellect)
- "coupling" with the thought (considering acting on it)
- assent
- action
- the development of a sinful passion

The earlier in the process one is able to gain control of the thought, the better. Evagrius noted eight basic evil thoughts: gluttony, lust, avarice, dejection, anger, despondency or listlessness, vainglory, and pride. By keeping watch over our heart we acquire watchfulness and discernment. We are able to detect the thoughts, to discriminate between good thoughts and evil thoughts, and to guard the heart by rejecting evil thoughts. This wrestling should be accompanied by grief, sorrow for our sins and the gift of tears (Ware 1989; Climacus 1991).

Purification also has a positive aspect, the putting on of virtues and the development of communion with God. The cardinal virtues to develop are faith, hope, love and humility. By faith we draw near to God, endure hardships and tribulation, and obey the commandments of Christ and of our spiritual guide. Hope looks toward the completion of the whole process of salvation and does not disappoint (Rom 5:5). For some of the Fathers (Maximos the Confessor and St. Simeon the New Theologian, for example) love is the highest virtue and the expression of union with God. "God is love, and he who abides in love abides in God, and God in him" (1 Jn 4:16). Purifying the heart will lead to an abundance of love for God, for his creation and for our fellow humans. Humility is seen as a fountain of other virtues. "The remedy for all the passions . . . is humility. Those who possess that virtue have won the whole battle" (Climacus 1982:236). Without humility we are unable to see our sin, unable to repent, therefore unable to be purified, illumined and deified. Humility is built by denying our own will and submitting to the direction of our spiritual father. "Humility can come only when you have learned to practice obedience. When a man has a self-taught skill, he may start having high notions of himself" (Climacus 1982:239).

Illumination. The second stage of spiritual development is illumination. We begin to experience dispassion and grow through contemplation of the mysteries of God revealed in this world. We begin "to see God in all things and all things in God—to discern, in and through each created reality, the divine presence that is within it and at the same time beyond" (Ware 1989:398). So we contemplate the glory of God in nature, meditate on the meaning of the Scriptures and nurture prayer in the heart.

In the Orthodox tradition, the key practice of this stage is the development of constant, unceasing prayer in the heart. The usual method is to practice the Jesus Prayer. This is a brief prayer that is repeated over and over throughout the course of the day. The prayer in its usual form is "Lord Jesus Christ, Son of God, have mercy on me." Sometimes the phrase "a sinner" is added to the end of the prayer. This may be said according to one of two patterns. One may concentrate one's heart and attention and say the prayer thoughtfully to the exclusion of any other activity. For those in the monastic life this is possible for extended periods of time. For those who have to carry out the responsibilities of everyday life, however, this may be impractical. So the prayer is said as frequently as possible, leading ideally to a state of unceasing inner prayer.

Union. The final stage of spiritual development is union with God. Ultimately this state will be the experience of all believers in heaven (1 Jn 3:2). In the state of mystical union, consciousness of the act of prayer and even the words themselves fall away. All that remains is a union of love between God and the deified human soul. St. Isaac the Syrian said, "When we have reached love we have reached God and our journey is at an end" (Ware 1989:402). The light of transfiguration that was seen in Christ on the mountain is now shared with us.

St. Nikitas Stithatos, a disciple of St. Simeon the New Theologian, describes this well:

> Deification in this present life is the spiritual and truly sacred rite in which the Logos of unutterable wisdom makes Himself a sacred offering and gives Himself, so far as is possible, to those who have prepared themselves. . . . In this way all of them, joined together in the union of love, are unceasingly united with the one God; and God . . . abides in the midst of gods (cf. Ps. 82:1, LXX), God by nature among gods by adoption. (Stithatos 1995:148)

This experience will never end, though it may last only a time on the earth.

Orthodox spirituality knows no fundamental distinction between the monk and the layperson, at least in terms of the nature of the process of salvation. All are called to purification, illumination and ultimate union with God. All are called to be transformed, to acquire the Holy Spirit, to become partakers of the divine nature. All are called to pray. The station of life may be different, the challenges may be different, but the goal is the same: the healing of the soul and the restoration and fulfillment of the image of God in the human being.

THE ROLE OF THE SPIRITUAL DIRECTOR

In the monastic context there are few roles more important than that of the spiritual father. St. Theodore the Studite asks, "What is more to be desired than a true father—a father-in-God?" (quoted in Ware 1990:vii). St. Simeon the New Theologian urges his hearers, "Brother, constantly call on God, that he may show you a man who is able to direct you well, one whom you ought to obey as though he were God Himself, whose instruction you must carry out without hesitation, even if what he enjoins on you appears to you to be repugnant and harmful" (Symeon the New Theologian 1980:232).

What role does the spiritual father or mother play in the life of his or her spiritual children? Bishop Kallistos Ware (1990) notes five basic roles of the spiritual father: doctor, counselor, intercessor, mediator and sponsor.

First, the spiritual father is a doctor, one who is to bring healing to the soul that has been sickened and injured by its sinful separation from God. St. John of the Ladder says that the shepherd is to acquire spiritual medicines and instruments to use in healing the souls of his charges. "A plaster is a cure for visible, that is, bodily passions. A potion is a cure for inner passion and a draining of invisible uncleanness. . . . An eye salve is a caustic chastisement which speedily brings healing" (Climacus 1991:232). The spiritual guide must be able to accurately diagnose the spiritual ills of his disciples and to prescribe remedies that will bring about their cure. One of the chief ways to be healed is to confess one's sins to one's spiritual guide—and frequently, for "a fresh, warm wound is easier to heal than those that are old, neglected, festering, and in need of extensive treatment, surgery, bandaging, and cauterization. Long neglect can render many of them incurable. However, all things are possible with God" (Climacus 1982:130).

Confession is not a legalistic recital of sins, nor a simple seeking of absolution, but an appeal to God for transformation and renewal. In the Orthodox tradition, confession is both sacramental (made before a priest, who by virtue of the grace of ordination prays for and restores the penitent) and personal. One's confessor could be a layperson, according to St. Simeon the New Theologian, provided that this person had experienced directly the grace of the Holy Spirit in her or his life. Generally, the nonpriestly confessor would point the penitent to the priest for the sacrament.

The spiritual father is also a counselor—but not in the modern sense of counseling as listening in a nonjudgmental fashion and nondirectively. The spiritual guide is to teach and advise, to answer specific questions and give specific directions for how we are to live our life. The teaching may be verbal ("Speak a word to me, father"), or it may be in silence, or simply by example.

Another aspect of this counsel has to do with the disclosure of thoughts. As noted earlier, mastery of the passions and purification of the *nous* require that the thoughts, whether good or evil, be recognized and controlled. To further this process, the monk was encouraged to reveal to his spiritual father everything that happened in his mind. "Indeed, you should also confess the thoughts of your heart to your spiritual father every hour, if possible. But if not, do not put if off till evening,

but after the morning office examine yourself and confess all that has befallen you"
(Simeon the New Theologian 1980:283). In this way the young ascetic learned to
know himself, to discern the nature of his thoughts and the process of controlling
them, and developed the quietness of spirit requisite for true prayer. This was
never done under constraint but in an atmosphere of mutual trust and faith.

One of the most important roles of the spiritual father is that of intercessor. To
lead one's charges to God, one must pray for them. St. John of the Ladder says, "A
shepherd is preeminently he that is able to seek out and set aright his lost, rational
sheep by means of guilelessness, zeal, and *prayer*" (Climacus 1991:231, italics
added). This of course grows out of the general obligation Christians have to pray
for one another. But the spiritual father is especially interested in bringing the
grace of God to bear on the life of his spiritual children. Intercessory prayer is the
direct invocation of the power of God upon them.

When asking for advice, a disciple would often ask his guide to also pray for
him. The prayers of the fathers were said to follow the disciples everywhere and
protect them from harm and temptation. The prayers of a spiritual guide are powerful. St. Simeon attributes all of his spiritual accomplishment to the prayers of his
spiritual father (St. Simeon the New Theologian 1980:245-46). But this does not
excuse the seeker from praying on his own behalf. Negligence on behalf of the disciple can interfere with the efficacy of the prayers of the spiritual guide. And because of the communion of the saints, the prayer of the spiritual father on one's
behalf can continue even after death.

The spiritual guide is also a mediator between God and the seeker. Of course
in the ultimate sense there is *one* mediator between God and human beings, the
incarnate Word of God, Christ himself. But if we are to learn how to draw near to
God, the Fathers believed, we need one who knows God to show us the way. *The
Ladder of Divine Ascent* is instructive in this regard:

> Those of us who wish to get away from Egypt, to escape from Pharaoh, need some
> Moses to be our intermediary with God, to stand between action and contemplation,
> and stretch out his arms to God, that those led by him may cross the sea of sin and
> put to flight the Amalek of the passions. Those who have given themselves up to God
> but imagine that they can go forward without a leader are surely deceiving them-
> selves. (Climacus 1982:75)

To be a mediator first means that the spiritual guide knows and has experienced
God himself. This points to the single most important qualification of the spiritual
guide: the inspiration of the Holy Spirit. St. Simeon says, "Do not seek to be media-
tors on behalf of others until you have yourselves been filled with the Holy Spirit,
and until you have come to know the King of all through the conscious experience
of your soul" (Ware 1990:xix-xx). The spiritual guide must have practiced the as-

cetic disciplines, brought the passions under control and advanced to the vision of God. Thus she is able to lead her spiritual children to that exalted relationship.

The spiritual guide is also to be a sponsor for his or her spiritual children. The word *sponsor* is reminiscent in Orthodox practice of those who present a person for baptism. The sponsor takes responsibility for the newly illumined before God, committing himself or herself to make sure that progress is made in the spiritual life. As sponsor, the spiritual guide takes responsibility for his spiritual children. The spiritual guide, further, is to help the seeker carry part of his spiritual burden. This can take several forms. The spiritual guide can patiently listen to the struggles of his disciple, giving counsel, support and correction, even when it becomes burdensome. The spiritual guide can even take to himself a portion of the penance for sin. According to St. Gregory the Theologian, "The norm of all spiritual direction is to always neglect one's own interest for the profit of others" (Hausherr 1990:142). The spiritual guide is called upon to manifest the sacrificial love of Christ for his disciples, to bear their burdens with them and "lay down one's life for his friends" (Jn 15:13 NKJV).

This section has focused on the practice of spiritual direction in the monastic context. Is there a difference between that arena of life and that of the ordinary layperson, living in the world and trying to find salvation? At root, in the Orthodox understanding there is only one spiritual life, which is to lead to the healing of the soul through the stages of purification, illumination and union. If spiritual direction is essential in the monastic calling, it would make sense that it would be necessary at some level for all.

In the modern Orthodox context, laypersons can go to monasteries to find spiritual direction appropriate for their lives. That, of course, presumes that there is a lively and genuine monastic life available, one that has indeed transformed the lives of those who would give direction. The first level of spiritual direction is still the priest, the confessor and provider of the sacraments. Ideally, he will be able to instruct the penitent in the way of salvation. By faith and the grace of God, all can find someone to point the way to heaven. Though it is far from ideal, we can even learn from those who are just a step or two ahead of us on the path, drinking from the well of the fathers of the church and trusting the Holy Spirit to guide us.

INDICATORS OF MATURE SPIRITUALITY

What is spiritual maturity? St. Paul sets the goal very high: perfection, the "measure of the stature of the fullness of Christ" (Eph 4:13), to become by grace what he is by nature. St. Nikitas Stithatos says that the "sign of perfection" is "the unerring knowledge of God," from which flow superior wisdom, foresight, visions and knowledge. From knowledge of God comes ecstasy of mind and longing for the vision of God (Hausherr 1990:43). The process of growth in Christ is unending. It will take us until our last breath, indeed even into eternity, to become fully what he wants us to be. Still, there are certain indicators that will appear in our heart and life as we grow from glory to glory.

One of the key indicators of spiritual maturity in the Orthodox tradition is *dispassion*. Dispassion, according to St. John of the Ladder, is "the health of the soul." When one is dispassionate, one has overcome the passions, transforming them into instruments of the love and power of God. "Impassibility does not consist in mortifying the passionate part of the soul, but in removing it from evil to good, and directing its energies towards divine things . . . and the impassible man is one who no longer possesses any evil dispositions, but is rich in good ones, who is marked by the virtues, as men of passion are marked by evil pleasures" (Palamas 1983:54). Dispassion is to unite the mind *(nous)* to God through contemplation and prayer and to place the illumined mind as a ruler over the soul, with the appetitive part (desire) embracing love and the incensive part (the emotions) practicing patience. The person close to dispassion is freed from attachment to material things of this world "and is wholly absorbed in the spiritual things of God" (Nikitas Stithatos, quoted in Vlachos 1994a:302).

Growth in virtue is also an indicator of mature spirituality. I have earlier noted humility, faith, hope and love as characteristics of the illumined heart. The flowering of these virtues is an indication of spiritual maturation. Of course, the greatest of these virtues is love. The closer we get to God, who is love, the more our heart will be filled with love for God and for our neighbor. The one who truly loves will not judge her brother or sister, will love the righteous and the sinner with the same divine love, and will have compassion on the weak. She will harbor no rancor toward the one who has injured her; she suffers with and prays for her neighbor. She will provide materially as she is able for the poor and needy and will sacrifice her own benefit for that of others.

Another indicator of mature spirituality is how we endure suffering. Suffering will come, a guarantee of life in this world. St. Theophan the Recluse says, "There is but one road to the kingdom of God—a cross, voluntary or involuntary" (Igumen Chariton of Valaam 1966:231). This cross trains our will so that we can yield our heart and life into the hands of our loving God. The one who bears sufferings with patience, even with joy, as St. Paul indicates (Rom 5:3), is being trained by the Holy Spirit. St. Theophan the Recluse believed that bearing suffering with faith can be as effective at building humility as having a spiritual guide. "For in such instances it is God Himself who acts as director, and He is certainly wiser than man" (Igumen Chariton of Valaam 1966:231).

The final indicator of spiritual maturity I will mention is inner peace. A person who has vanquished the passions, who has faith in Christ, who rejoices in tribulation, who is filled with godly sorrow and repentance yet knows the forgiveness of God, whose heart is lifted up continually in prayer to God will know peace, the "peace which passes all understanding." St. Seraphim of Sarov said, "Acquire the spirit of peace, and thousands around you will find their salvation" (quoted in Moore 1994:126). This peace is not absence of turmoil around; it is calmness and quietness within. "Be still, and know that I am God" (Psalm 46:10 NKJV). The one who is still, who has quieted the raging of the passions, who has communion with God within, who is mature, knows peace.

CONTRAST TO TRADITIONAL PSYCHOTHERAPY AND PASTORAL COUNSELING

Orthodox spiritual direction is quite different from traditional psychotherapy. To begin with, Orthodox teaching rests on a different foundation from that of many of the perspectives used by modern psychologists. At the risk of oversimplification, psychology is anthropocentric, while Orthodox spiritual direction is theocentric. The goals are different, the view of the fundamental problems are different, and the methods are different.

First, let us look at goals. Depending on the school of psychological thought and the problem presented by the patient, the goal of therapy could be to help one adjust to life circumstances, to find release from feelings of guilt, to obviate a psychological disturbance of the emotions or personality, to modify behavior, or to help the patient feel a sense of love, worth and purpose.

Now, these may be worthy proximate goals, but they fall short of what Orthodox spiritual direction envisions as a successful conclusion to the therapeutic process. The goal of the Orthodox therapeutic process is deification, the transformation of the human person into the fullness of the image and likeness of God that is possible for created beings. In Orthodox thinking the soul is ill because it has been darkened through separation from God. Healing comes from purifying the soul of its corruption through repentance, ascetic discipline and the grace of God.

Some schools of psychological thought (Freudian and Skinnerian, for example) would simply reject the idea of trying to come into relationship with God. "Excessive religious devotion" or a sense of guilt caused by an "overdeveloped superego" may in fact be seen as the root of the psychological problems an individual struggles with.

This points to the difference between psychology's and Orthodox theology's understanding of the basic human problem. For Orthodox Christianity the problem is indeed sin, not merely guilt from breaking the "law" of God or the moral precepts of society, but the darkening or corruption of the soul because of separation from God. For some schools of psychology, guilt is a false feeling to be rejected.

Rules are made by society and may be repressive of human freedom. There are no moral absolutes in these ideologies, just better or worse adjustments to the circumstances of life. For Orthodoxy, sin is real, and the cure is not to pretend that it doesn't exist or is a mere neurosis. The cure is repentance, the sorrow for our actions and for our separation from God that leads to a radical reorientation of the life from self-indulgence toward God.

Psychologists also see the problem in terms of response to the traumatic experiences of life. Healing, in this case, involves recognizing the source of the problems and coming to terms with what happened, adjusting and building a life that is not controlled by the unresolved conflicts of the past. The therapist leads the patient to reflect on traumatic experiences to find the roots of present conflicts. Once the patient understands the root of a problem, its hold over his emotions can be lessened, and he can become better adjusted to life in the world. This can be beneficial. What needs to be added, from the point of view of spiritual direction, is the healing grace of God, repentance, forgiveness and spiritual strength. Further, spiritual direction can help the individual see traumatic experiences in the context of the love of God and the development of godly character in imitation of Christ. For Christians, union with the God who has "borne our sorrows" and trust in the One who "causes all things to work together for good to those who love him" brings great healing. The wise spiritual director can point the seeker along this way.

The therapeutic method used by traditional psychologists also differs from that used by Orthodox spiritual directors. The psychotherapist questions and listens to the patient, pointing and prodding to make her aware of the problem and suggesting ways she can mature psychologically. In behaviorist therapy, rewards and punishments may be suggested as means of modifying behavior. Reality therapists would seek to help patients construct plans to responsibly meet their needs for love and self-worth. All of this can be valuable. It is excellent to be able to overcome destructive patterns of behavior and build new ones. The Orthodox spiritual director locates the problem in the darkening of the *nous,* diagnoses the particular struggles of the seeker, and leads her through the process of purification (controlling the passions, guarding the thoughts, repentance and building virtues), illumination (contemplation and prayer) and union with God. His methods will incorporate the appropriate spiritual disciplines and encourage participation in the sacramental mysteries of the church.

One final point of difference: the traditional psychotherapist sometimes denies the reality of the spiritual world, or at least finds it irrelevant to the process of healing. In Orthodox understanding, God is active in the life of people, and so is the devil. An experienced spiritual guide is able to recognize the work of both and lead the seeker to resist the devil and yield to God.

Table 2.1 summarizes the differences in approach.

Table 2.1. Differing Approaches of Orthodox Spiritual Direction, Secular Psychotherapy and Pastoral Counseling

Dimension	Spiritual Direction	Psychotherapy	Pastoral Counseling
Presenting Problem	sin; passions (anger, despair, lust, pride, avarice, etc.); desire to know God; desire to develop in virtue	trauma; emotional needs; mental illness; problem behaviors; guilt; depression; alcohol/drug dependency; etc.	concerned with states of emotional distress.
Goals	overcome specific passions; attain dispassion; overcome sin; build virtue (faith, hope, love, humility); learn to know God	adjust to circumstances; change behavior; take responsibility; overcome illness	work through the specific emotional crisis. If the goal becomes transformation, pastoral counseling has spiritual direction.
Procedure	listen to seeker; hear confession; diagnose specific needs; prescribe appropriate disciplines (fasting, rule of prayer, etc.); give direction as needed	listen; develop joint plan of action; behavior modification; etc.	listen; assist with emotional distress, drawing resources from modern counseling literature or classic pastoral wisdom
Resources	spiritual writings (Scriptures, lives of saints, inspirational books; prayer books); liturgical and sacramental life of church; monasteries; retreats; etc.	books and literature; medical professionals; seminars; support groups; etc.	books and literature; spiritual writings (Scripture, lives of saints, inspirational books, prayer books); training in pastoral counseling

Not all counseling is secular, however. Over the past several decades Christian pastors and counselors have adopted various insights and methodologies from the world of psychotherapy and applied them to the pastoral situation. The major difference from secular counseling in this case would be the use of additional resources grounded in the faith tradition of the pastoral counselor and the client. From an Orthodox Christian perspective this is preferable to secular psychotherapy and would have useful applications, but there remain some important differences between the pastoral counseling approach and Orthodox spiritual direction.

In contrasting spiritual direction with pastoral counseling, Kenneth Leech (1977) notes three major differences that may be helpful. First, the pastoral counselor tends to be concerned primarily with states of emotional distress. A condition or event leads the client to seek help with a specific situation. The counselor, using the resources of the tradition, helps the client work through the crisis. In Orthodox spiritual direction, the encounter between seeker and guide is not necessarily connected to a crisis moment. The goal is the transformation of the individual into the likeness of Christ, a process that is gradual and lifelong. Progress may be made in dramatic and pivotal moments, or it may be made one step at a time. Direction may be given and sought in the moments of everyday life, without emotional sickness or upheaval as a precipitating factor. Further, prayer and one's relationship with God are to be cultivated at all times. The emotionally healthy and the saint still need direction. So the relationship between spiritual director and seeker is long term and less crisis driven.

Second, Leech notes that pastoral counseling is often clinic- or office-based rather than community- or church-based. Generally, the Orthodox spiritual director knows the seeker from interaction in the life of the church and in the warp and woof of everyday life. This is particularly true when one's priest is one's spiritual director. In Orthodox spiritual direction, the believer is served within the context of the sacramental life of the church. Direction presupposes regular participation in worship, confession and Communion.

Leech (1977) also notes that pastoral counseling has been focused excessively on the individual, missing the larger connection with society. To merely seek for peace in one's soul, he argues, is to miss the connection to others and ignore injustice in the world. Orthodox spirituality is nuanced in this regard. For Orthodoxy, prayer is not disconnected from others but unites us to others in God. Intercession is one of the highest expressions of love. Further, the experience of peace with God, of deified union with him, will flow out in service of others and even be the catalyst for bringing others to God. Yet the Orthodox spiritual director will always point toward love of neighbor.

This point is well illustrated by a story from the desert fathers. "A brother questioned an old man, saying, 'Here are two brothers. One of them leads a solitary life for six days a week, giving himself much pain, and the other serves the sick. Whose work does God accept with the greater favour?' The old man said, 'Even if the one who withdraws for six days were to hang himself up by his nostrils, he could not equal the one who serves the sick'" (anonymous, quoted in Allen 1986:173). Orthodox spiritual direction will lead the individual in love toward God, toward transformation. And the highest level of transformation is to become love as God is love.

From an Orthodox perspective, pastoral counseling must avoid the dual errors of reducing the goal of spiritual life to solving an individual's presenting problem and to focus so exclusively on theology or spiritual practice that grace is not brought into the circumstances of everyday life.

HELPFUL BOOKS ON SPIRITUAL DIRECTION
FROM THE ORTHODOX TRADITION

From a historical perspective, the best book on Orthodox spiritual direction is Irenée Hausherr's *Spiritual Direction in the Early Christian East* (1990). Hausherr examines in great detail the practice of spiritual direction in the Orthodox world, particularly in the monastic context of the early Christian centuries.

Of recent Orthodox writings on the process of spiritual growth and development, the most complete is *Orthodox Psychotherapy: the Science of the Fathers,* (1994) by Archimandrite (now Bishop) Hierotheos Vlachos, translated by Esther Williams. Vlachos, a Greek monk and theologian, analyzes in great detail the process of the cure of the soul in the Orthodox tradition.

CIRCUMSTANCES FOR REFERRAL TO A MENTAL HEALTH PROFESSIONAL

As noted in the last section, there are substantial differences between Orthodox spiritual direction and traditional psychotherapy. However, sometimes a mental health professional might be better equipped to work with one who has come for spiritual direction. In fact, the achievement of some of the more limited, proximate goals of psychotherapy may ultimately help the spiritual seeker to attain spiritual maturity.

Under what circumstances should the Orthodox spiritual director consider referral? First, referral should be considered when the person coming for direction evidences serious psychological problems. These problems may have a root in some traumatic event (abuse, grief, injury or the like) or may have a biochemical genesis. Persons with schizophrenia, bipolar disorder or obsessive-compulsive behaviors, for example, need help simply getting to the place where they can cope with the everyday challenges of life. First restore the ability to function, then point the way to God. Often these problems can be helped by a mental health professional, sometimes using the medications that are increasingly available.

There has been much discussion in recent years about whether medications are appropriate for treating Christian believers, particularly with regard to depression. Some argue that these illnesses are signs of spiritual weaknesses and should be dealt with through counseling and prayer alone. I take a different view. If a mental illness is caused by a biochemical defect and can be treated by drug therapy, it is appropriate to do so. There is little intrinsic difference between treating a biological illness of one part of the body (a cancer or an infection, for example) with drugs and treating a biological condition of the brain with medication. Sometimes drug therapies are overused and prescribed when not necessary. But for those with serious mental illnesses, a course of drug therapy may be effective in reestablishing their ability to be rational and function on a day-to-day level.

A second reason for referral arises when the spiritual director does not have the strength and knowledge necessary to help the individual. This may occur on a couple of levels. First, the time constraints and energy needed to work with a very involved case may be more than the director can give. A referral to a mental health professional could allow the person to deal with some of the basic human struggles that he or she has without inordinately taxing the director. When those issues are resolved, the director could help the seeker deepen her relationship with God. Second, some situations are simply beyond the director's knowledge, experience and ability. For some directors, these situations may include serious mental illness, child abuse, sexual molestation, or alcohol or drug rehabilitation. To be sure, each of these situations needs the healing touch of God, with which the spiritual guide can help. But for full healing an experienced professional is invaluable.

The third reason for referral would be if the seeker was not willing or desirous of embracing the Orthodox faith and membership in the sacramental community of the Orthodox Church. The Orthodox spiritual director, to be effective, has to build from a common theological and spiritual foundation.

To be sure, for the Orthodox spiritual director, no referral to a mental health professional will be fully effective for the healing of the soul of the seeker. From the Orthodox perspective, without communion with God, no matter how balanced, functional or adjusted one is, an emptiness will remain inside, a nostalgic longing for Eden, our heart's true home. The Orthodox spiritual director seeks not only psychological balance but fullness of life—a fullness found only in God.

Summary

Orthodox Christian teaching sees as the goal of human life the fulfillment of the image and likeness of God within us, to become by grace "partakers of the divine nature." The Orthodox spiritual director leads the seeker along the path toward purification, illumination and ultimate union with God. The seeker learns with the aid of the director to gain control of the passions, to live and grow in virtue and, most important, to pray.

This essay has examined the history and practice of Orthodox spiritual direction and compared it to conventional methods of psychotherapy and pastoral counseling, noting circumstances under which referral to a mental health professional may be necessary. Further, I have indicated some of the characteristics associated with spiritual maturity in the Orthodox tradition, particularly the attainment of dispassion and the development of virtue. The constant theme has been the cultivation of communion with God, prayer and the transformation it brings. In the Orthodox tradition, this is true healing for the soul.

References

Allen, Joseph J. 1986. *The ministry of the church: the image of pastoral care.* Crestwood, N.Y.: St. Vladimir's Seminary Press.

Chariton, Igumen of Valamo. 1966. *The art of prayer: An Orthodox anthology.* Ed. Timothy Ware. Trans. E. Kadloubovsky and E. M. Palmer. London: Faber & Faber.

Chryssavgis, John. 1990. *Repentance and confession in the Orthodox Church.* Brookline, Mass.: Holy Cross Orthodox.

Climacus, John. 1982. *The ladder of divine ascent.* Trans. Colm Luibheid and Norman Russell. New York: Paulist.

————. 1991. *The ladder of divine ascent.* Trans. Lazarus Moore. Boston: Holy Transfiguration Monastery.

Fedotov, George P. 1948. *A treasury of Russian spirituality.* New York: Sheed and Ward.

Hausherr, Irenée. 1990. *Spiritual direction in the early Christian East.* Kalamazoo, Mich.: Cistercian.

Jurgens, William A. 1970. *The faith of the early fathers.* Vol. 1. Collegeville, Minn.: Liturgical.

————. 1979. *The faith of the early fathers.* Vol. 3. Collegeville, Minn.: Liturgical.

Leech, Kenneth. 1977. *Soul friend: The practice of Christian spirituality.* San Francisco: Harper & Row.

Meyendorff, John. 1974. *A study of Gregory Palamas.* Trans. George Lawrence. New York: St. Vladimir's Seminary Press.

Moore, Lazarus. 1994. *St. Seraphim of Sarov: A spiritual biography.* Blanco, Tex.: New Sarov.

Nazianzen, Gregory. 1978. In defense of his flight to Pontus. In *A select library of Nicene and Post-Nicene fathers of the Christian church,* 2nd ser. edited by Phillip Schaff and Henry Wace, 7:204-27. Grand Rapids, Mich.: Eerdmans.

Nikodimos of the Holy Mountain and Makarios of Corinth, eds. 1995. *The Philokalia: The Complete Text.* Vol. 4. Trans. and ed. G. E. H. Palmer, Philip Sherrard and Kallistos Ware. London: Faber & Faber.

Palamas, Gregory. 1983. *The triads.* Ed. John Meyendorff, trans. Nicholas Gendle. New York: Paulist.

Sayings of the desert fathers, The. 1984. Trans. Benedicta Ward. Kalamazoo, Mich.: Cistercian.

Sparks, Jack, ed. 1978. *The apostolic fathers.* Nashville: Thomas Nelson.

Symeon the New Theologian. 1980. *The discourses.* Trans. C. J. deCatanzaro. New York: Paulist.

Theophan the Recluse. 1995. *The spiritual life and how to be attuned to it.* Trans. Alexandra Dockham. Platina, Calif.: St. Herman of Alaska Brotherhood.

Vlachos, Hierotheos. 1993. *The illness and cure of the soul in the Orthodox tradition.* Trans. Effie Mavromichali. Levadia, Greece: Birth of the Theotokos Monastery.

————. 1994a. *Orthodox psychotherapy: the science of the fathers.* Trans. Esther Williams. Levadia, Greece: Birth of the Theotokos Monastery.

————. 1994b. *Orthodox spirituality: A brief introduction.* Trans. Effie Mavromichali. Levadia, Greece: Birth of the Theotokos Monastery.

Ware, Kallistos. 1989. Ways of prayer and contemplation: Eastern. In *Christian spirituality: Origins to the twelfth century,* ed. Bernard McGinn, John Meyendorff and Jacques LeClercq, pp. 395-414. New York: Crossroad.

————. 1990. The spiritual father in Saint John Climacus and Saint Simeon the new theologian." In *Spiritual direction in the early Christian East,* ed. Irenée Hausherr, pp. vii-xxxiii. Kalamazoo, Mich.: Cistercian.

The way of a pilgrim and *The pilgrim continues his way.* 1965. Trans. R. M. French. New York: Seabury.

3

SPIRITUAL DIRECTION IN THE ROMAN CATHOLIC TRADITION

Gene Barrette

To trace spiritual direction in the Roman Catholic tradition is to try to harvest fields rich with produce almost beyond measuring, a bounty sprung from charisms of the Holy Spirit seeded over centuries. It is a daunting task, but one that can leave us rejoicing and praising the Lord for variety, as well as for staple and at times exotic fruit. Blessed the one who fears not the diversity nor the surprises. Blessed the one who is willing and able to plunge into the harvest and revel in its feeding places. These pages are an attempt to bundle and share some of the traditions of Roman Catholic spiritual direction.

DEFINITION AND DESCRIPTION

Christian spiritual direction may be defined as the help or guidance that one person (directee) seeks and another (director) gives over a period of time in the process of growing in a loving relationship with God. This process unfolds under the continual impulse, inspiration and action of the Holy Spirit. Spiritual direction, therefore, involves three persons: the directee, the director and the Holy Spirit.

Effective Christian spiritual direction helps a person (1) to understand and live out their unique relationship with God, who calls and continues to interact with each of us, (2) to live this relationship as a disciple of Jesus Christ, putting on the mind and heart of Christ, (3) to know and use the means of nurturing and strengthening this relationship, such as methods of prayer, meditation and asceticism, (4) to recognize and disarm or eliminate whatever internal or external forces or sinful attitudes and behavior diminish or destroy this relationship, and (5) to experience the power and fruits of this relationship by responding to Jesus' gospel imperative of witness and mission in everyday life. Spiritual guidance or direction is human/divine assistance for translating discipleship into a life journey of trans-formation. Called to be a disciple, sent to be an apostle: this is the fundamental vocation of all baptized Christians. This process of change has always benefited from the guidance of others.

Christian spiritual direction becomes specifically Roman Catholic when it is done within the context of the Catholic Church's understanding of Scripture, is connected to its sacraments, and draws on the teaching and guidelines that have protected and fostered a variety of spiritualities over the centuries of the church's history.

Spiritual direction is a relational process in which the director and directee develop attentiveness to the actions of the Holy Spirit in the person seeking direction. It is not a program or activity aimed at mastering mystical/ascetical theology, nor an exploration of theories about spirituality or spiritual growth, nor training in the practice of virtues or moral discipline.

Spiritual direction focuses on discovering what hinders and what promotes attentiveness and response to the Spirit's action in this particular directee. It is not simply the skilled application of techniques and strategies mapped out for the achievement of holiness or a deeper spiritual life, although one could easily assume this from reading some of the guides and textbooks on spiritual direction. Spiritual direction is not a speculative venture but an *experiential process* focused on one's lived relationship with God. Spiritual direction is grounded in the experience of the divine.

As William Barry and William Connolly describe it, "Religious experience is to spiritual direction what foodstuff is to cooking. Without foodstuff there can be no cooking. Without religious experience there can be no spiritual direction" (Barry and Connolly 1982:8). "Spiritual direction is not an escapist head-trip that tries to intellectualize reality, but a patient effort to recognize God in all the complexity of His presence to us, on all the levels of our being" (Carlson 1996:73). Theology, concerned with understanding, is an "eyebrows-up" process; spiritual direction, concerned with a loving response in faith, is very much an "eyebrows-down" process.

The fundamental requirement for true spiritual direction is belief and trust that the Trinity is at work in the world and in each of us *here and now*. The spiritual director helps the seeker to be attentive, open and responsive to the Spirit's presence and constant invitation to transformation. Spiritual direction helps us acquire a new way of seeing, of being aware, leading to a new way of personally responding to this self-communicating God.

Multiple and diverse spiritualities can be found in the Catholic heritage, a heritage shared by many Christians. These spiritual ways of life often came from men and women inspired, gifted, given a charism by the Holy Spirit. From these spiritualities emerged schools, movements and religious communities focusing on a particular aspect of Christ's life or message, stressing different theological perspectives, reflecting historical, cultural and philosophical mindsets, as well as developments in the sciences and arts of understanding the person. Spiritual direction often took shape in the light of these different spiritualities. There never has been, nor will there ever be, a one-size-fits-all approach or technique of spiritual direction in the Catholic Church. But all valid Christian spiritual direction has biblical roots.

History of Spiritual Direction in the Catholic Church

Spiritual direction in Scripture. Is spiritual direction biblical? Without hesitation, yes! Scripture gives evidence of spiritual guidance in the time of Jesus and the earliest days of the Christian community. People were not just taught about the Way; they were helped to live the Way.

Those nights Jesus spent with Nicodemus, leading him into the mysteries of being "born again" (Jn 3), were times of guidance. And how else to describe those times "apart" when Jesus slowly revealed to his disciples *how* to "follow me"? It is fair to use the term *spiritual direction* to describe what Ananias did to help Paul translate his blinding insight into a whole new way of being and doing (Acts 9:10-19). Paul himself became a spiritual guide, drawing from his own powerful experience that had brought him to the declaration "yet I live, no longer I, but Christ lives in me" (Gal 2:20). To discover and proclaim Jesus as our Lord and Savior, to be baptized by water and anointed in the Spirit, to join a particular Christian denomination, are only the beginning, the initiation, into *living* the Way.

Paul's pastoral letters to Philemon, Timothy and Titus are filled with spiritual advice, guiding the recipients into responsible adult faith. "Everything in Paul, from his explanations, even dissertations on sin and nature, through his moral teachings, through his instructions on Christian discipline within the family, the Church, the community, shows his understanding of the same *process* that Jesus used in his ministry, the *process* we call, in a more narrow form, spiritual direction" (Schroeder and Meyers 1996:43). "Finally, brothers, we earnestly ask and exhort you in the Lord Jesus that, as you received from us how you should conduct yourselves to please God—and as you are conducting yourselves—you do so even more" (1 Thess 4:1). For Paul it is all the question of being transformed into the image of Christ, to "put on the Lord Jesus Christ" (Rom. 13:14; Gal. 3:27).

With three words, the evangelist John defines God, and the reverberations have never and will never cease to move hearts and the world: God is Love (1 Jn 4:8). His letters spell out the consequences this truth has on life. James's letter, insisting on the necessary integration and interaction of faith and works, urges Christ-followers to be moving always from believing to living (Jas 1:23-25; 2:14-17). Spiritual direction is a graced process that helps an individual to believe in, seize and appropriate the reality of the hope-filled gift proclaimed by the One seated on the throne, "See, I make all things new!" (Rev 21:5). And thus a practice with biblical roots passed into the life of the Christian community.

Early practice. As one reads the New Testament, the history of the early church and the directives of the apostles and fathers, it is evident that spiritual direction and development was once the norm for all Christians. It was the task of the apostles, priests and pastors to provide spiritual food and guidance for their people (Schroeder and Meyers 1996). The members were "formed" and "guided" by their participation in the community's sacramental and liturgical life, through mutual prayer, edification and correction (Rossi 1996). People were motivated and inspired by the community's sharing of its experience of growth in Christ and guidance by the Holy Spirit. Some of the formation included "informal admonitions by one's parents, spouse, friends and fellow Christians" (Merton 1960:11-12).

In the fourth century persecution and martyrdom in the church came to an end. Christianity was accepted and sanctioned by Emperor Constantine. This acceptance, however, robbed Christians of dramatic occasions to manifest a total gift of self to God by suffering or dying because of their faith in Christ. Many still desired to give powerful, living witness of their commitment to Christ. They felt that life in the world was incompatible with authentic Christian living and so turned their backs on the world (*fuga mundi*—flee the world) and in a sense died to it. They began to live austere lives of intense prayer and penance.

Many believed such self-isolation was necessary to be able to accept on an ongoing basis the salvation won for them by Christ. They also wanted to witness to the power of God's hold on them. Seeking a radical kind of life, many gravitated to the desert, especially in Egypt and Syria. Some lived as hermits, others lived near one another in small gatherings or communities. Here are the beginnings of the monastic movement in the church. The seeds of future religious life were present in the burning desire these men and women had to surrender their will, their possessions and their procreative powers to God. This total offering of self developed into the profession of the religious vows of poverty, chastity and obedience.

As some of these men and women gained reputations for holiness, others sought them out for spiritual guidance, asking them to be their spiritual fathers or mothers. In such cases these holy men and women, to some extent, replaced the bishops and presbyters who were the people's ordinary spiritual guides. The great spiritual figures in the Egyptian and Syrian deserts were often not priests, and some were women. This predominantly lay movement was a manifestation of the charismatic dimension of the church, the Holy Spirit powerfully at work, but at some distance from the church's hierarchical structure.

The spirituality born in these desert experiences was marked by austerity and starkness. To work on one's spiritual life meant to combat demons trying to snatch or drive the soul away from Christ. These demons were encountered in the desert but also in the individual's dwelling, imagination or heart. The spiritual skill or gift most needed in this work of combat was *discernment,* the capacity to discern between good and false spirits. John calls us to this task in his first letter (1 Jn 4:1-6). Very few felt adequate to do this by themselves, and therefore they sought help and guidance from men and women of noted spiritual experience.

The desert fathers and mothers gave advice to the neophytes concerning prayer, fasting, work, discipline, virtues, and other skills and practices needed to discern the spirits at work in them and to respond effectively. Their directives were often short statements. This material became known as the "Wisdom of the Desert." The interaction, often rather authoritarian, between these desert guides and seekers gave shape to spiritual direction as it has been most commonly recognized in the Christian tradition. Some notable names of this period are St. Anthony of Egypt (d. 356), John Cassian (d. 435) and Evagrius Ponticus (d. 400).

Spiritualities are always contextual. Before we continue to explore spiritualities and spiritual direction, it is important to understand that spiritualities are always contextual. They reflect theological, philosophical, cultural and historical biases. Another context is the *locus:* was this spirituality linked to monasticism, religious life or the laity? Certain contexts have influenced spiritualities in the Catholic Church up to the present day.

The Platonic view of the soul as imprisoned by the body can be found in many writings from the early church. This Greek influence is evident, for example, in St. Augustine. Drawing from Paul's teaching that we all share in Adam's sin, Augustine developed his theology of "original sin." From original sin comes the basic disorder found in all humans, *concupiscence:* the body and its desires, instincts and passions, usually perceived as at war with the soul.

Introduced into the mix were Manichaeism and Gnosticism, world and religious views later condemned by the church. These philosophies portrayed life in dualistic terms: the material is evil, the spiritual is good. Life therefore is about the conflict and struggle between the two.

One can find biblical support for this vision in a particular reading of John's Gospel declarations about the "world" and also in Paul's references to life in the "flesh" in contrast to life in the "spirit." Within this perspective, the focus of the spiritual life became the civil war within each person between the body and soul, flesh and spirit. Such influences have re-emerged from time to time over the centuries, as seen in Jansenism in sixteenth- and seventeenth-century France.

Biblical theology, however, does not deal in such dichotomies but considers the human person as one. The division comes not in the person, or the world, in itself, but rather in the attitude or the direction and goals of the person or the world. A healthy spirituality is grounded in the Genesis assertions "And God saw how good it was" (Gen 1:4, 10, 12, 18, 21, 25) and "God looked at everything he had made, and he found it very good" (Gen 1:31). To some it may seem a stretch, but a healthy spirituality also keeps in mind, "What God has joined together, no human being must separate" (Mt 19:6).

Within the view that the body is bad and the soul is good, spiritual development became mostly concerned with the soul. The earnest spiritual seeker did everything possible to ignore, denigrate or even destroy the body. Much spiritual direction thus focused on overcoming bodily urges or concupiscence. This resulted in a great emphasis on asceticism and mortification in spiritual direction.

Asceticism involves physical and spiritual practices aimed at conditioning individuals so that the soul may conquer and control all nonspiritual forces. There are interior ascetical practices: control of thoughts, struggle against gluttony, lust, avarice, anger, boredom, vainglory, pride, *acedia* (lack of commitment to spiritual values), listlessness, unconcern, depression. External ascetical practices included set prayer times, fasting, bodily mortification (Muto 2000), vigils, renouncing legitimate joys and pleasures, custody of the eyes (not of negligible value in today's image-saturated culture), and other activities aimed at reining in fleshly needs, desires and tendencies. This approach was reflected in the sayings of the early desert fathers and mothers and also in the rules for monastic or religious life. Such a negative spirituality, however, can run the risk spelled out in the Gospel parable of the man who swept out one demon only to have his house invaded by seven others (Mt 12:43-45; Lk 11:24-26).

If the theological focus is on works, on gaining one's salvation rather than accepting the salvation gained for us by Christ, then spirituality is also skewed. The focus becomes "saving one's soul," and the result is the burden of many spiritual activities, devotions and works to be accomplished. This can even give rise to spiritual competitiveness, which has not always been foreign to monastic and religious life, nor to small groups or coteries in the church. Any direction that focuses on our efforts rather than on the Spirit at work in us steers us in the wrong direction. There is the risk of adopting a semi-Pelagian, "we try harder" mentality in the spiritual life (Wallace 1996).

Classic monastic and religious rules provided the foundation for much spiritual direction. Among these were the Rule of St. Augustine, the oldest surviving rule for religious in the West, and the Rule of St. Benedict. Benedict is considered the father of Western monasticism, and his Rule is the basis of many monastic communities, including the Trappists and the Rule of the Carmelites (1200s).

In the Middle Ages theology became something of a speculative science. The spiritual life also became the object of scientific scrutiny. Manuals of ascetical or mystical theology and books on "the science of the saints" made their appearance. The spiritual life was analyzed. "Maps" and "stages" of spiritual life were developed and used by spiritual directors, unfortunately often in a very Procrustean way.

Reactive pockets always exist in the church, and to counteract some of the too abstract and speculative content of theology and spirituality, mystical movements arose which focused on the experience of God, Jesus and the Spirit. Mystical writings flowed from hearts bursting with the experience of divine love, feverishly setting the imagination in motion. The ravishing experience of God's presence and love and the near-death sense of God's absence and silence both became subjects of spiritual writings.

Spiritual directors often turned to these writings to understand spiritual experiences. These works could help guide seekers to a contemplative and affective surrender to the mystery of God. The institutional church, however, looked on mystics and their writings with suspicion and wariness, because mystics were not as containable or controllable as speculative theologian. Some notable mystical writers of the fourteenth through sixteenth centuries are Julian of Norwich (*Showings* or *Revelations of Divine Love*), Walter Hilton (*The Stairway of Perfection*), St. John of the Cross (*The Dark Night of the Soul, The Spiritual Canticle, The Living Flame of Love*), St. Teresa of Ávila (*The Way of Perfection, The Interior Castle*) and the author of *The Cloud of Unknowing*.

The locus, as well as the focus, of spirituality has a notable influence. For many centuries "the spiritual" was seen as the privileged domain of those in monastic and religious life or the priesthood. Therefore spiritual direction was for a spiritual elite. This definitely influenced the means that were promoted for holiness. Most spiritual exercises or activities were connected to the vowed state and community life of religious orders. There was little regard for the married and single states of life. Prayer was understood almost exclusively as "times apart" with definite cycles, often linked to the recitation of the Divine Office and the Psalms, in a monastic or cloistered setting.

But religious life itself eventually shifted from the monastic setting and became more apostolic. Religious men and women began to respond to the needs of laypeople living ordinary lives in the world. Thus spiritual direction became more open and connected to the everyday life of the Christian. A number of leaders arose as strong promoters of apostolic and lay spirituality:

- St. Francis of Assisi, founder of the Franciscans, and St. Dominic, founder of the Dominicans, both established mendicant religious orders whose pastoral task was to preach Christ to the laity, especially to counteract some dangerous teachings of the times, and to work for the care of souls.

- Thomas à Kempis's classic *The Imitation of Christ* was written to help ordinary people on their spiritual journey and is considered the most widely read spiritual book after the Bible. Thomas was part of the Devotio Moderna movement of the 1300s and 1400s, which promoted the mystical life, prayer, meditation and piety for the laity and sought to combat the purely humanistic values of the day.

- St. Ignatius of Loyola, founder of the Jesuits, was author of the *Spiritual Exercises,* one of the most insightful guides for spiritual direction, especially regarding the discernment of spirits. The Ignatian exercises are still a very powerful and popular form of retreat. They can be done over thirty days, on an eight-day retreat or on an ongoing daily basis.

- St. Francis de Sales, lawyer, bishop of Geneva and renowned spiritual director, wrote *Introduction to the Devout Life* and *Treatise on the Love of God.* "My purpose," Francis says in *Introduction to the Devout Life,* "is to instruct those who live in town, within families, or at court, and by their state of life are obliged to live an ordinary life." He once observed, "The measure of love is to love without measure" (quoted in Muto 2000:81).

It should be kept in mind that all these spiritualities were focused primarily on Christ and how to live out the mystery of Christ-in-you. At times devotions to Mary or the saints played a part in certain spiritualities, but their authenticity always was assessed on the ultimate connection with Jesus.

In the modern era, a shift in philosophical thought resulted in a new worldview. From the classical, Greek, static view of life, science and other empirical observations opened a worldview that is fluid and evolutionary. Life and the universe began to be thought of in terms of process, which connects better with the biblical sense of history and spirituality as pilgrimage and journey. The twentieth century also brought the impact of psychology, sociology and anthropology. Science has created unimagined new frontiers and has traversed them almost as quickly. Communism, socialism, existentialism, capitalism, secularism, feminism and other new "isms" all had impact. Faith, religion and spirituality were naturally influenced by it all. Some reactions were exploratory, accommodating, adapting, finding mutual ground; others were reactionary, condemnatory, rejecting, setting up enemy lines. Some faiths and religions entered the dance, others blocked off new ghettos.

The greatest seismic shift in the Catholic Church happened in the early 1960s, when Pope John XXIII convoked an ecumenical council, a gathering of Catholic bishops from around the world. From 1962 to 1965 they met in Rome for three sessions. This event became known as Vatican II. There had been a Vatican I Council in 1869-1870. John XXIII desired to open windows and allow a breath of fresh air in the church and to establish a genuine, loving, open dialogue and interaction between the church and the modern world. Led by the Holy Spirit, the pope called for a new pouring out of the Holy Spirit in the church. He wanted a "new Pentecost." *Aggiornamento* was the buzzword, meaning "bringing up to date" or "renewal." Renewal was sought through return to the roots of the church: the Scriptures, the liturgy, the church's teachings, and especially the power and guidance of the Holy Spirit.

The council, and the period following it, marked a strong reappropriation of the Holy Spirit in the Roman Catholic Church. There was even a name change. No longer was the third Person of the Blessed Trinity called the "Holy Ghost"; now the name was "Holy Spirit," with all the biblical resonance of life, power, vivifying force, breath, inspiration, movement and transformation.

There was never a denial of the Holy Spirit in the Catholic tradition. Catholics have always believed they receive the Holy Spirit at baptism and that the Spirit's presence is reinforced in the sacrament of confirmation. Catholics believe in the gifts of the Holy Spirit as described in Scripture (Is 11:2; 1 Cor 12:8-11) and often pray that these powers be released in them. The Spirit of Truth has been present in the church throughout its history (Jn 14:26; 15:26). This Spirit ensures that revealed truth is preserved from error, inspired the articulation of the creeds and tradition, guided the establishment of the canon of Scripture, and raises inspired men and women who have led the church, reformed it and founded religious communities. There is no doubt that the Holy Spirit is at the heart of the church.

Some of the major Vatican II contributions are as follows:

1. The church is defined as "the people of God" rather than a hierarchical institution to which people belong for the sake of certain spiritual benefits.

2. There is a "universal call to holiness." No longer is there a "higher" spirituality for the ordained and the religiously professed than for the laity (McBrien 1994).

3. The liturgy is the summit and fountain of life and holiness in the church and therefore was made more accessible for fuller participation of the laity through the use of the vernacular instead of Latin.

4. Liturgical reforms reinstated the importance of the liturgy of the Word and thus gave renewed prominence to the Scriptures.

5. The altar now would face the people, emphasizing that the priest and people are celebrating Mass *together,* highlighting the "priesthood of the faithful" conferred at baptism.

6. The laity could now exercise the ministries that are rightfully theirs through baptism, making use of the variety and diversity of gifts or charisms the Holy Spirit showers on *all* (1 Cor 12:4-11).

Vatican II encouraged recognition of the signs of grace in other religions and faiths, even non-Christian ones. Instead of fearing and decrying what is wrong or dangerous in other faiths, the challenge is to discover what is right, affirm it, recognize what we have in common, and when possible celebrate it. The spiritual director must have a great openness and capacity to mine the graces within different spiritual traditions.

One cannot underestimate the influence that the horizon shifts caused by Vatican II have had on the approach to spiritual direction in the Catholic church. Theoretical textbook approaches became inadequate when faced with the dynamism of the renewing power of the Holy Spirit and the acceptance of that same Spirit at work in the "spiritualities" of the various religions of the world. The "playing field" of spiritual direction for Catholics became seemingly "sans frontiers."

THE PROCESS OF AUTHENTIC TRANSFORMATION

One of the principal settings for spiritual direction throughout the centuries has been the sacrament of confession, penance and reconciliation. In confession, penitents were assured of God's forgiveness in the words of absolution spoken by the priest. The priest also gave advice on how to avoid sin. In the fifth and sixth centuries Irish monks produced "penitentials," books filled with remedies for sins, and confessors used them as guides in their care of souls. Because of the sacramental context, much spiritual direction focused on moral living.

The ultimate goal of Christian spiritual life, however, is to "put on the Lord Jesus Christ" (Rom 13:14). The goal of Christian spiritual direction is to help a person "become sensitive to God's presence, deepen the personal relationship with Christ and attend to the action of the Spirit in one's life" (McCready 1996:113). Anything and everything that contributes to that work may be included in the process of spiritual direction.

Direction most often occurs in a one-on-one situation between a director and a directee. A first step in the process is to explore the desires and motivations of the person seeking direction. Are they seeking help to deal with a present crisis or problem, or are they seeking guidance for their long-term life pilgrimage? What is their understanding of the gospel way of life? How do they define a spiritual life? What are their present spiritual goals? Do they have a prayer life? What is their experience of God in prayer?

Classically, spiritual growth has been described in three stages: purgative, illuminative and unitive. While there is a rich history within the Roman Catholic Church concerning the meaning of each of these classic categories and their place in the journey to spiritual maturity, each of these stages has already been discussed in the two preceding chapters in this book. Therefore I will not try the patience of the reader by echoing that information here.

HELPFUL BOOKS ON CATHOLIC SPIRITUAL DIRECTION

In my judgment, the two most helpful books regarding spiritual direction in the Roman Catholic tradition are William A. Barry and William J. Connolly, *The Practice of Spiritual Direction* (1982), and David Fleming, ed., *The Christian Ministry of Spiritual Direction: The Best of the Review 3* (1996), a collection of articles from *Review for Religious*.

It is important to observe, however, that in the context of Vatican II and contemporary psychological focus there is a growing emphasis on a "holistic" approach to spirituality and spiritual direction. The goal of Christian holistic spirituality is to unite *all* parts of one's life into the Christian call and response. "A holistic spirituality helps to develop Christians who can overcome the pernicious schizophrenia between soul and body, brain and heart, and thus become more whole" (Au and Wilki 1993:490).

Holistic spirituality opposes pitting the body against the soul, the sacred against the secular, "this world" against "that world," the spiritual against the material. It counters the dualism that has plagued Western, Christian spirituality over the centuries (Au 1993). Holistic spirituality is rooted in the incarnational belief of the pervasive presence of God in all reality. We live in a divine milieu (Au 1993). Our God is not one of territorial imperatives but a God who is *everywhere* "at home." Although sin and its impact are not denied, in this focus, consciousness of "original blessings" is preferable to an insistence on "original sin."

Holistic spirituality embraces the totality of a person's existence, relationships with others, with her work, with the material world. It finds every human concern relevant. "Holiness is not an otherworldliness which dims the radical goodness of the created order. . . . The holy person is the one who is fully what God created that person to be, and who has been recreated in the Holy Spirit" (McBrien 1994:104). Fullness is wholeness is holiness.

The appropriate religious question is, How is God leading and loving me in *all* aspects of my life? Spiritual direction helps "discover the personal God in the dark moments and the secularly nonvalued or 'throw-away' experiences of life. . . . God more literally becomes acknowledged as the God of my *whole life*" (Fleming 1996:8). Nothing is outside of God's breath.

A powerful tool at any level of spirituality is the "examination of consciousness." At different intervals during the day a person takes two minutes, reviews the previous three or four hours—the people, places, events, thoughts—and simply asks the question, "Where were you, Lord, in those moments? How did I respond to you?" With such God-consciousness one becomes able to truly follow Paul's challenge to "pray at every opportunity" (Eph 6:18; Col 4:2). Ultimately, authentic transformation leads to, and actually occurs through, the most fundamental of spiritual action, "letting go and letting God." Or as more commonly stated, "Thy will be done."

THE ROLE OF THE DIRECTOR

Spiritual directors are to ally themselves consciously with the indwelling of the Spirit of the living God, because this indwelling Spirit is the source of the directee's powerful desire for "more" in the way of life and union with God (Barry and Connolly 1982). Anchored in God as much as possible and completely open to the Holy Spirit, the director must love the seeker unconditionally and respect his or her unique freedom (McDowell 1996). Thomas Merton elaborates, "The director is not to be regarded as a magical machine for solving cases and declaring the holy will of God beyond all hope of appeal, but a trusted friend who, in an atmosphere of sympathetic understanding, helps and strengthens us in our groping efforts to correspond with the grace of the Holy Spirit, who alone is the true Director in the fullest sense of the word" (Merton 1960:6).

The director's primary function is *clarification* and *discernment,* to clarify what God wants in the person's life and discern between the evil and the good spirits creating movement in the person's emotional and spiritual life. Put more poetically, the director is to "assist in helping the person read the breathings of the Spirit . . . read the writing on the walls of the soul" (Carlson 1974:89). Discernment gives the capacity to do this.

As early as the desert fathers and mothers, discernment has been recognized as one of the major tasks of spiritual direction. Discernment involve discerning not only the movements of the Holy Spirit but also the presence of the "enemy," blocking the Spirit's work. St. Ignatius's *Spiritual Exercises* is the classic source for the rules of discernment. The Exercises were based on the "conviction that God can and wants to be met in dialogue" (Barry and Connolly 1982:27). Discernment helps to know who is speaking.

Ignatius gives two sets of rules for discernment. One set is to help understand, interpret and deal with desolation and consolation, part of everyone's spiritual life. The other set helps distinguish what are God-inspired thoughts and movements and what comes from the devil. Decisions need discernment: choosing between good and evil and choosing between two goods. Ignatius's focus on the loving experience of God in dialogue was quite a departure from the emphasis on rational knowledge of God that dominated spirituality at the end of the Middle Ages (Barry and Connolly 1982).

Spiritual direction is to be a free relationship, not a master-disciple relationship. The director is companion to the pilgrim and offers guidance. But he or she needs to revere the spiritual freedom of the pilgrim and not foster dependence, because it is the Lord who is the director of life's pilgrimage (McCready 1996).

A Catholic spiritual director needs an informed and intelligent understanding of the Bible, the faith of the church and modern theology because initial work in spiritual direction often involves the healing or correcting of false images of God. The director needs knowledge of modern psychology and the diversity of Christian religious experience and should also have a sympathetic awareness of non-Christian religious experience (Barry and Connolly 1982). Today, with the greater emphasis on holistic spirituality, it is ever more imperative that a director have knowledge and understanding of the multiple facets of being human.

A director must be a person of love, broad human and spiritual experience, competence, prayer, insight, vision, balance, prudence, reverence, patience, compassion, trustworthiness, discretion, sympathy, sincerity, warmth, simplicity, encouragement and *lots of common sense.* The director may be a powerful "wounded healer" because of his or her own life experience of struggle, passion, conflict, spiritual darkness and light.

Patience to respect God's timetable for the seeker's spiritual growth is very important in a director. A director has to know how to live in *kairos,* God's time, and not simply in *chronos,* human time. There is always a danger of wanting to "push ourselves beyond the pace of grace" (Muto 2000:153). It takes "patient effort to recognize God in all the complexity of His presence to us, on all the levels of our being" (Carlson 1996:73). Some claim that *encouragement* is the most significant help that a director gives (Carlson 1996).

It is also important for the director to have a healthy respect for the unique shape of each individual's holiness. As each person has a physical DNA, so too each has a unique spiritual DNA. The Enneagram, the Myers-Briggs Inventory and other psychological inventories can help illuminate one's personality type and the influence this inner structure has on one's way of praying, meditating, processing experience and being involved in the apostolate.

To correct an at-times overemphasis on the director's authority, today the director is described in less authoritarian images:

- God's usher, aware of God coming, of God present (Wallace 1996:82)

- midwife, linked to the great patristic theme of the "birth of God in men's hearts" (Carlson 1996:83)

- instrument of the main Artist, who is the Holy Spirit, "engaged in the one work of art, which is to change us into the image of Christ" (Sheets 1996:57)

- soul friend (Leech 2001)
- doctor of the soul exercising *cura animarum*—cure or care of the soul.

Another role of the spiritual director is not often mentioned: that of "intercessor in the night." The director, in quiet moments of prayer, consciously prays for the seeker (McDowell 1996).

A final note that may be disconcerting to people who are involved in the ministry of spiritual direction is that the director should be looked at as a model. "Ideally, in looking at the director, the seeker understands what it is like to live the spiritual life more fully. The director's interior joy and peace, effortlessness in movement, powerful presence, dynamism and effective modes of action can provide the hope and determination the directed one needs to persevere in traveling the spiritual path" (McDowell 1996:211).

INDICATORS OF SPIRITUAL MATURITY

Spiritual maturity builds on human, psychological and emotional maturity but stretches past the boundaries of what common sense may understand as maturity. Christian spiritual maturity finds its criteria in Scripture, often in the paradoxes of Christ's teachings.

St. Paul lists some of the characteristics of the person who has put on Christ (Rom 13:14), who is conscious of the Spirit dwelling in him (1 Cor 3:16, 19). The spiritually mature individual does "not conform to this age" but is "transformed by the renewal of mind, so that he may judge what is God's will, what is good, pleasing and perfect" (Rom 12:2). That person is able to cut through illusion and false desires and manifests a fresh, spiritual way of thinking (Eph 4:22-24). This in itself sets that person apart and makes him countercultural.

Christian maturity is more than living by "code and cult." Mature holiness must surpass that of the scribes and Pharisees (Mt 5:20). It lives in the conviction that it is mercy that God desires and not sacrifice (Mt 12:7) and that "the Sabbath was made for man, not man for the Sabbath" (Mk 2:27).

Mature spirituality knows "the kingdom of God is not a matter of eating or drinking, but of justice, peace and the joy that is given by the Holy Spirit" (Rom 14:17). The mature spiritual Christian never loses sight of Jesus' bottom line: "Love one another as I have loved you" (Jn 15:12; see also Mt 22:34-40; Rom 12:8-9).

Mature Christian spirituality "follows the way of love, even as Christ loved" (Eph 5:2) and "loves in deed and in truth, and not merely talks about it" (1 Jn 3:18). This love is incarnate in ways indicated by Jesus himself: feed the hungry, give drink to the thirsty, clothe the naked, visit the sick and those in prison (Mt 25:31-46). The command to love "as I have loved you" leads the mature to sacrificial love, to laying down one's life for another (Jn 15:13), to loving and forgiving one's enemies (Mt 5:43-45). This love is compassionate and forgiving (Eph 4:32) and seeks every kind of goodness, justice and truth (Eph 5:9). This love has no room for fear; it casts out all fear (1 Jn 4:18), because fear is useless when what is needed is trust (Lk 8:50). Fear is also taken away because the mature Christian knows that "God makes all things work together for the good" (Rom 8:28).

Mature Christian spirituality orbits around the Paschal Mystery. It does not shrink away from following Jesus into death. It does not try to avoid or deny the cross. Mature spirituality knows we must die in order to live, that we must take up the cross and can only save our life by losing it (Mt 16:24-25). Even when the spirit cries out, "My God, my God, why have you forsaken me?" (Mt 27:46), mature spirituality is not crushed or overwhelmed, because it knows resurrection follows, new life, new beginnings. Mature Christian spirituality recognizes and expects the rhythm of Good Friday and Easter in life and therefore sees meaning at the heart of suffering.

Mature Christian spirituality is also observed in those who manifest the gifts and fruits of the Holy Spirit in their life: their love is sincere, they detest what is evil and cling to what is good, they are fervent in spirit, rejoice in hope, are patient under trial and persevere in prayer, they are generous in hospitality, they rejoice with those who rejoice, weep with those who weep and live peaceably with everyone (Rom 12:9-18). Through the power of the Holy Spirit they have hope in abundance (Rom 15:13). Their love is shown not only in big ways but also especially in the small choices and attitudes that fill every day. Their love is kind and patient, does not put on airs, is not snobbish, not jealous, never rude nor self-seeking, not prone to anger nor to brood over injuries, does not rejoice in what is wrong but rejoices with the truth (1 Cor 13:4-7). The mature Christian has a steadfastness about her (Lk 9:62), and sin no longer has controlling power over her (Rom 6:14). Such a person radiates the fruit of the Spirit: love, joy, peace, patience, endurance, kindness, generosity, faith, mildness and chastity (Gal 5:22-24).

The fundamental criterion for mature Christian spirituality remains a gospel criterion: "By their fruits you shall know them." And the fruit of having "put on Christ" is the character of Christ.

SPIRITUAL DIRECTION, PASTORAL COUNSELING AND PSYCHOTHERAPY

Religion and psychology have not had the best of relationships, since psychology came on the scene at the beginning of the twentieth century claiming the status of a science and generally challenging, if not outright dismissing, matters of faith or spirituality. At times faith was not merely dismissed but seen as dangerous and the source of many psychological problems. Naturally, religion reacted. It condemned psychology as a sick, sex-obsessed science that was destructive of faith, negated free will and personal responsibility, and was pernicious to the health of family and society.

But the science grew. Emotional and psychological problems were diagnosed and categorized. Treatments were developed and applied. Some churches responded by drawing up lists of Scripture texts that held God's answer to every illness, every discomfort, every crisis, every question. Many texts were linked to demons and possession. Read it, pray it, repeat it: here is your solution.

Other churches baptized a particular psychological or therapeutic approach, especially the humanistic theories focusing on the "actualizing of one's potential." Here, in these movements, the grail could be found. Weekend workshops and retreats were almost ritualized.

A more middle-of-the-road church response that developed was pastoral counseling, a specific modality of pastoral care. Pastoral counseling takes the insights of psychology and behavioral sciences, explores and understands them in the light of theology and a faith tradition, and applies them to the needs of an individual, group or community, usually in a crisis situation, with the intention of arriving at a life-giving or life-enhancing resolution. It is pastoral because it is connected to the ministry of Christ, done in the spirit of the gospel and oriented toward *metanoia* or conversion. Like spiritual direction, pastoral counseling strives to help individuals cooperate and respond to God's grace—the Holy Spirit at work in their present, particular situation. (See Underwood 1985; Blanchette 1985; Conn 1985; Wicks 1993).

Most will see a difference between pastoral counseling and spiritual direction. As I have observed, one's relationship with God, the putting on of Christ and attentiveness to the Holy Spirit in one's experience are the central elements in spiritual direction. In pastoral counseling, the focus is on presenting problems such as difficulties in a marriage, domestic violence, addictive patterns, sexual or emotional abuse, vocational discernment, grief processing and the like. This is "strategic problem-solving" in faith, using faith (Rossi 1996). While spiritual direction may also focus on the here and now, it never loses sight of the then and always.

Spiritual direction is a more timeless and continuing activity than pastoral counseling. One can almost apply Gabriel Marcel's famous insight: life is not a problem to be solved but a mystery to be lived. It might be helpful in making a distinction to view spiritual direction as falling more on the mystery side of life while pastoral counseling falls more on the problem-solving side.

Spiritual direction and pastoral counseling both build on the process of psychological development toward human maturity but take the process further than does psychotherapy. The material and goal of psychotherapy is healthy relationship with self, others and the world. The material and goal of spiritual direction and pastoral counseling is ultimately one's relationship to all the above, *plus* the relationship with God, with Christ, in the Holy Spirit. The freedom achieved in the human maturation process is used to listen and respond to God. It's a response-ability (i.e., ability to respond) in a realm broader than the simply human. The major difference between psychotherapy and spiritual direction and pastoral counseling is that the latter two bring a person in contact with a reality that is beyond the realm of mere human common sense. That reality is the Paschal Mystery of Jesus. The Christian lives within this Paschal Mystery, and a spiritual director or pastoral counselor seeks to help the person recognize that rhythm.

Table 3.1. Distinctions Between Spiritual Direction, Pastoral Counseling and Psychotherapy

Dimension	Spiritual Direction	Pastoral Counseling	Psychotherapy
Presenting Problem	Desire to make one's faith an experiential, heartfelt relationship with the Lord that will truly guide and motivate	A specific life crisis with desire for input from wisdom of Scripture and tradition	Desire to overcome some addictive/maladaptive pattern of behavior, thoughts or emotional functioning
Goals	To translate a notional faith into a felt faith, an "eyebrows-up" faith into an "eyebrows-down" faith, a faith that is woven into every aspect of this specific, unique individual	To apply wisdom from Scripture and tradition to reduce impact of crisis and improve the possibility of living more in harmony with God	To develop an understanding of what lack or loss or need the maladaptive patterns are attempting to fulfill; to develop strategies to regain control and freedom in one's life
Procedure	Take the content of one's faith and after each statement, simply ask, "What difference does it make?" or "So what?" Do this within the context of prayer, conversation with God and keeping tabs of one's feelings. Learn and practice the "examination of consciousness."	May involve skills designed to facilitate exploration of problem area and promote insight. Will guide in applying sacred wisdom. Depending on specific problem, other procedures such as grief counseling may be used.	Examine the behavior and explore the related feelings. Attend to the concrete life consequences of problem. Possible need for medical assessment and further professional consultation or treatment.
Resources	Scriptural context of the faith truths; Ignatian form of meditation on the scriptures; autobiographies of faith seekers; holistic Christian spiritual writers	Encouragement toward increased faith, church support systems; resources from spiritual direction and psychotherapy commensurate with level of training	Literature on treatment options

Jesus' teachings are filled with paradoxes, especially the central wisdom of the cross, that we must die in order to live. There is also Jesus' command to forgiveness (Mt 6:15, 18:21-22, 35)—what Philip Yancey calls an "unnatural act" (1997). Jesus also throws in the command to love one's enemies (Mt 5:43-4). These Christian basics must be grappled with in spiritual direction and pastoral counseling. They certainly are beyond the scope of most approaches to psychotherapy.

Robert Rossi captures some of the fundamental difference between spiritual direction/pastoral counseling and psychotherapy. "What the director knows about Jesus Christ, his Father and the Spirit of Jesus steadily becomes more important than what he knows about human feelings and interaction, although the two areas of knowledge will never become totally separated" (Rossi 1996:14). As you move across the spectrum—psychotherapy, pastoral counseling, spiritual direction—the importance of the work of the Trinity in a person's life generally increases. Table 3.1 may provide help by clarifying these differences.

The words of Ann Belford Ulanov and Barry Ulanov relate to pastoral counseling but apply equally to spiritual direction:

> x What is urgent is some serious recognition of just how powerful the spirit really is in our lives, to discover, for scientific reasons among others, how much human interiority wears the colors, speaks in the accents, moves in the gestures and postures of the numinous. . . . The Christ still gets born in a stable—though now it looks like a consulting room—in the muck and an obsessive complex, a dogging anxiety, the pain of realizing how much our hate and passivity have detoured us. (Ulanov and Ulanov 1985:18-19)

Although pastoral counseling began and grew primarily in Protestant churches, it has found a respected and strong place in the Catholic Church in the last several decades. Many leaders in the Catholic tradition have been diligently working to forge approaches to spiritual direction that respect the developments and discoveries in psychology and hold those findings in creative dialogue with sound biblical, ecclesial, theological and spiritual understanding of the human person. There are many respected psychology departments in leading Catholic universities and Catholic institutes and centers of psychology, spirituality and pastoral counseling.

Today anyone working in the field of spiritual direction and pastoral ministry is negligent if he or she ignores the findings of psychology, just as that same person is negligent if he or she tries to do the ministry independent of the centrality of God's Word (Schroeder and Meyers 1996).

REFERRAL TO A MENTAL HEALTH PROFESSIONAL

Catholic spiritual directors hesitate to attribute evidence of strong psychological or emotional disturbances to demonic possession. Even though Catholics have the tradition and the ministry of exorcism, this is rarely utilized. Spiritual directors today have enough wisdom or knowledge to know when the mental and emotional state and behavior of a person is beyond the director's competence and needs professional psychological help.

The following would be examples of such cases: (1) morbid anxiety without discernible cause, or out of proportion to its apparent cause, (2) painful or intolerable sadness without reasonable cause, that is, depression, (3) loss of normal adaptation, for example, a student cannot study, a mother cannot take interest in her children, (4) psychosomatic disturbances such as severe headaches, localized anesthesia, paralysis, fainting, nausea, (5) obsessive-compulsive behaviors, (6) any threat of suicide (Rossi 1996). Spiritual directors need to know mental health professionals who espouse and understand Christian spiritual values or at least are not antagonistic to them.

Catholics do not deny God can and does directly intervene at times, but we also have a strong belief in the sacramental dimension of life and believe God most often mediates his power and work. Therapists, counselors and medication are channels and instruments of God's miraculous work. They deserve acknowledgment, respect and use.

SUMMARY

Spiritual direction in the Roman Catholic Church today has been greatly influenced by the theological perspectives of Vatican II and its reemphasis on the role of the Holy Spirit in the church. Rediscovering and experiencing the charisms of the Spirit and the lay ministries that flow from these charisms have led to real changes in the ministry of spiritual direction. Once the domain of priests and religious leaders, spiritual direction is now also an area of training for laypeople. Pastoral counseling has definitely broadened the field, but when seen as identical to spiritual direction, it runs the risk of diluting the focus of spiritual direction. Recent developments seem to indicate a clarification of specific goals and objectives for each discipline or art.

There is presently a tremendous revival of this ministry in the Catholic Church. In the United States alone there are over three hundred centers established for the training of spiritual directors, and a very large number of participants are laypeople. The titles of some of these programs reflect the renewed emphasis on the role of the Holy Spirit in spiritual direction. In the archdiocese of Atlanta a formation program for spiritual direction is called Ru'ah, the Hebrew word for the Spirit, the breath of God. In Orlando a program is called Audire, which means to listen, highlighting one of the main tasks in spiritual direction—to listen and discern the Spirit at work.

The core of spiritual direction is the *experience* of God, explored in prayer. The spiritual director helps the individual discern his or her feelings during prayer and encourages the individual to bring every part of his or her life to these conversations with God. Such authentic encounters with the divine are transformative and help the seeker to "put on Christ." Pastoral counseling, while usually dealing with a specific situation, ultimately hopes to lead to the same grace conclusion.

References

Au, Wilkie. 1993. Holistic spirituality. In *New dictionary of Catholic spirituality*, ed. Michael Downey, pp. 488-91. Collegeville, Minn.: Liturgical.

Barry, William A., and William J. Connolly. 1982. *The practice of spiritual direction*. New York: Seabury.

Birmingham, Madeline, and William J. Connolly. 1994. *Witnessing to the fire*. Kansas City, Mo.: Sheed and Ward.

Blais, Madeleine. 1971a. Seeking the will of God and the permanent nurturing of one's vocation. In *Spiritual counseling*, ed. Canadian Religious Conference, pp. 22-28. Ottawa: Canadian Religious Conference.

————. 1971b. A sense of values in one's personal life. In *Spiritual counseling*, ed. Canadian Religious Conference, pp. 29-32. Ottawa: Canadian Religious Conference.

Blanchette, Melvin C. 1985. A philosophical foundation for professional and ethical issues in pastoral counseling. In *Clinical handbook of pastoral counseling*, exp. ed., ed. Robert J. Wicks, Richard D. Parsons and Donald Capps, 1:614-31. Mahwah, N.J.: Paulist.

Blastic, Michael. 1993. Franciscan spirituality. In *New dictionary of catholic spirituality*, ed. Michael Downey, pp. 408-18.

Buckley, Michael J. 1993. Discernment of spirits. In *New dictionary of Catholic spirituality*, ed. Michael Downey, pp. 274-81. Collegeville, Minn.: Liturgical.

Caligiuri, Angelo M. 1996. Spirituality and ordinary human experience. In *The Christian ministry of spiritual direction*, ed. David Fleming, pp. 12-18. St. Louis, Mo.: Review for Religious.

Carlson, Gregory. 1996. Spiritual direction and the Paschal mystery. In *The Christian ministry of spiritual direction*, ed. David Fleming, pp. 72-81. St. Louis, Mo.: Review for Religious.

Chorpenning, Joseph F. 1993. Salesian spirituality. In *New dictionary of Catholic spirituality*, ed. Michael Downey, pp. 850-54. Collegeville, Minn.: Liturgical.

Cloud of unknowing, The. 1973. New York: Doubleday-Image.

Conn, Joann Wolski. 1985. Spirituality and personal maturity. In *Clinical handbook of pastoral counseling*, exp. ed., ed. Robert J. Wicks, Richard D. Parsons and Donald Capps, 1:37-57. Mahwah, N.J.: Paulist.

Cusson, Gilles. 1971. The Christian spiritual man of today. In *Spiritual counseling*, ed. Canadian Religious Conference, pp. 40-46. Ottawa: Canadian Religious Conference.

Doyle, Charles Hugo. 1956. *Guidance in spiritual direction*. Ridgefield, Conn.: Roger A. McCaffrey.

Egan, Harvey D. 1993. Ignatian spirituality. In *New dictionary of Catholic spirituality*, ed. Michael Downey, pp. 521-29. Collegeville, Minn.: Liturgical.

Egan, Keith J. 1993. Carmelite Spirituality. In *New dictionary of Catholic spirituality*, ed. Michael Downey, pp. 117-25. Collegeville, Minn.: Liturgical.

Edwards, Tilden. 1980. *Spiritual friend.* New York: Paulist.

————. 2001. *Spiritual director, spiritual companion.* New York: Paulist.

Empereur, James. 1997. *The enneagram and spiritual direction.* New York: Continuum.

Flannery, Austin, ed. 1992. *Vatican Council II: The conciliar and post conciliar documents,* vol. 1. Grand Rapids, Mich.: Eerdmans.

Fleming, David L. 1993a. Reconciliation and spiritual direction. In *New dictionary of Catholic spirituality,* ed. Michael Downey, pp. 1037-39. Collegeville, Minn.: Liturgical.

————. 1993b. Spiritual direction and liturgy. In *New dictionary of Catholic spirituality,* ed. Michael Downey, pp. 1220-24. Collegeville, Minn.: Liturgical.

Fleming, David. 1996a. Models of spiritual direction. In *The Christian ministry of spiritual direction,* ed. David Fleming, pp. 106-12. St. Louis, Mo.: Review for Religious.

————. 1996b. Spiritual direction: Charism and ministry. In *The Christian ministry of spiritual direction,* ed. David Fleming, pp. 3-9. St. Louis, Mo.: Review for Religious.

Fortier, William. 1993. American spirituality. In *New dictionary of Catholic spirituality,* ed. Michael Downey, pp. 34-38. Collegeville, Minn.: Liturgical.

Francis de Sales. 1962. *Treatise on the love of God.* Trans. Henry B. Mackey. Westminster, Md.: Newman.

————. 1972. *Introduction to the devout life.* Trans. John K. Ryan. New York: Doubleday-Image.

Ganss, George E. 1993. Discretion. In *New dictionary of Catholic spirituality,* ed. Michael Downey, pp. 284-85. Collegeville, Minn.: Liturgical.

Glendon, Lowell M. 1993. French school of spirituality. In *New dictionary of Catholic spirituality,* ed. Michael Downey, pp. 420-23. Collegeville, Minn.: Liturgical.

Goldbrunner, Josef. 1964. *Holiness is wholeness and other essays.* Notre Dame, Ind.: University of Notre Dame Press.

Gratton, Carolyn. 1993. Spiritual Direction. In *New dictionary of Catholic spirituality,* ed. Michael Downey, pp. 911-17. Collegeville, Minn.: Liturgical.

Groeschel, Benedict. 1980. *Spiritual passages: The psychology of spiritual development.* New York: Crossroad.

Hilton, Walter. 1979. *The stairway of perfection.* Garden City, N.Y.: Image.

Hunter, David. 1993. Patristic spirituality. In *New dictionary of Catholic spirituality,* ed. Michael Downey, pp. 723-32. Collegeville, Minn.: Liturgical.

Ignatius of Loyola. 1951. *The spiritual exercises of St. Ignatius.* Trans. Louis J. Puhl. Chicago: Loyola University Press.

Jette, Fernand. 1971. Spiritual direction today. In *Spiritual counseling,* ed. Canadian Religious Conference, pp. 5-13. Ottawa: Canadian Religious Conference.

John of the Cross. 1991. *Collected works.* Trans. Kieran Kavanaugh, ed. Otilio Rodriguez. Washington, D.C.: Institute of Carmelite Studies.

Julian of Norwich. 1978. *Showings*. In *The classics of Western spirituality*. Trans. Edmund Colledge. New York: Paulist.

Kardong, Terrence G. 1993. Benedictine Spirituality. In *New dictionary of Catholic spirituality*, ed. Michael Downey, pp. 84-91. Collegeville, Minn.: Liturgical.

Kinerk, Edward. 1996. Toward a method for the study of spirituality. In *The Christian ministry of spiritual direction*, ed. David Fleming, pp. 19-35. St. Louis, Mo.: Review for Religious.

Komonchak, Joseph A., Mary Collins and Dermont A. Lane, eds. 1991. *The new dictionary of theology*. Collegeville, Minn.: Liturgical.

Leech, Kenneth. 2001. *Soul friend: An invitation to spiritual direction*. Harrisburg, Penn.: Morehouse.

Lonergan, Bernard. 1972. *Method in theology*. New York: Herder and Herder.

May, Gerald. 1982. *Care of mind, care of spirit*. New York: Harper & Row.

McBrien, Richard P. 1994. *Catholicism*. San Francisco: HarperSanFrancisco.

McCready, James. 1996. Spiritual direction as pilgrim and companion. In *The Christian ministry of spiritual direction*, ed. David Fleming, pp. 113-21. St. Louis, Mo.: Review for Religious.

McDowell, Alice. 1996. The three dimensions of spiritual direction. In *The Christian ministry of spiritual direction*, ed. David Fleming, pp. 95-105. St. Louis, Mo.: Review for Religious.

Merton, Thomas. 1960. *Spiritual direction and meditation*. Collegeville, Minn.: Liturgical.

Milligan, Mary. 1993. Apostolic spirituality. In *New dictionary of Catholic spirituality*, ed. Michael Downey, pp. 51-56. Collegeville, Minn.: Liturgical.

Muto, Susan. 2000. *Catholic spirituality from A to Z*. Ann Arbor, Mich.: Servant.

Neuman, Matthias. 1996. Am I growing spiritually? In *The Christian ministry of spiritual direction*, ed. David Fleming, pp. 36-47. St. Louis, Mo.: Review for Religious.

Nuth, Joan M. 1993. English Mystical Tradition. In *New dictionary of Catholic spirituality*, ed. Michael Downey, pp. 337-47. Collegeville, Minn.: Liturgical.

Pennington, Basil. 1993. Monastic Spirituality. In *New dictionary of Catholic spirituality*, ed. Michael Downey, pp. 665-70. Collegeville, Minn.: Liturgical.

Principe, Walter. 1993. Spirituality, Christian. In *New dictionary of Catholic spirituality*, ed. Michael Downey, pp. 931-38. Collegeville, Minn.: Liturgical.

Rossi, Robert. 1996. The distinction between psychological and religious counseling. In *The Christian ministry of spiritual direction*, ed. David Fleming, pp. 123-47. St. Louis, Mo.: Review for Religious.

Ruffing, Janet K. 2000. *Spiritual direction: Beyond the beginnings*. New York: Paulist.

Russell, Kenneth. 1993a. Anglo-Catholic spirituality. In *New dictionary of Catholic spirituality*, ed. Michael Downey, pp. 41-45. Collegeville, Minn.: Liturgical.

―――. 1993b. Ascetical theology. In *New dictionary of Catholic spirituality*, ed. Michael Downey, p. 638. Collegeville, Minn.: Liturgical.

―――. 1993c. Asceticism. In *New dictionary of Catholic spirituality*, ed. Michael Downey, pp. 63-65. Collegeville, Minn.: Liturgical.

Schroeder, Frederich, and Craig Meyers. 1996. *Spiritual direction for today's Catholics.* New Jersey: Catholic Book.

Sheet, John R. 1996. Spiritual direction in the church. In *The Christian ministry of spiritual direction,* ed. David Fleming, pp. 54-71. St. Louis, Mo.: Review for Religious.

St. Michel, Vianney. 1971. Of values and mentalities. In *Spiritual counseling,* ed. Canadian Religious Conference, pp. 33-39. Ottawa: Canadian Religious Conference.

Stinissen, Wilfred. 1999. *The gift of spiritual direction.* Liguori, Mo.: Liguori.

Studzinski, Raymond. 1993. Feelings. In *New dictionary of Catholic spirituality,* ed. Michael Downey, pp. 392-94. Collegeville, Minn.: Liturgical.

Teresa of Ávila. 1980. *The collected works.* Trans. Kieran Kavanaugh, ed. Otilio Rodriguez. Washington, D.C.: Institute of Carmelite Studies.

Thomas à Kempis. 1989. *The imitation of Christ.* Notre Dame, Ind.: Ave Maria.

Tickerhoof, Bernard. 1991. *Conversion and the enneagram.* Denville, N.J.: Dimension.

Ulanov, Ann Belford, and Barry Ulanov. 1993. Reaching to the unknown: Religion and the psyche. In *Clinical handbook of pastoral counseling,* exp. ed., ed. Robert J. Wicks, Richard D. Parsons and Donald Capps, 2:7-26. Mahwah, N.J.: Paulist.

Underwood, Ralph. 1985. Pastoral counseling in the parish setting. In *Clinical handbook of pastoral counseling,* exp. ed., ed. Robert J. Wicks, Richard D. Parsons and Donald Capps, 1:332-48. Mahwah, N.J.: Paulist.

Wallace, Frank. 1996. Spiritual direction. In *The Christian ministry of spiritual direction,* ed. David Fleming, pp. 82-94. St. Louis, Mo.: Review for Religious.

Wicks, Robert J. 1993. Introduction. In *Clinical handbook of pastoral counseling,* exp. ed., ed. Robert J. Wicks, Richard D. Parsons and Donald Capps, 2:1-3. Mahwah, N.J.: Paulist.

Woods, Richard. 1993. Spirituality, Christian (Catholic), history of. In *New dictionary of Catholic spirituality,* ed. Michael Downey, pp. 938-46. Collegeville, Minn.: Liturgical.

Yancey, Philip. 1997. *What's So Amazing About Grace?* Grand Rapids, Mich.: Zondervan.

Zawilla, Ronald J. 1993. Dominican spirituality. In *New dictionary of Catholic spirituality,* ed. Michael Downey, pp. 286-94. Collegeville, Minn.: Liturgical.

4

SPIRITUAL DIRECTION IN THE EPISCOPAL TRADITION

Gray Temple

Spiritual direction as an expectation of ordained pastors goes back to the very beginnings of Anglicanism. The traditional wording of the service used for several centuries for the ordination of persons to the priesthood contained the following description of a priest's duties:

> Ye have heard, Brethren, as well in your private examination, as in the exhortation which was now made to you, and in the holy Lessons taken out of the Gospel, and the writings of the Apostles, of what dignity, and of how great importance this Office is, whereunto ye are called. And now again we exhort you, in the Name of our Lord Jesus Christ, that ye have in remembrance, into how high a Dignity, and to how weighty an Office and Charge ye are called: that is to say, to be Messengers, Watchmen, and Stewards of the Lord; *to teach, and to premonish,* to feed and provide for the Lord's family; to seek for Christ's sheep that are dispersed abroad, and for his children who are in the midst of this naughty world, that they may be saved through Christ forever.
>
> . . . Wherefore consider with yourselves the end of the Ministry towards the children of God, towards the Spouse and Body of Christ; and see that ye never cease your labour, your care and diligence, until ye have done all that lieth in you, according to your bounden duty, *to bring all such as are or shall be committed to your charge, unto that agreement in the faith and knowledge of God, and to that ripeness and perfectness of age in Christ,* that there be no place left among you, either for error in religion, or for viciousness in life. (Book of Common Prayer 1928, italics added)

The ministry of spiritual direction is implicit all through this service.

Bishop Jeremy Taylor in *A Letter to a Person Newly Converted to the Church of England* unselfconsciously assumed the role of spiritual director: "Pray frequently and effectually; I had rather your prayers should be often than long" (quoted in More and Cross 1951:615). He assumed it as his duty, not thinking to ask permission.

The last century has added several important contributions to spiritual direction, some of which I shall detail. Recent developments include the inclusion of qualified laypersons as spiritual directors. Negotiation of the boundaries between spiritual direction, pastoral counsel and psychotherapy has received much recent attention. Feminism has had a discernible and salutary impact on spiritual direction in the Episcopal Church, especially as clients are encouraged to examine their own needs to dominate or be dominated by others. The reapprehension of Celtic spirituality among Episcopalians has been a merry recent development, occasionally skirting the neighborhood of the much-maligned heresiarch Pelagius (late fourth to early fifth centuries). The expression of our love of Christ in service to others and in care for the earth has come in for much recent emphasis. This evolution has added flavor to an Anglican tradition previously distinguished by its instructional component, chiefly in the practices of prayer.

DEFINITION OF SPIRITUAL DIRECTION

In the Episcopal Church, spiritual direction is a purposeful, disciplined relationship between two (sometimes more) Christians. It aims to help one or both participants identify and cultivate practices that link their individual lives to God. Spiritual direction could be thought of as the next step after evangelism. That is, once a soul enjoys an experience of the saving grace of God in Jesus Christ, that soul must pursue spiritual growth. A previously worldly soul must become holy. Spiritual direction assists a soul in pursuing holiness.

Growth in holiness can be helpfully compared to art. They have various elements in common.

Each requires honest, courageous self-disclosure. Self-protection makes for second-rate art. Self-deception is self-protection's spiritual equivalent, and it cancels spiritual growth utterly. Self-protection in art keeps the would-be artist cautious and imitative. Self-deception while attempting spiritual growth inclines the soul to pat answers and shallow understandings of the human condition. Spiritual directors keep us honest—or try to. A wise spiritual director can spot the difference between mere earnestness and actual honesty—and knows that legalism serves our fear of the abyss more than our love of God.

Each requires submission to tutelage. Few artists advance without submitting their work to the critical scrutiny of superior artists. This is agonizing but necessary. The growing artist needs to be able to view her own work objectively, as though it were the work of another. Likewise, the soul attempting spiritual growth must embrace her own *ordinariness* before her uniqueness can hope to emerge. There are spiritual directors who know God's ways and the "devices and desires of our . . . hearts" better than we do. We get "honest to God" faster in their company. It assists our spiritual growth to have another objectively view it with us. A spiritual director likely knows as much about different approaches to prayer as an art teacher would know about different approaches to, say, pigmentation.

Each requires struggling over a hump of tedium. Anyone who has ever struggled with a painting, a sculpture, a piece of music or a poem knows the point at which the original vision is no longer accessible or exciting. At such times one is tempted to walk away from the creative work in disgust or even to destroy it. A fellow artist can often "recall us to our first love," artistically speaking. The same tedium occasionally sets into our life with Jesus Christ. We get assaulted with periods not just of lassitude but also of actual disgust. The assault has other sources than simply the devil and is more complex than the simple fruit of sin. Our relationship with Jesus is a human relationship just like our marriage—which, in the normal course of things, goes through peaks and valleys. A wise spiritual director understands the dynamics of a complex relationship at a depth beyond mere deviltry or human badness. Such a director, for example, might discern that a soul's sense of being repelled or bored by Jesus likely reflects panic in the face of our Lord's growing importance in her life. If we are to clear the hump of tedium that occasionally blocks the spiritual pilgrimage, it is enormously helpful to enjoy (or be made to tolerate) the company of those who have mapped such humps in their own and others' lives.

Each leaves us feeling larger, freshly born. An authentic artistic achievement leaves our powers of perception and discernment across the whole of life greatly enhanced. It washes away our competitiveness with other artists and confers a sense of collegiality with erstwhile rivals. In the same way, the fruit of the Spirit is "love, joy, peace . . ." (Gal 5:22-23). It offers us joy and peace even in the midst of turmoil; it leaves us humbly self-accepting and accepting of others. Again, spiritual direction can help us focus this internal phenomenon at points where we might hesitate to trust its reality.

Each conveys life and hope to others. An authentic work of art stretches and deepens the way we, the recipients, perceive the world around us. The presence in our life of an authentic saint has much the same transforming power. A saint can be understood as one who has survived self-disclosure, the tutelage of superior critics, the tedium of relational intensity and frustration, the terror of rebirth. There are few Kierkegaards among us, capable of achieving sanctity in isolation from spiritual community. Most of us need incisive fellowship. Spiritual direction is one of the most intense forms of fellowship available to us. It is not for sissies.

Spiritual direction usually takes the form of periodic meetings. These can resemble the periodicity of pastoral counseling—perhaps hourly sessions with the director in an office—or they could consist of retreats together for a stretch of days. If we but knew, probably much spiritual direction takes place these days by e-mail; that would not have surprised Baron Friedrich von Hügel or Evelyn Underhill, who often used the postal service.

Components of a typical session can include sacramental confession; review of a spiritual journal or dream journal; the formation, monitoring and adjustment of a "rule of life"; instruction in and practice of different forms of prayer; suggesting and directing a course of spiritual reading; and informal conversation in which the directee is encouraged to share her or his story with the director, linking that story with the gospel story. It can occur as a one-to-one relationship or in a group devoted to the purpose.

There is a strong instructional component to spiritual direction in the Episcopal Church. Many of our members came into the church trailing images and notions of God sufficient to provoke nightmares, images inculcated when they were children in more restrictive church settings. It is difficult to love a god whom you fear and resent. So a director will likely spend time up front introducing the directee to the God of Jesus Christ.

Many people entering the Episcopal Church have no notion of the richness and variety of the life of prayer; their images of prayer may be confined to talking at God, with no experience of *listening*. For many the Bible, if it is known at all, is simply the compendium of Christian belief and morals; they bring no notion of the Bible as a launching pad for intimate prayer.

So a director must be a teacher. That teaching can take the form of supervising a directee's readings in the area of prayer. Or it can take the form of coaching or modeling various methods of prayer.

Some practitioners of spiritual direction in the Episcopal Church would object to my use of the terms *direction* and *director*. They would argue (effectively) that the most nourishing spiritual engagement between two Christians is companionate and authoritatively "horizontal." "There is a ladder of spiritual maturity," a friend once told me, "and on it we each occupy a separate rung; that ladder is stretched *flat on the ground* before God."

Others would report great fruit from a more traditional relationship, vertical and semi-professional in nature. In the Episcopal Church, you are as likely to find one as the other—and if you have an initial preference, you'd be wise to ask in advance.

This polarity reflects the close relationship between spiritual pursuit and psychotherapy within the Episcopal Church. The nondirective counseling methods associated with Carl Rogers made their way into our discussions of spiritual guidance in the 1950s and 1960s and for more than a decade virtually amounted to a fad. This contrasted strongly with the previous stereotypic image of the stern, high-collared priest assigning spiritual homework from behind a desk. As could have been predicted, the discussion has proved pendular; today Episcopal spiritual mentors tend to seek a characteristically Anglican middle way between the two extremes.

Like the scribe trained in the kingdom of God (Mt 13:52), a director in the Episcopal Church will share with you treasures both old and new—as old as the Scriptures, as new as (perhaps) current brain research. Though spiritual directors distinguish what they do from psychotherapy, some wear both hats on different occasions, and most are familiar with psychotherapy, either as therapists or as consumers. Directors are expected to be sufficiently clinically astute to recognize psychopathology when it rears its head and to refer the sufferer to a qualified clinician.

HISTORY OF SPIRITUAL DIRECTION IN THE EPISCOPAL CHURCH

Spiritual direction in the Episcopal Church benefits from several tributaries. If Episcopal spiritual direction has a primary foundation, it would likely be the Books of Common Prayer. The present Prayer Book (1979) used by Episcopalians is the eleventh since the first edition of 1549. All editions of the Prayer Book share in common the sacraments (expressed in timeless Tudor English in some cases), the Daily Office (devotional services focused on Scripture reading, derived from the monastic Hours), the Psalter, Pastoral Offices (e.g., Ministry to the Sick), the Episcopal Offices (e.g., Ordination), wonderfully worded prayers and thanksgivings for all occasions, catechisms and historical documents (e.g., the Athanasian Creed, the Thirty-nine Articles of Religion). One primary task of any Episcopal spiritual director is to acquaint directees with the riches the Prayer Book offers.

As a branch of the Catholic Church independent of Rome since the Reformation, with our own monastic tradition alive and well, the Episcopal Church draws on the treasures of traditional Catholic spiritual practices. It should not surprise you to find an Episcopal director who is intimately familiar with, say, Ignatian spirituality. Many of us are deeply fond of St. Francis de Sales, whose *Introduction to the Devout Life* (translated 2000) was written to a laywoman encouraging her to find in her "secular" life materials for sanctification equal to those found in convents. This is a project richly descriptive of what many of us understand spiritual direction's goals to be. On a director's bookshelves do not be surprised to find Teresa of Ávila, John of the Cross, *The Cloud of Unknowing* (fourteenth century), Brother Lawrence's *Practice of the Presence of God* (translated 1958), and any and all of the great spiritual classics. It is not only feminists who treasure Julian of Norwich. There are distinctly Episcopal forms and applications of the Rosary which some of our directors can teach you.

Spiritual direction was part of the armamentarium of the Anglican priest/pastor from the very beginning. The so-called Anglican Divines, including the poet/priests John Donne (1571-1631) and George Herbert (1593-1633), theological writers of the sixteenth and seventeenth centuries when we had first separated from obedience to Rome whose writings helped Anglicanism find its voice, took the ministry of spiritual direction as a matter of course and left us much that we still use today. Anglicanism from the beginning had its own distinct *Seelsorge*[1] tradition. Indeed all of the successive Books of Common Prayer from 1549 to 1979 have been crafted to shape individuals and families in their life of personal prayer as well as large congregations.

As the Church of England separated from the oversight of the Roman pope during the Reformation, it contained two distinct parties of thought and practice. The High Church tended to stress the church's abiding catholic essence in worship, church order, practice and doctrine. Doctrinally, the High Church party tends to concentrate on the mystery of the incarnation. The Low Church party (from which eventually grew the Puritans) gratefully appropriated all it could from the continental Reformation, especially from Geneva. Doctrinally, the Low Church party tends to concentrate on the mystery of the atonement. These two emphases can be felt among us to this day, even in the ways spiritual direction is practiced. Incarnational spiritual direction tends toward meditation and contemplation, an appreciative, nonjudgmental posture toward life. Atonement-based spiritual direction concentrates on getting one's life in order.

A robust expression of the Episcopal Church/Anglican Communion goes by the name Anglo-Catholicism, born of the Oxford Movement in nineteenth-century England. Both spiritual direction and monasticism have always been familiar elements of this sector of our church. Anglo-Catholicism forms the foundational substrate of spiritual direction in the Episcopal Church.

In England—though not, regrettably, in America—the evangelical (Low Church) wing of the church made distinct contributions to the practice and theory of spiritual direction. One thinks of the Wesleys in this connection, for example. Evangelicals have been Anglicanism's most robust foreign missionaries, an outgrowth of their concern that humanity be reconciled to God.

In the early 1980s spiritual direction achieved academic expression in the Episcopal Church as Alan Jones established the Center for Christian Spirituality at the General Seminary in New York. The center's example was quickly copied by our other theological schools.

During the 1970s and 1980s the spiritual life of people in the pews was deeply

---

[1]*Seelsorge* is the "care of souls"—a separate academic discipline in Continental theological curricula.

enriched by the importation of the Cursillo movement into the Episcopal Church from Roman Catholicism. Thousands of Episcopalians returned to their parishes from life-changing weekends to ask their rectors, "What's this 'spiritual direction' thing all about?"

Oddly, the charismatic movement in the Episcopal Church has had no detectable impact on the practice of spiritual direction. Though charismatic influences are visible in a more flexible approach to worship and more energy for evangelism and are audible in recent hymnody, the movement has not shaped the average director's approach to spiritual growth.

There are likely two reasons for this neglect. The first is that the charismatic movement (for reasons I don't entirely understand) gravitates toward an uncritical embrace of premodern theological and hermeneutic epistemologies. Consequently the movement has produced no theology or biblical scholarship worth the name. (The one happy exception, in my opinion, is Suurmond 1994.) Episcopalians tend to think that trying to live in a mental frame of reference from several centuries back is bad for you. Spiritual maturity involves making some sort of treaty with present-day reality, including cultivating the ability to discern the presence of God within our own intellectual terms.

Second, Episcopalians tend to think of the Rock of our Salvation as sedimentary, not igneous. Ask an Episcopalian when she was saved, and she will likely reply, "Two thousand years ago." Dramatic experiences of conversion are notoriously difficult to maintain. (For a full discussion of this difficulty, see Temple 2001.) Any number of classical spiritual writers warn us against reposing too much consolation in dramatic spiritual breakthroughs. Episcopal spiritual directors think of mature spirituality as within the grasp of all, not just the "reborn." So there is a suspicion toward and bias against dramatic spiritual conversion experiences.

I personally view that lacuna as regrettable. For all of its frivolity, the charismatic movement developed some of the best and fastest "connectivity software" we possess for launching an intense relationship with God. And our people find their way to it without our tutelage. We would do well to know what they are excited about when they report those experiences to us. A fair amount of miscommunication gets reported back from freshly "born again" Episcopalians who bounce off their attempts to get spiritual direction.

Another important tributary into the practice of spiritual direction in the Episcopal Church has been psychotherapy. This combination of medical practice and pastoral care found a home among Episcopalians decades earlier than among more conservative denominations. That psychotherapy plays a proper role in anyone's personal growth is an accepted notion among us. Familiarity with psychothera-

---

Two helpful books from the Anglican tradition

F. P. Harton's, *The Elements of the Spiritual Life* (1950) is an Anglo-Catholic classic. Though some find its categories precious, it is as full a compendium of the classical spiritual wisdom of the Western Catholic tradition as I know.

I'd also recommend *A History of Christian Spirituality* (1980) by my old friend the late Urban T. Holmes III. Terry, as his friends and students called him, exemplified as well as presented much that Episcopalians are most proud of in our spiritual tradition. In that little book you will engage a mind that took our life with God utterly seriously, from a platform of deep knowledge of the human psyche.

---

peutic vocabulary and procedures among Episcopalians is not so much a professional qualification as a cultural expectation.

It should be mentioned here that many Episcopalians find the psychology of C. G. Jung to be especially attractive. The Episcopal Church embraces among its members any number of skillful lay analysts whose attraction to Jung expresses the same interest others confine to spiritual direction. An Episcopal spiritual director is likely quite familiar with the Myers-Briggs Personality Type Indicator (or at least the Keirsey-Bates version) and will be able to bring it fruitfully to bear on the task of spiritual self-cataloging. Morton Kelsey's name towers over this emphasis in the Episcopal Church, but one could mention John Sanford as well.

Some of our most distinguished spiritual directors—notably Tilden Edwards, the founder of the Shalem Institute—came to their current modes of practice through lengthy periods of study in Asian spiritual traditions. The Sufi tradition within Islam has enriched the direction of some, while Zen is evident as an element in others' offerings. There are Episcopal directors who find the Kabbalah a nourishing resource. Taoist receptive, nonresistant sensibilities readily find a home in some courses of direction.

That Asian ascetical practices should enrich Christian spirituality ought not to surprise us. There is evidence of yogalike practices in early Eastern Orthodox hesychastic monasticism. In fact, a friend once explained to me something I have not been able to substantiate otherwise—so take this next suggestion *cum grano salis,* with a grain of salt. He reported that yoga was carried through India into China by Nestorian Christian missionaries on the way to the imperial court in the fifth century C.E. He went on to say that there is little evidence of these practices in Asia prior to the fifth century. That would mean that some of the practices that we associate with Buddhism and Hinduism have Christian roots, and recently the Asians have returned the favor.

Of course not all of the Asian contributions to Episcopal spiritual direction have come from heterodox religions. Some Episcopal spiritual directors cherish the Greek Orthodox *Philokalia* and the Russian Orthodox "Prayer of the Heart" or "breath prayer." When I was just starting out, my director gave me Anthony Bloom's *Beginning to Pray* (1970), a Russian Orthodox treasure.

I should acknowledge that spiritual direction has had its coldest reception in the American Episcopal Church within our Low Church evangelical sector. This tension is more American and Australian than, say, British. Evangelicalism is a positive force within the Church of England, both for spirituality and for social justice, whose root system reaches back to our very Reformation beginnings. English evangelicals are at the spiritual direction table alongside their Anglo-Catholic colleagues, just as they work shoulder to shoulder in the slums. Unhappily that has not been the case in the United States. Why?

The reason goes deeper than the simple partisan tension that has always been present between evangelicals and Anglo-Catholics in the Episcopal Church. Evangelicalism in North America tends to be distinctly Calvinist, sometimes even blurring into fundamentalism. Consequently Episcopal (American) evangelicalism attributes ultimate importance to Christ's atoning work on the cross by which we are justified before God. Approaching God by cultivating our mystical proclivities appears to them to bypass the cross, as though a sinful human being could achieve intimacy with God simply by strenuous self-refinement. Jonathan Edwards (with whose theology many evangelical Episcopalians are in agreement) warned against being misled by visions and emotional raptures in his (splendid) treatise on the religious affections (see Edwards 1997). Spiritual direction can appear to be a flirtation with that danger.

The Anglo-Catholic response to that objection tends to take two forms. First, the High Church party (Anglo-Catholics) would make the following theological assertion. The atonement is already a present reality in the beginning of creation; paraphrasing Athanasius, "There was never a time when the Word was not," they would maintain, "There was never a time when *the atonement* was not." That is, the cross does not so much effect the atonement as call it into clear focus to be grasped gratefully. Among Anglo-Catholics and even the Broad Church party (the group in the middle between Anglo-Catholics and evangelicals), the incarnation subsumes the atonement within itself. Second, advocates of spiritual direction would argue from personal experience that the hard work of sanctification does not bypass the cross; indeed, the strenuousness of the effort lies in its requirement that we embrace the cross tightly.

Let me also mention that spiritual direction has had a most difficult time in its dealing with classically liberal Episcopalians. The latter have viewed it as suspiciously otherworldly and consequently evasive of the demands of here-and-now justice.

Against that suspicion, our spiritual direction community would maintain (and, at best, demonstrate) that a sacrificial devotion to justice, especially for the poor, is an indispensable element of any nourishing "rule of life." Justice is the *fruit* of piety, not its rival.

THE PROCESS OF AUTHENTIC TRANSFORMATION

What transforms a directee? How does growth in holiness happen? By the operation of the Holy Spirit, surely. Yet that truth by itself is not a complete answer. We know the wind only by its effect on the leaves, the dust, the temperature of our skins. We know the presence of Spirit only within our flesh. If there is a single factor that makes spiritual direction effective as a change agency for the soul, it is this: spiritual direction *holds our shame at bay* long enough for us to see ourselves as God sees us in Christ.

We would not be so prone to self-deception if we did not hope by that means to avoid shame. The director can serve as a virtual sacrament of God's own presence by receiving a directee's most anxious (or indeed appalling) disclosures without betraying disgust, thus requiring that the directee apply our Lord's command "Judge not" to herself. The fruit is a more candid self-confrontation and consequently speedier spiritual growth.

That dikelike function against the tsunami force of personal shame takes various forms in Episcopal spiritual direction. The regular practice of sacramental confession (the sacrament of penance or reconciliation) gradually transforms its practitioner.

My first confession feels as if it will be the worst. That's when I finally dump all the stuff I'm most deeply ashamed of in front of God and another human being and encounter mercy, understanding and forgiveness. The one that feels best is the second time I confess formally. I've not had time since the last confession to get into much spectacular mischief, so this time my sin list is subtler, more discerning, more "spiritual." Again I meet mercy, understanding and pardon. My third, fourth and fifth are actually the worst—because each of them is identical to the second. I am not making any progress; I know it, my confessor knows it, God knows it.

And yet I meet mercy, understanding and forgiveness no matter how often I confess the same tired stuff. It finally occurs to me that I cannot wear out God's mercy; I can't even wear out my confessor's patience. My daily life begins to feel subtly different. I realize that at every moment I am both coming from being forgiven and walking toward it. And remarkably, I gossip less; I abandon resentments faster; I put up with and enjoy those around me with growing discernment. I change.

Or growth in holiness may occur as I tell my life's story in detail to one who listens without judging—one who is *for* me. As I love my director and trust her judgment, I come to sense the possibility of being personally lovable. All of us at some time harbor the fear that if we become known accurately, we will be abandoned. Spiritual direction proves that fear false.

Or it may occur as I discover that I am not a contemplative apophatic[2] spiritual type, that mere garden-variety vocal prayer works best for me, not wordless images embraced in hesychastic[3] stillness! How humiliating. Until my director points out that Jesus' own prayers were kataphatic[4] (talkative) and self-referential.

In some form or another, that discovery will occur—and I will change. God's own acceptance of me, sacramentalized in my director/companion, will relax something deeply within me. And as Bernard of Clairvaux predicted, my period of lengthy purgation gives over to a period of lengthy illumination and service to God and my fellows—with the promise of a limitless unity with God and all creation awaiting fulfillment.

At this point in the process an Episcopal director may offer an advantage not always found in other denominations. That is, an Episcopalian is slightly less likely to impose a one-size-fits-all sin-based doctrine of humanity on you. Real spiritual direction takes you deeper than guilt-inducing revivalism, because the consolations of God go even deeper than the relief of forgiveness. God's love has other operations—even profounder operations—than forgiveness alone.

When our notion of God is confined to the nightmarish enraged Parent so many pretend to love, it is difficult to imagine God's love as other than barely tolerant pardon for ourselves and apparent favoritism toward others. But when we meet the God and Father of Jesus Christ, God's love emerges as a kaleidoscope of wonderful, merry and different operations. And your sin, while real, proves not to be the most important or interesting thing about you. At least as important as being forgiven by God is having God explain you to yourself.

The discovery that God is willing to employ your service *before* you have achieved moral or spiritual perfection results in a rapture superior to the relief of being pardoned. Incarnation-based theology and spirituality are more likely to take you to those depths, heights and breadths—where real change takes place—than theology or spirituality confined to the atonement alone.[5]

---

[2]This term refers to methods of prayer and spirituality that do not rely on words or images to apprehend divine truth or that reject them altogether. I believe that if you distinguish between meditation and contemplation, the latter tends toward apophaticism.

[3]A form of monasticism rooted in practices that involve stillness and the attempt to contemplate divine uncreated light. The term comes from the Greek *hesychos,* which means "quiet."

[4]Kataphatic prayer and spirituality repose more confidence in words and images, vocal prayers, prayer books and the like, and find creeds and doctrines helpful supplements to the life of prayer.

[5]For a fuller discussion of that comparison, see Temple (2001).

THE ROLE OF THE SPIRITUAL DIRECTOR

There is disagreement in Episcopal circles about the correct nomenclature—and, by extension, the proper or most helpful relationship—for spiritual direction. There is a strong current of opinion in favor of a peer relationship and a companionate process. As noted above, this sensibility was at one time focused in the therapeutic procedures of Carl Rogers. Promoting oneself as a "director" can sound like a bumptious power trip. My own observation is that there are two types of Episcopalian likely to introduce themselves with the title *director.* One would, of course, be a nervous beginner whose self-consciousness and fear of failure benefit from any prop he can grab. The other has been at it so long that she's learned that spiritual direction is not much affected by what you call it—and that, finally, titles don't matter much.

The companionate "spiritual friend" exponents certainly have a point: our equal preciousness before God. It is quite moving to have a respected figure whom we would expect to assume power over us demit that power in order to seek intimacy with us. Yet that point can lead to a category confusion: equal preciousness to God may not always be the same thing as equal experience in the life of the Spirit. Consulting an obvious superior can save time. Disingenuousness and false modesty waste time. I have myself sometimes refused the term *director,* insisting on being known as "companion," at points when I had not yet mastered impulses toward power-striving and competitiveness which I wished to mask. On those occasions my insistence on a companionate model did not signal superiority to another director who was clearer about the value of what she could teach.

The distinction between the directing and the companionate models also pertains to what might be called "air time." In a classical direction, the directee gets the full attention of the director at all times. In companionate relationships, the seeker gets less than full attention. It takes considerable maturity on the part of both parties to assign the proportions comfortably. The director who decides he's really a "companion" may confuse elements of his own life with the gospel—and share those elements at resentable length.

INDICATORS OF SPIRITUAL MATURITY

How do we recognize mature spirituality in the Episcopal Church? I don't know that our discernment differs greatly from that of other denominations. Most devout Christians, confronted with worldly versions of "spirituality" (deliberately separate from churches) which concentrate primarily on self-love and self-refinement, understand the underlying truth shrouded in such an approach. Our Lord, after all, did say to love your neighbor as yourself—a dubious commandment if we despise ourselves. Devout Christians also detect the limitation of these "secular" approaches: their avoidance of personal sacrifice, their evasion of the command to take up our own cross on behalf of others, and their occasionally casual approach to personal morality. There are popular forms of spirituality which (inadvertently, we hope) traffic in moral "free lunches"—permission to despise people who do not share our anguish over, say, the environment or the consumption of meat.

Authentic spiritual maturity shares this in common with psychological maturity: both involve and require the endurance of discomfort in the service of growth. Again, I think something like that understanding of spiritual maturity will be found in any of the traditions represented in this journal.

Rather than offer a necessarily incomplete analysis of spiritual maturity (pretentious on my part, at any rate), let me suggest what is obvious. We have the human pattern of spiritual maturity in Jesus Christ. To the extent that our lives come to resemble his, to the extent that our kinship with him becomes more conspicuous, to that extent we are spiritually mature.

But again, though that's clearly the right answer, it's hardly that simple. What complicates our looking to Jesus as the model of spiritual maturity is the thick overlay of distorted images and teachings about Jesus that cloak his humanity. To grasp him as the Gospels present him, we have to acknowledge his occasional outbursts of anger, his occasional rudeness, his evident delight in flouting respectability when it collided with righteousness. All of those individual characteristics flowed from the fact that Jesus had somehow got his death over with a long time before he faced Golgotha. So Jesus could speak to us about the necessity of death to self: death to the world and to our status within it.

Jesus was not able to accomplish any of that until the Spirit of God clearly persuaded him that God loved him. It follows that we can't, either. Until we encounter grace in its inexhaustible totality, we dare not contemplate death to ourselves, to the world, to anything at all. Only when I know God loves my life can I think of risking it, of clutching it more loosely. Incarnation-based spiritual directors agree with the four Gospels that the actual *life* of Jesus is at least as important and interesting as his death.

If that is true, growth into spiritual maturity takes time—lots of it. I commented earlier on the gradual impact of the director's (and by extension, God's) love and acceptance on our ability to "accept acceptance" (in Paul Tillich's haunting phrase). For many of us, reaching such a state feels like the goal. How can we begin to embrace the realization that achieving this goal is, quite literally, the *beginning* of our real spiritual journey? The least we can say is "Give it time—lots of time."

A director once told me, "If you want a friendship with somebody that feels like you've been friends for twenty years, invest twenty years in it." To expect less from the one who calls us "no longer servants, but friends" imposes a naive consumerist mentality onto God. We see little evidence that God feels obliged to quote us such a low price.

CONTRAST WITH TRADITIONAL PSYCHOTHERAPY AND PASTORAL COUNSELING

It is difficult to know how to contrast spiritual direction with traditional psychotherapy. The problem is that psychotherapy is a wriggling target, one that does not hold still. It is not always clear what will actually happen in a psychotherapeutic setting. Will it be an actual conversation with a discerning interlocutor? Or will I be asked to ramble about whatever comes to mind in the presence of a deliberately nonresponsive analyst? Will I be told to talk to an empty chair as though my mother were in it? Will I be hypnotized or asked to track the therapist's moving fingers with my eyes? Might I be forcibly restrained by fellow group members as I bellow my way through an iatrogenic near-psychotic regression? Will "therapy" constitute taking pills and reporting on the side effects a month later? Must I fingerpaint?

It does not help that for many decades various exponents of psychotherapy have called the therapeutic practitioner community the "new priesthood," as though the only elements of spirituality worth discussing were those reducible to psychological ("soulish") categories. Some psychotherapies unblushingly assume spirituality is within their proper province; one thinks of Jungian analysis or transpersonal psychotherapy in this connection. Compared with the mercurial nature of psychotherapy, spiritual direction seems palpably monolithic.

Kenneth Leech, a leader in spiritual direction within and beyond the Church of England, understands psychotherapy or counseling as a meeting between two human beings in the presence of God to pursue a human goal (better relations with self, others, world), while spiritual direction is a meeting between a person and God in the presence of another person for a divine goal (to solidify one's relationship with God). That perception is widely embraced among Episcopal spiritual directors.

To that distinction I would add three additional elements. First, psychotherapy is normally administered in exchange for a fee. Spiritual direction tends to be offered *ad maiorum Dei gloriam* (to the greater glory of God)—which is how Episcopalians say "free."

Second, many forms of psychotherapy aim to alter a person's unconscious mental processes, using various tools to gain access to zones of the client's heart which are not consciously available to them. Spiritual direction addresses conscious material that is vulnerable to the will of the client.

Third, the task of spiritual direction is to examine every detail of the client's life *sub specie aeternitatis*—in the light of the presence of God. A psychotherapist may not find that point of view rigorous enough to be helpful.

I know a priest who is also a competent psychotherapist. I asked him how he tells which one he's doing. His cryptic reply was, "When I find myself playfully ironic and paradoxical, I discover I'm doing psychotherapy; when I'm spontaneously serious and attentive to what the other person is saying without the need to go paradoxical, I think I'm doing spiritual direction."

A spiritual director will normally ask at the outset whether a person is engaged in psychotherapy—and will normally greet a positive answer as friendly. Experience indicates that psychotherapy is an effective way to generate an accurate agenda for prayer.

Table 4.1 may convey some of the differences between psychotherapy and spiritual direction.[6]

Table 4.1. Comparison of Spiritual Direction, Pastoral Counseling and Psychotherapy

Dimension	Spiritual Direction	Psychotherapy	Pastoral Counseling
Presenting Problem	Wish to grow in one's relationship to God	Wish for relief from emotional pain, aberrant thought processes, or relational discord with self or others	Wish for help with problems in living and is either open to or seeking growth in relationship to God
Goals	Assisting directee to employ the resources of the Christian faith in her life in order to live more closely in Jesus' company	Assisting client to address her life circumstances in fresh ways, leading to better adjustment, greater life satisfaction	Assistance in encountering life circumstances in the light of the resources of faith and thereby living with better adjustment and fulfillment
Procedure	Prayer, instruction, vocal counsel, directed reading and writing projects, etc.	Concentrated conversation, "reframing," recommendation of medication and a host of additional techniques	Regularly scheduled individual and group conversations
Resources	A vast spiritual literature, retreat facilities, spiritual communities	Medical backup, professional supervision, a vast professional literature	Combines resources of spiritual direction and psychotherapy with reliance on client's faith commitment

Somewhere between these two disciplines we should observe the function-turned-profession of pastoral counseling. As the name of the discipline implies,

---

[6]To those in either discipline who howl objections to the gross oversimplification such a table constitutes, I can only protest with Mother Eve, "The Editor tempted me and I did comply."

pastoral counseling grew out of the clergy's practice of counseling parishioners within the context of a congregation.

Most Episcopal pastoral counselors discovered their interests as parochial priests in something like a "call to the ministry." God calls men and women to the Episcopal priesthood laterally rather than vertically. That is, God's direct call on all of us is to discipleship; the call to ordination comes to some of us through church members who keep asking us, "Did you ever think of becoming a priest?" until we finally realize it's God calling us. Similarly, a priest moves into the profession of pastoral counseling when enough parochial counselees say, "You're really good at this."

Some proceed back to graduate school for a degree in counseling or some form of psychotherapy. Many get credentialed through the American Association of Marriage and Family Therapy. Pastoral counselors may staff a counseling center housed by a large congregation or cathedral. Others may attach themselves to private therapeutic practices. In large cities there may be one or more pastoral counseling associations that certify and deploy ordained counselors.

A pastoral counselor assists people with their difficulties, paying attention to the client's consciously available material and resources. The value system of an Episcopalian Christian is presumed to be ego-syntonic to the client and is relied on to a greater or lesser extent by the counselor.

REFERRAL TO A MENTAL HEALTH PROFESSIONAL

At what point do spiritual directors refer clients to psychotherapy? A friend reports that her trigger for referral is any point at which she catches herself trying to "fix" the client. That's a signal that she is being drawn into a conversation that belongs between the client and God, not between herself and the client.

There are a couple of obvious triggers. First, if the client divulges that he is a danger to himself or others, the director is mandated by law to alert appropriate medical and law enforcement personnel. Unless those disclosures occur within the context of a sacramental confession before an ordained confessor, such communications do not enjoy legal privilege. Related to that trigger is the mandate to report physical or sexual abuse of underage persons or the elderly to the appropriate authorities. Even were this information to come up during the sacrament of penance, most clergy would insist that self-reporting and reparation be part of the penitent's penance.

Should a person exhibit bizarre behavior, that is a clear trigger that it's time to refer. Should the client report visions, voices or visitations as spiritual experiences which strike the director as incongruent with the faith of Christ as found in the New Testament and the church's teaching, it is likely time to refer. Spiritual direction is rarely if ever an emergency ministry. In the Episcopal Church, most clergy have been through at least one quarter of Clinical Pastoral Education; that is often sufficient to hone their perceptions to sort out psychopathology from spiritual phenomena.

Summary

Spiritual direction is defined as a disciplined relationship intended to assist at least the client to a richer relationship with God. In the Anglican churches spiritual direction has always been implicit in the role of a parish priest. In the Episcopal Church spiritual direction nestles comfortably into teaching (especially prayer and friendlier images of God) and is conversant with psychotherapy and pastoral counseling. The transformation of the client results from an alliance against the client's shame. Episcopalians gauge spiritual maturity by the degree of one's growth into Christlikeness. Distinguishing spiritual direction from conventional psychotherapy and pastoral counseling is somewhat tricky in view of the latters' fluidity in practice. Alert directors can sense a client's need for other disciplines, such as psychotherapy, medicine, accountancy or law.

While spiritual direction in the Episcopal Church gratefully draws from too many extra-Anglican treasures to be able to claim uniqueness, I believe the blending of those resources amounts to a discipline that is distinctive.

First, Anglican/Episcopal spiritual direction is deeply rooted in our denominational history. No longtime Episcopalian is ever surprised to learn of this resource, even when hearing the term for the first time. It has a legitimacy among us that is distinctive.

Second, like Jesus' scribe in the kingdom of heaven, an Episcopal spiritual director "draws from the storehouse treasures both old and new." Classics from Roman Catholicism, continental Pietism, other faith traditions and psychotherapy all find their way into the mix.

Third, Episcopal spiritual directors tend to be open to other areas of knowledge and regard many as germane to the directee's spiritual growth. Our directors tend to be conspicuously open to the insights derived from the behavioral sciences. A fascination with quantum physics as likely as not will be incorporated into wonderment and worship. Art will be embraced as an assistance to spiritual growth, not as its rival.

Fourth, to the extent that it makes sense to distinguish between major doctrines, spiritual direction in the Episcopal Church rests more weight on our Lord's incarnation than on the atonement. At the risk of gross generalization, Episcopal theological thinking tends to subsume the atonement within the incarnation, seeing the first as already implicit in the second. The result is an approach to the state of the soul before God that assumes that God is really *for us*.

REFERENCES

Bloom, Anthony. 1970. *Beginning to pray.* Mahwah, N.J.: Paulist.

The book of common prayer. 1979. New York: Church Hymnal Corporation.

Cloud of unknowing, The. 1978. Trans. Clifton Wolters London: Penguin.

Donne, John. 1959. Devotions upon emergent occasions; together with Death's duel. Ann Arbor: University of Michigan Press.

Edwards, Jonathan. 1997. *The religious affections.* Carlisle: Banner of Truth Trust.

Francis de Sales. 2000. *Introduction to the devout life.* Trans. and ed. John K. Ryan. London: J. M. Dent and Sons.

Harton, F. P. 1950. *The elements of the spiritual life: A study in ascetical theology.* London. SPCK.

Herbert, George. 1981. *The country parson, the temple.* New York: Missionary Society of St. Paul.

Holmes, Urban T., III. 1980. *A history of Christian spirituality.* New York: Seabury.

John of the Cross. 1901. *The works of John of the Cross of the Order of Our Lady of Carmel.* Trans. David Lewis. London: Thomas Baker.

Julian of Norwich. 1952. *Revelations of divine love, recorded by Julian, Anchoress at E. Norwich Anno Domini 1371.* London: Methuen.

Kelsey, Morton. 1972. *Encounter with God.* Minneapolis: Bethany Fellowship.

Lawrence, Brother. 1958. *The practice of the presence of God.* Westwood, N.J.: Fleming H. Revell.

More, Paul Elmer, and Frank Leslie Cross. 1951. *Anglicanism: The thought and practice of the Church of England, illustrated from the religious literature of the seventeenth century.* London: Society for the Promulgation of Christian Knowledge.

Philokalia. 1995. Trans. G.E.H. Palmer, Philip Sherrard and Kalistos Ware. London: Faber & Faber.

Sanford, John. 1970. *The kingdom within.* Philadelphia: J. B. Lippincott.

Suurmond, Jean-Jacques. 1994. *Word and Spirit at play: Towards a charismatic theology.* London: SCM Press.

Temple, Gray. 2001. *The molten soul: Danger and opportunities in religious conversion.* New York: Church Publishing.

Teresa of Ávila. 1964. *The way of perfection.* Trans. E. Allison Peers. New York: Doubleday/Image.

———. 1979. *The interior castle.* Trans. Kieran Kavanaugh. Mahwah, N.J.: Paulist.

SPIRITUAL DIRECTION IN THE REFORMED TRADITION

Ben Johnson

Without question the Reformed tradition and one of its constituent denominations, the Presbyterian Church USA, possess a deep interest in spirituality, though the word is seldom used. John A. Mackay affirms this concern most enthusiastically.

> For deep in the heart of Calvinism, and in Presbyterianism, in its truest and most classical form, resides a profound piety, that is, a passionate experience of God linked to a profound devotion to God. . . . It is piety in this sense that provides the requisite dynamic for the conduct of church affairs and the application of Christianity to life in all its fullness. (Mackay 1960:9)

In this tradition the cultivation of the devout and dutiful practice of the faith springs from gratitude to God. The preferred methods of developing piety have been preaching, teaching, pastoral care and the administration of the sacraments.

We can only speculate about the omission of spiritual direction from the agenda of the Reformers. Perhaps they failed to address this issue because of the newfound freedom that flowed from justification by "grace alone" and "faith alone." Structured efforts toward growth and change would have had the scent of "works righteousness." Or in an effort to cut away all the barnacles acquired by the church for fifteen centuries, they may have ignored this ancient practice because it did not stand at the center of biblical teaching. Yet another possible reason was that the doctrine of the priesthood of all believers made the practice of submitting one's life to another—especially a priest—reek of clerical authority. But while spiritual direction was not emphasized, it was not lost: another person in the same era was giving thoughtful consideration to it.

While Calvin was writing the *Institutes of the Christian Religion,* Ignatius of Loyola was constructing the *Spiritual Exercises.* These exercises aimed at helping men and women contemplate Christ by reading Scripture and imaginatively participating in the life of Christ. So powerful were these exercises that they evoked deep feelings of affection for Christ and profound revelations of the self. The exercises so profoundly affected participants that they required the help of a director.

In the modern era various persons have sought to recapture this emphasis on spirituality within the Reformed tradition. In his *Spirituality in the Reformed Tradition,* Howard Rice, for example, has given particular attention to spiritual direction. Under the heading "Consultation" he mentions a dozen forms of direction. He comes nearest to spiritual direction in the contemporary sense when he describes pastoral care, letter writing and personal guidance (Rice 1991:120-50). Others in the tradition have also sought to make contributions to the conversation about direction. Eugene Peterson has urged pastors toward spiritual direction. He writes about being a spiritual director, getting a spiritual director and practicing spiritual direction (Peterson 1987:130-31). Andrew Dreitcer and I have included a chapter on spiritual companionship in a recent volume on spiritual leadership (Campbell and Dreitcer 2001:81-98), and I have written two essays on spiritual direction in other places also (Johnson 1987:78-91; 1988:103-15).

WHAT IS SPIRITUAL DIRECTION?

Spirituality blows in the winds of renewal at the beginning of the twenty-first century. But the meaning of spiritual direction must be expressed in the context of a larger vision of spirituality. Urban Holmes offers a good working definition of spirituality when he says:

> I am defining spirituality as a human capacity for a relationship with that which transcends sense phenomena; this relationship is perceived by the subject as an expanded or heightened consciousness independent of the subject's efforts, given substance in the historical setting, and exhibits itself in creative action in the world. (Holmes 1982:12)

For the purposes of this book, making Holmes's generic definition specifically Christian can strengthen it: *Spirituality is the human capacity for a relationship with God as revealed in Jesus Christ through the Spirit.*

Spirituality is the faithful human response to divine providence. God is the Creator and sustainer of all creation, and nothing happens apart from God's initiative and presence. Perception of and response to the divine presence suggests the dynamic of all vital spirituality. The substance of this interaction with the divine must be formed to have meaning and continuing influence.

A kindred term to *spirituality* is *spiritual formation.* Spiritual formation encompasses spiritual practices that both provide a setting for the divine-human interaction and also form the dynamic life of the Spirit that leads toward maturity in Christ. The practices of prayer, Bible study, meditation, contemplation, journaling and guided reflection are illustrative of these practices. In prayer we become aware of, listen to and open ourselves to God. In Bible study or reading we listen for the voice of God addressing us in and beyond the text. Meditation refers to the practice of musing over the text, sifting out images of self and God and the contradictions. Contemplation calls for the cessation of our own efforts and leads to silently waiting in the divine presence. This presence at times comes spontaneously and with striking images, at other times with words of direction and assurance, and still at other times in no discernible manner. Journaling is an artful dialogue with God, not a chronological record of events. The journal becomes not only a partner in our dialogue with God but also a record of revelations, and it is a practice that invites further divine intervention in our life.

In addition to these individual formative practices, corporate practices aid in forming persons. Through the ages these practices have included worship in a vital community, shared life in small groups, and service with others in soup kitchens, food pantries and short-term missions. Formation through both individual and corporate practices shapes and transforms persons both consciously and unconsciously.

Spiritual formation and spirituality belong together. Without formation, spirituality has no focus. Where there is not form in which to hold the energy of the Spirit, it can be dissipated in meaningless activity—or worse, centered on the self. The dynamics of formation include worship, individual practices and choices.

The work of formation is greatly aided by spiritual direction. By this I mean one person's serving another through prayer, listening, discerning and responding to the presence of God in that person's life, to the end that she will grow in conformity to Christ. This relationship is clearly negotiated with respect to goals, roles, time, responsibilities and style.

THE PRACTICE OF SPIRITUAL DIRECTION

During the last few decades the practice of spiritual direction has grown in importance in the Presbyterian Church USA, one expression of the Reformed tradition. Evidence of this growth of interest can be noted in the number of clergy and laity who have sought spiritual directors, seminaries that have incorporated degrees or certificates of spiritual direction in their curriculum, the increasing numbers of ministers who have sought direction and who have also sought training in the art of spiritual direction. Prior to the last two decades of the twentieth century, the term would not have been recognizable in these venues. Since that time, however, spiritual direction has been introduced and practiced in a variety of settings in the PCUSA.

Introductory direction. In numerous settings like conferences, retreats and consultations, opportunities for short-term spiritual direction have been offered to participants. Generally, the practice has been described and offered to conferees for one or two sessions. As a consequence many have sought an extended time of spiritual direction, and others have enrolled in training to be come spiritual directors.

Institutional direction. Several institutions of, or related to, the PCUSA have introduced the practice of spiritual direction in recent years. The emphasis came first from San Francisco Theological Seminary in San Anselmo, California. The formal history of the Program in Christian Spirituality began in 1979, when noted author Morton Kelsey approached Professor Roy Fairchild with a proposal for a program to train pastors and therapists in spiritual direction. After considerable discussion, the SFTS board of trustees accepted a multiyear gift, named Fairchild as professor of spiritual life and psychology, and affirmed the creation of the Center for Christian Spiritual Disciplines. The center was launched in 1981, and public programming began with a series of lectures in 1982.

In 1987 Elizabeth Liebert was named professor of spiritual life and director of the Program in Christian Spirituality. In the early years of her directorship, she— in concert with Andrew Dreitcer—broadened the services to M.Div. students while continuing outreach to the church through conferences and retreats. Subsequently, spiritual direction was made available not only to students but also to the wider community.

In the last five years of the twentieth century, Columbia Theological Seminary in Decatur, Georgia, began a certificate in spiritual formation. One of the courses offered was in spiritual direction. A spiritual director was also always available to students in the various courses offered in the program.

In recent years the PCUSA has advanced the work of spiritual direction through its emphasis on discipleship. This arm of the church has emphasized spiritual direction through conferences and a newsletter.

Along with these efforts within the denomination, Fuller Theological Seminary, not a Presbyterian seminary but one that stands in the Reformed tradition, has developed Christian Spirituality Cohort seminars. These are a mix of lectures, discussions, media presentations, small groups, case studies and interactive dialogue. In a distance learning environment, electronic discussion groups enable cohort group members to stay in touch via e-mail. Faculty mentors participate in the seminars together. The seminars are held on the Fuller campus and at retreat centers in various locations. The doctor of ministry degree in Christian Spirituality prepares ministers to be a spiritual guide in the evangelical wing of the Reformed tradition.

Intentional direction. As a consequence of inner hunger and a quest for spiritual nurture, numerous pastors have received spiritual direction from a variety of places, many of them in the Roman Catholic Church. The spiritual growth these searching pastors have experienced has resulted in their getting training in direction and beginning to offer guidance to members of their congregation.

These emerging emphases in the Reformed tradition make it obvious that changes are beginning to occur. *Spirituality, spiritual formation* and *spiritual direction*—while not yet the common parlance of Reformed theologians and pastors—are terms that are seeping into the vocabulary of those in the Reformed community. The hunger of the people and the urgings of the Spirit seem to be working in harmony to nurture the practice of spiritual direction in Presbyterian and other Reformed families of faith.

THE PROCESS OF AUTHENTIC TRANSFORMATION

From the Reformed perspective all transformation comes from God. As Paul states to the Romans:

> I appeal to you therefore, brothers and sisters, by the mercies of God, to present your bodies as a living sacrifice, holy and acceptable to God, which is your spiritual worship. Do not be conformed to this world, but be transformed by the renewing of your minds, so that you may discern what is the will of God—what is good and acceptable and perfect. (Rom 12:1-2 NRSV)

We humans can present ourselves to God; we can seek conformity to Christ and not the world; but the transforming of the mind is the work of God, and it occurs through the Spirit at work in us.

What impact does this theocentric pursuit have on the transformation of the mind and spirit? The goal, in part, determines authentic transformation. In the Reformed perspective the goal of transformation will be "to become the person we were created to be" or "to do the will of God" or "to love God with our whole heart, soul, mind and body." These three explications of transformation aim at the same goal from an existential, a behavioral and a holistic affective point of view. All drive toward the biblical image of conformity to Christ.

Perhaps these goals warrant further clarification. First, the hope for conformity to Christ is a goal, not a destination. In the journey toward likeness to Christ, many of us have long detected a yearning for utopia. This strange word actually means "no place." Though there is no place of arrival, we still yearn for a state of being in which the contradiction between who we are and who we long to be is completely resolved. If the testimony of the saints is true, that is, that the closer we get to God the farther we feel from God, we fear our yearning has no place of fulfillment in this life. So as we continue on this journey, we should focus on the landscape through which we are passing on the way to our goal. Spiritual directors can help us recognize the journey nature of our conformity to Christ.

Second, there is no particular merit in reaching or claiming to have reached the goal. From a Reformed perspective such a claim would be unthinkable, and the utterance of it in testimony would smack of works righteousness, as if by our own efforts we had reached this exalted goal. Furthermore, the claim would sound far too boastful for a Presbyterian. It would have the scent of pharisaism.

A phrase that has been used to define the kingdom of God seems apropos to this issue. We are accustomed to saying the kingdom of God is "already but not yet." It is already achieved in the mind of God, but it is not fully evident in history. Even so we are already complete in Christ, we have died with him and are raised with him, but the full revelation of this gracious gift is not yet fully manifested in our lives. This already-but-not-yet dialectic creates a tension that gives birth to the existential yearning in the hearts of followers of Christ. The contradiction deepens our desire for holiness and fulfillment.

Recognizing this persistent tension not only fuels our yearning for greater conformity to God's intention but also liberates us from the guilt of not being perfect. How many of us have experienced crippling guilt when we have been embarrassed by this "not yet" side of the tension? When we recognize that this very tension is part of the process of conformity and that God sees us as "already" even before we reach that ultimate transformation, we can take heart and rejoice in God's grace. The spiritual director will always be laboring in this space between the "is" and "shall be" and accepting the ambiguity, as the human situation will enable both director and directee to respond more fully to God's immediate presence.

Third, the lack of precision with which to speak of the maturity we long for is also part of the process. The notion of Christlikeness defies measurement. Yet to speak of one person as like Christ and another as a contradiction of Christ still makes sense. In some manner we intuitively understand what is meant. Perhaps we could even go further and name some of the characteristics of persons who are like Christ and those who are not. But would any of us be willing to define the character of the person fully conformed to Christ? At the invitation most of us would shy away from this risky task.

This anxiety arises in part because we are not pursuing a tangible goal but a relationship. Relationships do not readily lend themselves to weight or measurement or formula. All three of these attributes can be fixed, defined or executed, but none of these is true of relationships. Relationships tend to be amorphous, open, changing and evolving. Our relation to Christ acquires many of the elements of human relations. Instead of being set or fixed, our relations are constantly in the process of development. Change in this sense does not mean improvement or deterioration, but difference. Even in our most treasured relations we experience change.

I think of my treasured relationship with my wife as an example. Our relationship today is different from the way it was in the first months we knew each other. It is different now because she has changed and I have changed. Our circumstances also are quite different with respect to work, children and schedules. We do not have the same relationship we had thirty years ago. Through all the changes we have faced issues, solved problems and negotiated differences, and as a consequence we have a mature, time-tested relationship. Is it better now than thirty years ago? No. It is different. We had a good relationship thirty years ago, and we have a good relationship today.

How do we define "good" in a relationship? Perhaps there are some categories that apply to each of the years, but the content of those categories changed from year to year. It seems that one would need to take a snapshot at some point on the journey and define "good" in that moment.

The metaphors of journey and relationship suggest the environment within which transformation occurs, and these snapshots of the Christian life deny all salvific achievement in the process. But neither of these engages the inner dynamics of transformation. In one succinct description of the amazing power of a human being, John Calvin offers a clue to the inward change and pointers that provide parameters for spiritual direction. Though he was certain of human sinfulness, he did not deny the amazing capacity of the human being to discover meaning and fulfillment through Christ. He said:

> Manifold indeed is the nimbleness of the soul with which it surveys heaven and earth, joins past to future, retains in memory something heard long before, nay, pictures to itself whatever it pleases. Manifold also is the skill with which it devises things incredible, and which is the mother of so many marvelous devices. These are unfailing signs of divinity in man. (Calvin 1960:57)

This bold assertion of human capabilities names specific acts involved in inward transformation. It begins with attentiveness. What is going on in the world, and what is occurring in the unfolding life of the individual? The presence of God may be active in persons' lives, but if they are unaware of it and do not attend it, no transformation takes place. Transformation begins with awareness.

Calvin then marvels that humans have the capacity to observe heaven and earth, that is, to notice both what is material and what is spiritual. If we divide perception between heaven and earth, quite clearly "heaven" refers to spiritual insight and "earth" points to sense perception. What we physically see, hear, smell, touch and taste provides the stimuli of earth. What we conceive, combine, imagine and create suggests the spiritual powers of the soul, heavenly attributes. So humans have the capacity to attend events and stimuli in the material world and the intuition and inspiration that erupt from their inner world. God reveals the divine self through both.

This ability to survey heaven and earth is complemented by the power to join past to future, that is, how one has perceived and interpreted past experience and intuitively connected it imaginatively with the future. Through this power of observation, interpretation and anticipation—"signs of divinity in man"—we have an important insight into the process of transformation.

When the human spirit has achieved this unity and sense of wholeness through its response to the data of sense and intuition, it is able to retain these creations in memory. Furthermore, human beings have the capacity to imagine alternative futures and live lives expressive of the fullness of Christ. Are not the miracles of human nature that Calvin names what we call sensory awareness, reason, memory, intuition, imagination and will? I think so. Furthermore, I see these as the very capacities we use to create, maintain and revise the narrative of our life. Our life experience, which we carry in a narrative, provides a goodly portion of the material for spiritual direction. Thus Calvin's view of humanness identifies the kinds of functions necessary for the transformation of a life in Christ.

The Role of the Spiritual Director

In earlier times when the social and cultural environment tended toward authoritarianism, the style of spiritual direction was also somewhat overbearing. But that has been changing in recent years. The role of the spiritual director is not that of the authoritative priest who interprets the will of God for believers and tells them the decision to make. Neither does the spiritual director serve as an authoritative interpreter of Scripture or life experience. Perhaps this image of the director as an authoritarian over the life of another has been the greatest hindrance to its embrace in the Reformed tradition. The Reformed emphasis on the priesthood of believers and their freedom in Christ to interpret the Scriptures and respond faithfully to God blinded the eyes of early Reformers to the value that could be derived from spiritual direction.

Perhaps the role of the spiritual director in the Reformed tradition can best be introduced through the variety of terms used for this practice. For example, the role of spiritual director has been referred to as a spiritual friend, which stresses the relational character of the role of the director: one person willingly befriends another on the spiritual journey. Or we may think of this role as that of a soul friend. *Soul* suggests depth, a guide who is willing to walk into the deep places of human life and listen to the persistent yearnings, explore the darkest fears and identify the dominant images of self or God.

Some have spoken of the spiritual director as a soul mate, a term that suggests the mutuality of the relationship. A soul mate must be one who gives as well as receives in a relationship of sharing. Though mutuality may be confusing by shifting the focus from the directee to the director, it need not do so. It is possible for a director to give information from his own life experience without becoming the center of the director-directee event.

Still another synonym for spiritual director is a companion on the inner way. The title suggests that the director companions persons on their journey, helping them sort out the meaning of their lives. Like soul friend, it suggests a journey toward one's depths.

The image of a midwife has also been used to describe the work of a spiritual director. One should not be fooled into thinking that this refers only to an evangelistic function of presiding over the "born again" experience. Though it certainly may include assistance at the beginning of a journey with Christ, it involves much more. The new creature in Christ Jesus is always "abornin'." God continues to come to souls in numerous ways, and each visitation holds the potential of newness—new life, new directions, new choices.

The spiritual director fills first one of these roles and then another—a spiritual friend who comes along beside another who begins the inner journey and then remains a companion as the directee continues to experience new life in the Spirit. While these images help suggest the identity of the spiritual director, they do not exhaust the role.

The spiritual director has responsibility for establishing the verbal contract with the directee. The opening exploratory conversation might include questions like: Where will we meet? How often? For how long? What are the expectations of the director, and what are the expectations of the directee? How can the relation be ended amicably? How will conflict be dealt with? Laying out these ground rules at the beginning of the relationship will save it from frustration and confusion later on.

The functions of the spiritual director begin with *listening*. The director forms one-third of the triad: God, directee and director. The most important task for the director is to listen for God in the words and behavior of the directee. As a listener, the director is always asking, *What is God saying to this life? What is God doing in this life?* The transactions in the session are between God and the directee, and the director must focus on that relationship and seek diligently to remain on the sideline, observing, asking questions and making suggestions sparingly.

Out of the listening role comes another function: questioning. As a careful inquirer, the director does not interrogate but functions as a skillful companion who poses enabling inquiries that grow out of sensitive listening. Good questions have roots in the conversation, and like a friendly finger, they point to areas that need to be noticed. Discerning explorations of the director enable the directees to discover and express new insights and to expand their awareness. Naturally, questions also carry suggestions, though the directee may lack clarity about what the questions point to. Obviously, the director does not inquire about matters that are of no consequence, so in a sense questions are subtle suggestions.

The spiritual director is also a discerner of spirits. Some people have an indescribable ability to "see through" a situation or an issue. How they see so consistently I am not sure. According to St. Paul, one of the Spirit's gifts is discernment. This gift seems to be at work when Peter discerns the call to accompany emissaries to Cornelius's house, and when Paul speaks to the young woman who followed him saying, "These men are slaves of the Most High God, who proclaim to you a way of salvation" (Acts 16:17). Maybe this gift functions today in spiritual directors.

If discernment is a gift, when is it given? Is it transferred to us when we are born of the Sprit or when we are filled with the Spirit? Or is the gift given in creation and later awakened through the Spirit? Possibly the awakening of the gift develops in spiritual directors as they listen to God in and through the lives of people. Perhaps we should stay open to all these ways that the gift of discernment may become operative in a director's life. Some anxiety about the exercise of this gift is appropriate, as we are not always sure whether our impressions and hunches are from God or from ourselves. But we must not deny the gift so crucial for the task.

The gift of discernment does not give us authority to tell others what is going on in their lives. Nor does it give us authority to answer their questions or solve their problems. An appropriate humility will always keep us cognizant of the distance between our discernment and the directee's experience. And this humility will help us to wonder about questions, search for answers and explore alternative possibilities. It will keep us from saying things like "God has shown me this about you," or "God has told me to tell you . . ." Great damage can be done to a trusting soul when we lose appropriate humility regarding our discernment.

A spiritual director prays. Maybe the director employs silent prayer. What better way to begin a session than a few minutes of silence with a directee? In the silence both the director and the directee open themselves to become aware of the presence of God. The director prays for the directee and the directee for the director. Both realize that without God nothing of value will come of the session. This posture of prayer established in the opening minutes of a session must pervade the time together.

To make prayer such a pervasive influence, the director assumes a contemplative posture. This means that the director images the session as being in God and thus continuously looks for the evidence of God's presence in the sharing of the directee, in the thoughts and images that come into her mind, and also in the interaction between herself and the directee. In our efforts to remain contemplative, we take care not to make it a pious work, so that when we are momentarily distracted from God, we can joyously return without self-condemnation or discouragement.

The director may also invite the directee into intentional prayer, even in the midst of a session. When the directee comes to confusing material or parts of life too painful to share, a reassuring prayer for him may lift the conversation to another level. The prayer may also be for the director to have discernment and guidance. She may not understand or he may not know the avenue to take and thus needs prayer. Silence serves the task of the director quite well at junctures like these.

Continuous prayer distinguishes spiritual direction from other caring experiences. Prayer transforms the sharing and lifts it to an intentional transaction in the presence of God. This is not to imply that other helping experiences do not also have transformative effects through the Spirit, but the spiritual director will always be quite intentional in seeking them.

The spiritual director also offers suggestions to the directee. These admonitions may be brief insights arising from the session or may point to a book to read or a spiritual discipline to practice. A director may even suggest the cessation of a practice that seems to come between the directee and God.

The spiritual director guides the session. She begins the session at the appointed time and ends it at the hour agreed upon. At the beginning of a session the director invites the directee into silence with her. The director continues the session with an opening question like, "What's going on in your life with God?" or, "How has your prayer been this month?"

Once the time together reaches this point, it must be open to flow as the director thinks best. Sometimes the director will ask several questions before discovering the best approach. Guided by the director and hopefully by the Spirit, the session continues until time to close. Likely the director will make a few suggestions, pray and end the session. Skillfully guiding the session is one of the most important tasks of the spiritual director.

Finally, the spiritual director must take care of his own needs. The axiom is true that we cannot take others where we ourselves have never been. Neither can we be sensitive to the Spirit in others if we are not attending the Spirit in ourselves. So the director must keep his life open and growing. He must also live before God if he would effectively help others to do the same. Most teachers and mentors of spiritual direction hold that those directing others should also be receiving direction. Doubtless wisdom also resides in this axiom.

All the roles, functions and responsibilities of the spiritual director have only one aim. Whether listening, questioning, discerning, praying, suggesting, contracting or keeping his own soul, the spiritual director aims at helping the directee to become the person she was created to be. This may sound very simplistic, but it does in fact comprise every role that a director plays in the life of another.

INDICATORS OF A MATURE SPIRITUALITY

Searching for indirect indicators of spiritual maturity is an intriguing quest. In times past those interested in spiritual maturity were often more specific than many of us are comfortable with today. When the character of mature spirituality has been reduced to specific behaviors or spiritual practices, serious souls have turned the indicators into goals and have approached maturity as a cause-and-effect achievement. For example, if humility suggests maturity, then wearing hair shirts, flagellating oneself, and accusing oneself should lead to humility. Cause-and-effect thinking leads to cause-and-effect practices, resulting in a self-generated spirituality that depends on us instead of God.

I take "indirect indicators of spiritual maturity" to mean the changes or trans-formations that occur in persons who have fixed their attention on Christ, who are on the journey and do not pretend to have arrived at the destination. Great wisdom lies in this approach to maturity, because it saves the pilgrim from the idolatry of perfectionism and of turning holiness into an achievement instead of a gift.

Quite easily we can say that the central indicator of maturity for a Christian is conformity to Christ. This does not mean that the believer seeks to imitate Christ in his actions but rather that he focuses his attention on Christ, so that Christ informs the true self through the free and spontaneous work of the Spirit. Though this comprehensive affirmation of Christ may lack enough specificity to be helpful, it points to one of Calvin's seminal statements regarding life with God. On the opening page of the *Institutes of the Christian Religion* he discusses the knowledge of God and begins with these affirmations:

> Nearly all the wisdom we possess, that is to say, true and sound wisdom, consists of two parts: the knowledge of God and of ourselves. But while joined by many bonds, which one precedes and brings forth the other is not easy to discern. In the first place, no one can look upon himself without immediately turning his thoughts to the contemplation of God, in whom he "lives and moves" (Acts 17:28). (Calvin 1960:35)

Calvin continues this discussion showing that this wisdom comes through an alternation of encountering self and encountering God. Spiritual maturity develops, then, out of a dialectical relationship of God and self. One side of this dialectic is the God who speaks to us in myriad ways; the other side is the self in its matu-rational dependency, looking to God and listening for God. Calvin makes it clear that this dialectical relationship is driven by the knowledge of God on the one hand and the knowledge of self on the other. When the soul looks at itself, it is immediately driven to God through a vision of its brokenness and need, and when the soul looks upon God it is driven to more fully see itself as a broken reflection of the holiness and majesty of God. The attention shifts from self to God and from God to self as point and counterpoint.

As this happens, signs of maturity begin to appear—usually when the soul is not looking. Perhaps indirect signs of maturity begin to be noted by the discerning spiritual director, but the task of the director is to work within the God-self dialectic with the confidence that if the directee attends to God and grows in the knowledge of self and God, maturity will occur.

Is there nothing that can be said about signs of maturity? Yes, we can speak of these if they occur within the God-self relationship and if they do not lead to an idolatrous or works-created maturity. We can speak of openness as a characteristic of maturity. Growing souls fearlessly open themselves to deeper insights into the self as made in the image of God. But they also increase in their openness to the revelations of God in the text of Scripture, in the events of their life and in their reflections.

Heightened awareness also suggests a growth toward maturity. Recall that Urban Holmes pointed to a "heightened awareness" as an aspect of spirituality. But we must not think of awareness in an absolute way. Perhaps we should think of a spectrum of awareness that ranges from unawareness, to cultural awareness, to an awakened consciousness, to a God consciousness and finally to a unitive consciousness. When persons focus on the God-self relationship, the dynamic interaction between God and the self receives the attention, and transformation occurs without the directee's seeking it or noticing it.

I have asserted that God engages human consciousness through the Word spoken in Scripture and through events from without and within from the imagination and intuition. If we take these manifestations of the divine to be somewhat constant and continuous, a growing ability to name these divine movements would suggest an increase in maturity.

The accuracy and promptness with which one recognizes the presence of God depends on spiritual discernment. So when the spiritual director recognizes a sharpened discernment in the directee, this also suggests growth in maturity.

The joyous exercise of Christian freedom—free to be who you are, free to do your tasks and free even to fail—suggests an enviable maturity. This freedom seems to be just the opposite of rule- and works-oriented maturity. Words like *spontaneous, habitual, guilt-free* and *authentic* point toward my meaning here. Joyous freedom—a gift that flows from a relation with a free and gracious God—indirectly announces an advance in maturity.

Increased conformity to the image of Christ becomes concrete in the fruit of the Spirit—love, joy, peace and the like. In the God-self dialectic God's people not only discern their dark, shadowy side but also discover their giftedness. Quite often

---

HELPFUL BOOKS FROM THE REFORMED TRADITION

Howard L. Rice, *Reformed Spirituality* (Louisville, Ky.: Westminster John Knox, 1991). This book develops a contemporary Reformed understanding of spirituality. It includes a discussion of spiritual direction, which the author calls "consultation." Marjorie J. Thompson, *Soul Feast: An Invitation to the Christian Spiritual Life* (Louisville, Ky.: Westminster John Knox, 1995). Written by a disciple of Henri Nouwen, this book presents a Reformed view of spirituality and an introduction to spiritual direction within the tradition.

---

these gifts of the Spirit point to a call. As the believer matures, the call to engage in the mission of Christ asserts itself. When the fruit of the Spirit, the gifts of the Spirit and the call of God develop in the directee, a wise director will recognize them as signs of growth in conformity to Christ. The directee, however, may not sense this as maturity and will often experience these changes as confusion or stress.

Maturity also begins to show itself in the consistency of the directee's pursuit of God and a life of integrity. Just as superficial judgment and alternating choices characterize immaturity, consistent choices and predictable action indicate a growing maturity. When a directee time and again chooses what she perceives as God's will, even in the face of personal risk or self-denial, this consistency indicates maturity in the love of God, a love that exceeds love of self. This might be recognized in the woman who stays in a marriage when her husband's vocation forces her to forgo her own dreams, or when she has an opportunity for financial gain but rejects it to keep time for her spiritual values. It could also be seen in a consistency of denying herself for the sake of the poor. While any of these behaviors might suggest increasing maturity, what is important is the consistency with which the choices are made. Repeated, predictable choices that are informed by a clear sense of identity suggest increasing maturity in Christ.

A list of indirect evidences of growth toward maturity should include a deeper immersion in life. Quite in contrast to the medieval goal of self-denial, escape from life and embrace of the monastic ideal, true maturity surely includes an engagement with life, all of life. The mature person neither denies the truth of his life nor runs away from life. Rather, the mature person faces life for what it is—joyous, painful, promising or depressing—and lives open to each moment. In choosing to live in the truth of each event, the mature person refuses to be laden with guilt or shame over the past or frightened by negative possibilities in the future. By accepting life and immersing himself in the possibility of the present, the mature person has the freedom to choose how to respond to life. When a spiritual director sees this posture toward life and the freedom it creates, she realizes that a high degree of maturity has been achieved.

Does not an expanding consciousness of kingdom concerns also express spiritual maturity? The person who has begun to focus on more than his relationship with God or achieving peace and joy and is reaching toward reconciliation of estranged persons shows another indirect form of maturity. A concern for kingdom issues of peace and justice, liberation of the oppressed, inclusion of the marginalized and witness to the nations also therefore suggests maturity in Christ.

Finally, the degree of ambiguity with which persons can comfortably live also hints at maturity. On the spiritual journey there is tension between what is and what we hope for. The ambiguity increases when our work demands that we violate principles of our faith, when we are confronted with two options, both of which are bad, when one act contradicts our foundational identity in Christ. The depth of our maturity determines how we handle the ambiguity of our situation.

RELATIONSHIP BETWEEN SPIRITUAL DIRECTION, PASTORAL COUNSELING AND PSYCHOTHERAPY

Spiritual direction. The spiritual director is a person of Christian maturity who has the gift and sense of call to assist others on their spiritual journey. The director seeks to aid the directee in paying attention to God. This assistance may be in the form of prayer, asking questions or making suggestions that arise out of the director's understanding of the directee's needs. The role of the spiritual director does not permit her to intrude in the life of another person, answer their questions for them or give them prescriptions for behavior. She does not function from a detached point of view but engages each aspect of the directee's life and experience. Inevitably, the director will be changed in the relation along with the directee.

Consider this typical example. A serious Christian seeking to grow finds a spiritual director and inquires about receiving direction. The director may ask what has awakened this interest. In response the inquirer describes a deepening interest in God, longing for a closeness that comes only occasionally, and a need for help in the discernment of a call. Quite clearly these desires flow from the life of a candidate for direction.

On the other hand, if the same person had responded that he was facing a serious marital problem and had failed in all his efforts to correct the problem, the spiritual director would refer him to a pastoral counselor. The pastoral counselor focuses on crisis management or conflict resolution. These matters, as important as they are, do not fall directly within the purview of the spiritual director.

Suppose the man who states his desire for spiritual direction enters into a relationship with a spiritual director. The first few sessions go well until the directee's image of God begins to surface. He alternately reports anger at and fear of God, until he finally describes his abusive father. Knowing that the corrupted image of God negatively affects his growth, the director will recommend a psychotherapist for assistance with the therapeutic issue while spiritual direction continues.

Even if the spiritual director happened to be a pastoral counselor with a Ph.D. in clinical psychology, he should not as a spiritual director seek to treat either the marriage crisis or the memories of abuse. Should he decide to employ other skills, he should negotiate this new relationship with the directee to avoid role confusion. It is my judgment that shifting roles might be rather simple for the director but would complicate the relation for the directee. Therefore a referral will generally prove more effective.

Pastoral counseling. The pastoral counselor is an ordained minister who specializes in helping persons deal with problems that arise in the normal course of life. These problems range from self-awareness and identity confusion to conflicted and broken relations. The problems may or may not have religious roots, but the client's faith or lack of faith always influences the cure.

The pastoral counselor aims to help the client find a way to resolve the issue at hand. Solutions to problems in the context of faith are appropriate for persons who are Christian believers. If the client is not a Christian, the pastoral counselor does not directly inject an evangelistic motive into the relationship unless the client asks for spiritual assistance.

Means available to the pastoral counselor include the relation with the client, testing, prayer, group therapy, and books or articles. The pastoral counselor also shares with the client information that multiplies the client's options. Issues in the client's life that have specific Christian answers—guilt, shame, sin or doubt—can be dealt with by the pastoral counselor with an understanding of forgiveness, acceptance and absolution.

The pastoral counselor assists the client in identifying the problem, understanding the contributing influences, seeing available options and anticipating consequences of various decisions. As the client deals with the problems at hand, the pastoral counselor offers herself in support and encouragement.

The pastoral counselor refers a person seeking clarity on a particular aspect of his spiritual life to a spiritual director. Evidence of a mental disorder would make it appropriate to refer the person to a psychotherapist. However, the dividing lines between these helpers are not as neatly drawn as this discussion suggests. Both prayer and discernment are required on the part of the pastoral counselor and the other caregivers.

Psychotherapy. The psychotherapist functions to heal symptoms that arise from the unconscious aspects of the personality. For the most part, spiritual directors and pastoral counselors work with human consciousness. The aim of the psychotherapist is to surface repressed materials in the unconscious that hamper the client's functioning. By means of specialized psychotherapeutic techniques, the therapist aims to cure the patient of her symptomatic behavior.

The psychotherapist is the doctor who diagnoses, treats and heals the client of symptoms. The psychotherapist does not seek a personal relationship with the patient but rather avoids it. He or she would refer a person searching for spiritual guidance to a spiritual director. Christian psychotherapists might sometimes provide spiritual direction themselves, but as a rule this has not been part of their training or experience. Most often people do not come to them for spiritual help but for the healing of bothersome symptoms.

Table 5.1. Comparison of Spiritual Direction, Pastoral Counseling and Psychotherapy

Dimension	Spiritual Direction	Pastoral Counseling	Psychotherapy
Presenting Problem	Desire for God	Personal problem	Emotional illness
Goals	Find God's will or conformity to Christ	Resolve the conflict or adjust to problem	Cure the disease
Procedures	Prayer, listening and directive responses	Testing, listening, giving information, group support	Testing, therapeutic listening, medication and other specialized therapeutic techniques
Resources	Prayer, the Holy Spirit, journaling, guide's experience, discernment	Tests, groups, body of experience, theological frame of reference	Testing, professional skills, medication, consultation with other professionals

Referrals. Spiritual directors, pastoral counselors and psychotherapists each have an area of expertise, and persons in need of care are best served when placed in the hands of those equipped to help with their particular need. When a person could be served either by spiritual direction or pastoral counseling, the situation will likely point more clearly to one rather than the other. The pastoral counselor will better serve the troubled person who has a religious orientation. On the other hand, the secular person who has eschewed religion may find more immediate help through the psychotherapist.

SUMMARY

Even though the Reformed tradition lacks an extensive body of literature on spiritual direction, it has important contributions to make to its understanding and practice. For example, belief in God's sovereignty lies at the heart of the tradition. God is the Creator and sustainer of all things and does not forsake the creation but constantly works providentially within it. This implies that all spiritual directors and directees are creatures of God and are under God's watchful care. God desires the fulfillment of directees more than they desire it for themselves. In seeking guidance they are working congruently with the will and intention of God. In these efforts they are not left to themselves but have God's constant support and encouragement. If God is sovereign, growth and transformation depend on God and not on us.

The Reformed view of providence also has an important contribution to make. For some persons in the Reformed tradition, providence has been tightly laced with a rigid doctrine of predestination, that is, God has willed whatever happens. If we can loosen this lace a bit and see that while God does *not* will whatever happens, God is certainly in it, we have a solid beginning point for spiritual direction. If God is not alien to the events of our lives but constantly is coming to us in them, all the data of life become grist for the spiritual direction mill. Every director should aim at helping the directee unmask the divine in the natural, that is, helping people name the acts of God in their lives.

Calvin's notion of two kinds of knowledge, neither of which is complete without the other, also provides a matrix for direction. Calvin says that true wisdom is of two kinds: knowledge of God and knowledge of ourselves. This dialectic is the setting within which all spiritual direction occurs. The spiritual director makes inquiry of the person, inviting self-discovery, and this new insight frames the directee's response to God. In other inquiries the director explores the directee's images and perceptions of God, and this revelation or quest brings the soul into bold relief. The oscillation between God and self and self and God creates the stage on which the spiritual director works.

The Reformed tradition emphasizes grace, the unmerited love of God. This understanding of the inclusive and inexhaustible love of God not only defines God's nature but also suggests the worth of persons in spite of their feelings of unacceptability. God loves the director and directee; both are recipients of a grace they do not earn or deserve. This grace is theirs because of the nature of God. Without this assurance of grace, who would have the courage to confront him- or herself? Without this love, who would dare to enter into the depths of another's life? Grace therefore must be the environment in which direction occurs.

Another commitment that stems from the Reformed tradition is the authority of Scripture. Calvin does not turn the Scriptures into dogma but holds the Spirit and Scripture together. The text of Scripture lies dormant on the page until the Spirit of God moves upon it. Quickened by the Spirit, the text becomes the voice of God to the hearer. God through the ancient Word currently addresses persons and reveals both God and the self. An encounter with God through the text often marks the beginning of newness for the hearer and provides data for direction.

By coupling the providence of God with the Scriptures, the spiritual director has two potent arenas in which to work—text and life experience. These provide both the stimulus and the content for reflection and conversation about the presence of God in the directee's life.

Semper reformanda (reformed and always reforming) is an important Reformational principle. No theology, creed or system of thought can fit all times and places. A change in context generally demands a restatement of faith that takes into account new and relevant influences. This principle, which opens the door of the Reformed tradition for rethinking the meaning and nature of spiritual direction, may also be an approach for other families of faith.

This principle gives broad permission to spiritual directors in the Reformed tradition to engage in constructing a form of direction that takes into account all the work that has been done in the field, especially in the last twenty years. In developing a Reformed perspective on spiritual direction, their tradition offers a deep well from which to draw. Though the seminal emphases in the tradition may be found in other communions, the sovereignty of God, the grace of God and the providential presence in our daily lives are foundation stones for a Reformed vision of spiritual direction.

REFERENCES

Calvin, John. 1960. *Institutes of the Christian religion.* Trans. Lewis Ford Battles. Ed. John T. McNeill. Philadelphia: Westminster Press.

Holmes, Urban T., III. 1982. *Spirituality for ministry.* San Francisco: Harper & Row.

Johnson, Ben Campbell. 1987. *To pray God's will.* Louisville, Ky.: Westminster.

———. *Pastoral spirituality.* 1988. Louisville, Ky.: Westminster Press.

Johnson, Ben Campbell, and Andrew Dreitcer. 2001. *Beyond the ordinary.* Grand Rapids, Mich.: Eerdmans.

Mackay, John A. 1960. *The Presbyterian way of life.* Englewood Cliffs, N.J.: Prentice-Hall.

Peterson, Eugene H. 1987. *Working the angles.* Grand Rapids, Mich.: Eerdmans.

Rice, Howard L. 1991. *Reformed spirituality.* Louisville, Ky.: Westminster John Knox.

6

SPRITUAL DIRECTION IN THE WESLEYAN-HOLINESS TRADITION

Wesley D. Tracy

As the nineteenth-century holiness movement in America matured, it formed itself into four clusters of churches: Wesleyan-holiness groups with Methodistic roots, those with a non-Methodist heritage who adopted the Wesleyan doctrine of holiness and its practice of revivalism, those who added tongues-speaking to the Wesleyan tradition, and those who embraced Keswick teachings (Tracy and Ingersol 1998).

This writer most directly represents the Wesleyan-holiness churches. These churches are nourished by roots that tap deep into the Wesleyan revival in eighteenth-century England. Their twenty-first-century witness can be seen in the Christian Holiness Partnership (CHP), formerly Christian Holiness Association (CHA). This is the oldest holiness association in the world. It began in 1867 as the National Camp Meeting Association for the Promotion of Holiness. Methodists controlled it at first, but today its membership and leadership include representatives from many churches. The CHP member churches include the Wesleyan Church, the Free Methodist Church, the Church of the Nazarene, the Salvation Army, nineteen other churches and two international mission societies. The Wesleyan Theological Society is an auxiliary of CHP and produces the *Wesleyan Theological Society Journal*. The Nazarene Publishing House is the largest Wesleyan-holiness publisher.

It is hard to speak with one voice about this dappled movement. But if there is one area of agreement, it is the idea that spiritual direction is not relevant. The holiness churches vigorously seek the goals of spiritual direction, but spiritual direction per se is not a common part of their vocabulary.

For example, the 543-page *Beacon Dictionary of Theology* published by the Nazarene Publishing House offers no definition of spiritual direction. Two professors at Nazarene Theological Seminary who have team-taught spiritual formation for eighteen years say that the only time spiritual direction comes up in their course is as a brief metaphor for pastoral ministry. These men have a new book, *Living the Lord's Prayer: Design for Spiritual Formation* (Weigelt and Freeborn 2001), and the phrase *spiritual direction* is not mentioned.

Given the democratic, free church, Protestant and individualistic elements in our cultural and ecclesiastical heritage, spiritual direction seems dictatorial and risky. However, if you speak of soul friends, spiritual companioning, spiritual guidance, small group ministry and faith mentoring, we feel so at home that we may lounge in your family room, even put our feet on the coffee table.

THE DEFINITION AND GOALS OF SPIRITUAL DIRECTION

The goal of spirituality in the Wesleyan mode is to bring the converted believer into the experience of sanctifying grace whereby inner sin is cleansed, the image of God restored, and the heart so filled with divine love that the believer can love God with all the heart, mind, soul and strength and the neighbor as one's self. The holiness movement uses such terms to describe sanctification as *perfect love, the deeper life, Christian perfection, holiness,* and *the fullness of* or *the baptism with the Spirit.* That state of grace is, however, not static but dynamic. The sanctified believer must continue to grow in Christlikeness, learning the skills of both being and living like Christ. The experience of sanctification has both gradual and instantaneous aspects.

When asked to define Christian perfection, John Wesley often quoted Matthew 22:37: "Thou shalt love the Lord thy God with all thy heart, and with all thy soul, and with all thy mind . . . [and] Thou shalt love thy neighbor as thyself" (KJV). In a letter to Walter Churchey, Wesley wrote, "Entire sanctification or Christian perfection is neither more nor less than pure love—love expelling sin and governing both the heart and life of a child of God. The Refiner's fire purges out all that is contrary to love" (1960:5:233).

Divine love conquering sinful self-centeredness is the goal of Wesleyan spirituality.

The "heaven of heavens is love." There is nothing higher in religion; there is, in effect, nothing else; if you look for anything but more love you are looking wide of the mark. . . . And when you are asking others, "Have you received this or that blessing?" if you mean anything but more love, you mean wrong; you are leading them out of the way, and putting them on a false scent. Settle it in your heart, that from the moment God has saved you from all sin, you are to aim at nothing more, but more of that love described in the thirteenth of Corinthians. You can go no higher than this. (Wesley 1978:2:430)

Wesley many times referred to the "Collect for the Communion Service" in the Anglican liturgy (the Book of Common Prayer) as the outline of his theology and thus the goal of spirituality:

> Cleanse the thoughts of our hearts
> by the inspiration of thy Holy Spirit,
> that we may perfectly love thee,
> and worthily magnify thy holy name,
> through Jesus Christ our Lord.

- *Cleanse the thoughts of our hearts* is heart purity, cleansing from inner sin.
- *By the inspiration of thy Holy Spirit* cites the agency of the sanctifying Spirit, the fullness of or baptism with the Spirit.
- *That we may perfectly love thee* salutes perfect love, perfection of intention, Christian perfection or "Christ-mindedness."
- *That we may worthily magnify thy holy name* points to the ethical, holy living that "full salvation" produces in the sanctified believer.
- *Through Jesus Christ our Lord* signifies the truth that such spirituality can come only through the grace of God in Christ (Tracy 1991:24).

The belief that sanctifying grace purges original sin and sets the sanctified believer free from self-domination in this life makes the Wesleyan-holiness people radical optimists. Though our Protestant forefathers taught that original sin would hang on our neck like an albatross all our life, holiness people teach that "you, even you, can be made inwardly pure and Christlike. . . . You can be freed from the inner sin nature, that fountain from which springs sinful acts and attitudes. We believe that you can be sanctified 'through and through' as 1 Thessalonians 5:23 declares" (Tracy 1993:5).

Thus the goal of spirituality—and therefore the goal of spiritual direction, spiritual friendship and spiritual guidance—is to help the believer live the life of love, that is, the life of Christlikeness. This is in harmony with Wesley's goals for his societies, which he called "a company of men having the form and seeking the power of godliness, united in order to pray together, to receive the word of exhortation, and to watch over one another in love, that they may help each other work out their salvation" (1872/1978:8:269).

HISTORY OF SPIRITUAL GUIDANCE IN THE WESLEYAN-HOLINESS TRADITION

Early in the Methodist revival, Wesley found the role of spiritual guide thrust upon him. "In every place people flock to me for direction in secular as well as spiritual affairs," Wesley wrote to a friend, "and I dare not throw . . . this burden off"

(1960:3:216). It was a role Wesley willingly embraced.

Steven J. Harper observes, "People looked to [John Wesley] for spiritual guidance for exactly the same reasons as Christians across the centuries have turned to spiritual directors, i.e., he personified the life they wished for themselves" (1985:92). Harper proceeds to cite the credentials of Wesley as a spiritual guide. He traces his upbringing in a devout home, his connection to historical spirituality, his adherence to Scripture and his spiritual writings. Wesley's fifty-volume *Christian Library*, published in 1755 and again in 1773, is a treasury of spiritual formation texts (see table 6.1; Harper 1985:91-94).

But Wesley's work as a spiritual director or guide is best seen in his correspondence. It is in the letters that we see his theology applied to life and the type of spiritual guidance he practiced. Wesley believed that all Christians need the support of spiritual friendship and guidance. To Frances Godfrey, whom he addressed as "My Dear Fanny," he wrote, "It is a blessed thing to have fellow travellers to the New Jerusalem. If you do not find any you must make them for none can travel this road alone" (1960:8:158). Even wealthy bankers like Ebenezer Blackwell needed spiritual friends. Wesley wrote to him, "I am fully persuaded if you had always one or two faithful friends near you who could speak the very truth from their heart and watch over you in love, you would swiftly advance" (1960:3:94-95).

Wesley's letter to Ann Bolton, written when he was eighty-two years of age, shows both the need and the qualities Wesley expected in a spiritual friend.

> My Dear Nancy,—It is undoubtedly expedient for you to have a friend in whom you can fully confide that can always be near you or at a small distance, and ready to be consulted on all occasions. The time was when you took *me* to be your friend; and (to speak freely) I have loved you with no common affection. I "have loved you"— nay, I still do; my heart warms to you while I am writing. But I am generally at too great a distance, so that you cannot converse with me when you would. I am glad, therefore, that Providence has given you one whom you can more easily see and correspond with. You may certainly trust her in every instance; and she has . . . understanding, piety and experience. She may therefore perform those offices of friendship which I would rejoice to perform were I near you. But whenever you can, give me the pleasure of seeing you. (1960:7:278)

Wesley seldom used the term *direction,* fearing that it put too much power in the hands of the spiritual guide. The spiritual guidance he taught was called "Christian conference," in which people experienced mutual spiritual guidance in classes, bands, societies, families, and "twin soul" and faith mentoring pairs. See figure 6.1, a diagram of Wesley's spiritual formation structures. What contemporary structure improves on this plan?

The society. The Methodist Connexion was at first an organization within the

Table 6.1. John Wesley's *Christian Library*

PATRISTIC SPIRITUALITY
Clement of Rome. *Epistle to the Corinthians.*
Ignatius of Antioch. *St. Ignatius's Epistles.* (Six are included.)
Macarius the Egyptian. *Homilies.* (Twenty three are included.)
St. Polycarp. *Epistle to the Philippians.*

SPANISH SPIRITUALITY
Don Juan D'Avila. *Spiritual Letters.*
Miguel de Molinos. *The Spiritual Guide Which Leads the Soul to the Fruition of Inward Peace.*
John Wesley. *The Life of Gregory Lopez.*

FRENCH SPIRITUALITY
Anthoniette Bourignon. *Solid Virtue.*
Jean Duvergier de Hauranne. *Christian Instructions.*
Jacques Joseph Duguet. *Letters on Morality and Piety.*
François Fénelon. *Explications of the Maxims of the Saints Regarding the Interior Life.*
John Wesley. *Conversations with Brother Lawrence.*
————. *An Extract of the Life of Monsieur De Renty.*

PURITAN SPIRITUALITY
Isaac Ambrose. *The Practice of Sanctification.*
Richard Baxter. *The Saint's Everlasting Rest.*
Robert Bolton. *A Discourse On True Happiness.*
Thomas Goodwin. *A Child of God Walking in Darkness.*
John Owen. *Of Communion with God the Father, the Son, and the Holy Ghost.*
Henry Scougal. *The Life of God in the Soul of Man.*
Richard Sibs. *The Fountain Opened; Or, The Mystery of Godliness Revealed.*

GERMAN SPIRITUALITY
Thomas á Kempis. *The Imitation of Christ.*
John Arndt. *True Christianity.*
August H. Francke. *Nicodemus; Or, A Treatise on the Fear of Man.*

AMERICAN SPIRITUALITY
Jonathan Edwards. *Distinguishing Marks of a Work of the Spirit of God.*
————. *The Life of David Brainerd.*
————. *Treatise on Religious Affections.*

ANGLICAN SPIRITUALITY
William Law. *A Serious Call to a Devout and Holy Life.*

Wesley's *Christian Library* contained translations and excerpts from two hundred works. He entitled the collection of fifty volumes *A Christian Library: Consisting of extracts from and abridgements of the choicest pieces of practical divinity which have been published in the English tongue.* Table 6.1 shows selected works from various categories included in the collection, which was first published 1749-1755. The *Christian Library* became required reading for student preachers.

Church of England. Societies held no meetings that would conflict with the Anglican worship schedule. Eventually the society became a sort of local congregation meeting in chapels, halls and homes. The society had four meetings open to the whole congregation: (1) a Sunday evening service of preaching, Scripture reading, testimonies and hymn singing, (2) a 5:00 A.M. meeting on a weekday morning, (3) the Watchnight service monthly on Saturday night, (4) the Love Feast, a service featuring a meal of bread and water and opportunities to mend relationships.

The class meeting. The society was subdivided into *classes* of about twelve persons each. Every member of the society was required to join a class that met weekly. The class meeting was a more or less democratic forum where rich and poor, the educated and the illiterate could meet as peers. At first "class-meetings met in homes, shops, school rooms, attics—even coal bins—wherever there was room for ten or twelve people to assemble" (Henderson 1980:140).

In the class meeting Methodist doctrines, sermons and practices were explained. But the class was also an arena of *koinonia,* love and mutual support. After an opening hymn, typically the class leader would share the problems and victories in his or her own spiritual life. Class members would then, on a voluntary basis, follow suit.

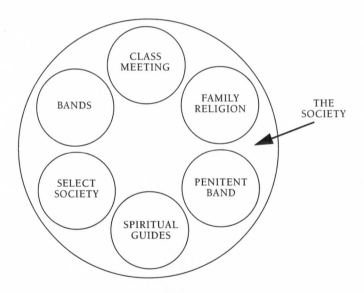

Figure 6.1. John Wesley's structures for spiritual formation

Wesley summarized the function of the classes in the *Arminian Magazine:*

The particular design of the classes is, to know who continue members of the society; to inspect their outward walking; to inquire into their inward state; to learn what are their trials; and how they fall by or conquer them; to instruct the ignorant in the principles of religion; to repeat, to explain, or enforce . . . what has been said in public preaching . . . [to ensure that] they have a clear, full, abiding conviction, that without inward, complete, universal holiness, no man shall see the Lord. (Henderson 1980:163)

When the Wesleyan revival jumped the Atlantic and came to America, rampant revivalism and the success of the Sunday school shoved the class meeting into the background. Today the heritage of the class meeting is expressed in Sunday school classes, small group Bible studies and membership classes.

The bands. The bands were same-gender groups of five or six persons committed to each other and to the holy life. Only about one-third of the typical society joined, or were invited to join, bands where they shared their spiritual journeys "without reserve and without disguise." Wesley felt that Methodism was closest to the New Testament ideal in the band meetings.

Before one could join a band, he or she was examined by means of eleven questions. Following are five of them:

1. Have you the forgiveness of sins and peace with God through our Lord Jesus Christ?

2. Have you the witness of God's Spirit with your spirit that you are a child of God?

3. Has no sin, inward or outward, dominion over you?

4. Do you desire to be told all your faults, and that plain and home?

5. Is it your desire and design to be, on this and on all other occasions, entirely open so as to speak everything that is in your heart without exception, without disguise, and without reserve? (Wesley 1978:8:272)

Wesley wrote five starter questions to be used in each band meeting. For Wesley's wording of the questions, see *The Works of John Wesley* (Wesley 1978). Following are these questions stated in contemporary style:

1. What spiritual failures have you experienced since our last meeting? What known sins, if any, have you committed?

2. What temptations have you battled with this week? Where do you feel the most vulnerable right now?

3. What temptations have you been delivered from this week? Please share with us how you won the victory.

4. Has the Lord revealed anything to you about your heart and life that makes you want us to join you in taking a second look at what might be sinful attitudes, lifestyle, or motivations?

5. Is there any spiritual problem that you have never been able to talk about—to us or even to God? (Tracy, Cockerill, Demaray and Harper 2000:133)

What Christian could not profit from meeting weekly with trusted "soul friends" to share answers to such questions?

The revival and camp meeting emphasis in America diminished the band meeting in the nineteenth century. And with the Sunday school then charged with almost all Christian nurture duties, the ministry of the bands faded. The genius of the band was, however, rediscovered when covenant groups surged through the religious and secular culture in the last three decades of the twentieth century. The Wesleyan and Wesleyan-holiness groups should have owned the franchise on covenant group work, but they had all but discarded the band ethos in favor of revivalism and Sunday school work and a lust to be like the super-successful Southern Baptists. Holiness churches had to relearn the covenant and support group ethos. Today covenant groups blossom like wisteria on the sunny side of the barn all over the Wesleyan-holiness movement.

The penitent band. This "backslider's band" was designed especially for sincere people who kept being recaptured by some besetting sin. They wanted to do right but had not found the strength and discipline to stay on the path to perfection. For them, the penitent band met on Saturday nights.

The Select Society. The Select Society was a small group for leaders in the Methodist Connexion. Only the most faithful and dedicated were invited. The Select Society had no rules, no set procedure and no official leader. Any concern of the leadership team could be discussed. Wesley's first experiment with this structure aimed at helping them advance in perfection and helping them love each other more, improving every leadership talent, and also "to have a select company, to whom I might unbosom myself on all occasions, without reserve" (Wesley 1960:8:261). Today church staff meetings and church board retreats do not draw on the Select Society heritage in any direct way.

Family religion. Those who write about Wesley's face-to-face groups almost always forget the family. Family worship and study was recommended twice daily, morning and evening. In addition, Thursday night was to be given to one-on-one parent-to-child instruction. On Saturday night the family was to review what had been learned during the week.

To help with family religion, Wesley provided *A Collection of Prayers for Families, Prayers and Devotions for Every Day of the Week, Prayers for Children, Lessons for Children* (two hundred Bible studies) and *Instructions for Children* (fifty-eight lessons on Christian living).

An insightful method of family worship was also provided:

Step 1: A short extemporaneous prayer.

Step 2: Psalm singing.

Step 3: Bible study. A parent was to read the scripture for the day and *explain* it. Then the children were to explain the Bible passage *back to the parents*.

Step 4: Family prayer using both written and spontaneous prayers.

Step 5: Singing of the Doxology.

Step 6: The Benediction given by a parent.

Step 7: The blessing. The parent lays his or her hand on the head of each child and blesses the child in Jesus' name. The blessing in Jesus' name, Wesley charged, was never to be omitted no matter how badly the child had behaved that day. (Tracy, Freeborn, Tartaglia and Weigelt 1994:197-99)

Twin Souls. Scholars have given the lion's share of their attention to Wesley's classes and bands. But a study of Wesley's letters reveals a lot of one-to-one spiritual guidance. Wesley frequently introduced "twin souls" to each other for the purpose of mutual spiritual guidance "without reserve and without disguise." The principle at work is "Our Lord . . . has given us to each other that we may strengthen each other's hands in Him" (Wesley 1960:2:115).

Faith mentoring. This is the term I am using to describe what Wesley called the service of "spiritual fathers" and "nursing mothers." Hundreds of times Wesley assigned a new or discouraged convert to the watch care of a seasoned saint. Serving as "God's usher," they would give whatever guidance they could. Sometimes Wesley made suggestions.

Ally Eden had gone against the fervent advice of her spiritual companions and married an unbeliever. Her life fell apart at the hands of a wicked husband. To Ann Bolton, the "nursing mother" to the classes and bands in the Witney are, Wesley wrote, "Do not forget poor Ally Eden. She has need of *comfort;* so we will not reprove her" (1960:8:246).

Many in the holiness movement today see faith mentoring as the most viable evangelistic method for the postmodern age.

THE PROCESS OF AUTHENTIC TRANSFORMATION

Authentic spirituality is a journey of grace. "By grace you have been saved through faith" (Eph 2:8 NIV). Though strenuous effort and vigorous discipline should be practiced in cooperation with grace, every stage of salvation is a gift of God's grace.

The saga of grace starts with *atoning grace,* with the Lamb slain before the foundation of the world. The story moves to *prevenient grace* (preventing and preparatory grace), operating before we even know it, giving us the capacity to choose God and good in spite of sin. *Saving grace* (which incorporates justification, regeneration and adoption) next rescues the believer from the guilt and power of sin. With Christ now living in the heart, the Christian discovers how serious God is about *sanctifying grace*. God will go on transforming the believer all through life by way of *refining* or *perfecting grace*. Even in *heaven*, the grace of God will likely be at work transforming us from one degree of glory to another.

Holiness people report experiencing the transforming grace of God in two ways. Both saving and sanctifying grace are experienced "in the twinkling of an eye." An instantaneous experience of conversion or "new birth" is the common testimony. Sanctifying grace, Wesleyan-holiness people believe, has both gradual and instantaneous aspects. John Wesley taught that although God makes the heart holy in an instant, there is no holiness that excludes "continual increase." The Scriptures speak of the act of sanctification (Acts 15:8-9) and the journey of sanctification (2 Cor 3:18).

The experiences of God's people through the centuries, Wesleyan-holiness pilgrims say, make us expect that God will cleanse our heart and fill us with the Holy Spirit "in the twinkling of an eye." Millions in the Wesleyan-holiness tradition claim that they didn't make up a second instantaneous work of grace that cleanses from sin. They have simply observed that this is the way God generally works.

John Wesley, between 1759 and 1762, personally interviewed some one thousand persons who had found the deeper life of holiness. He described the results of this research in the sermon "On Patience."

> Every one of them was exceeding clear in their experience. Every one (after the most careful inquiry I have not found one exception) . . . has declared that his deliverance from sin [entire sanctification] was instantaneous; that the change was wrought in a moment. Had half of these, or one-third, or one in twenty declared it was gradually wrought in them, I would have believed this in regard to them, and thought that some were gradually sanctified and some instantaneously.
>
> But as I have not found, in so long a space of time, a single person speaking thus: as all who believe they are sanctified declare with one voice that the change was wrought in a moment. I cannot but believe that sanctification is commonly, if not always, an instantaneous work. (1978:6:491)

In his classic *A Plain Account of Christian Perfection* Wesley said,

> Beyond all possibility of exception . . . my brother and I maintained . . . that this [sanctification] is received merely by faith . . . given instantaneously, in one moment. . . . There is a gradual work of God in the soul. . . . Generally speaking, it is a long time . . . before sin is destroyed. There is a gradual work both before and after that moment [of sanctification]. (1978:11:393, 423)

The saints in every age, Wesleyan-holiness people observe, have reported a crisis experience of God after conversion that ushered them into the deeper life.

The transformation of 2 Corinthians 3:18, on the other hand, continues throughout the long journey of faith and grace. "We . . . are being transformed into his likeness with ever-increasing glory" (NIV), the Bible says. That is the process of sanctification.

It isn't as though when you experienced the transforming moment of being filled with the Spirit you were given a lifetime supply of holiness. The Wesleyan tradition has always taught that sanctifying grace is a moment-by-moment experience. The cleansing of the Spirit goes on in the daily give-and-take of life. John Wesley called this spiritual breathing. As we live and breathe, the Spirit, the breath of God, cleanses and empowers.

The Spirit points out prejudices and unexamined practices and attitudes that need cleansing. As he guides us into more truth about ourselves, we learn of our lacks and lapses that need the refiner's fire. This transformation or sanctification goes on throughout life.

The cleansing and filling of the Spirit are not once and for all. John Wesley preached, "We feel the power of Christ every moment . . . whereby we are enabled to continue in the spiritual life and without which, notwithstanding our present holiness, we should be devils the next moment" (1978:5:167).

Moving beyond Wesleyan-holiness soteriology, the pastor, faith mentor or covenant group leader would look for evidences of Christlikeness as indications of authentic transformation. For holiness people, Christlikeness means love. Loving relationships and loving deeds are indications of spiritual transformation. Love is the fruit of the Spirit from which the others—peace, gentleness, joy, temperance—spring (Gal 5:22-23).

Wesleyan-holiness theologian H. Ray Dunning speaks of sanctification as providing four freedoms: (1) freedom for God (restoration of right relation and fuller restoration of the *imago Dei*), (2) freedom for others (self-sacrificing service), (3) freedom from the earth (restored balance with the creation and with "worldly things" such as wealth and possessions) and (4) freedom from self-domination (1988:485-98).

THE ROLE OF SPIRITUAL GUIDES

In a post-Christian, postmodern culture, faith mentoring emerges as the most promising method of passing the Light along to the next generation. We can no longer assume that Christian faith and values form the common ideals. To Wesleyan-holiness people, that means it is necessary to spend more time with fewer people and teach the faith by example, counsel, coaching and modeling.

In times much like our own, St. Paul urged Timothy, his son in the faith, "The things you have heard me say . . . entrust to reliable men who will also be qualified to teach others" (2 Tim 2:2 NIV). Christians established in prayer and the Scriptures, who are guided by the Spirit, known for holiness of life, patience, understanding, discernment, vulnerability and an ability to listen, will be our best evangelists and spiritual guides as they engage in one-on-one mentoring relationships (Tracy 1988:148).

Guide. The faith mentor is like a trail guide who has hiked this mountain before. He or she knows the hazards, challenges and happy surprises that lie ahead. The guide acts as God's usher, escorting the mentee into the Lord's presence in the various arenas of life.

Model. A model is, according to Sondra Matthaei, "a respected person who journeys with us, a living example of spirituality, lifestyle, values, sharing life experiences, vocation, intimacy, femininity/masculinity, and honesty" (1986:9). Laurent Daloz notes that as we observe our models, we do not slavishly try to "become *like* them, but . . . more fully ourselves *through* them" (1987:231).

Coach. The mentor-coach instructs on how to play the game. He or she then makes us watch spiritual game films—in painful slow motion—and shows us how to do better next time. Paul tells the Thessalonians that he wants to coach them face to face so that he can "perfect that which is lacking in your faith" (1 Thess 3:10 KJV).

In sports, it is often the coach who will not let us give up when the going gets tough. When Jane Hilton, a new convert, was devastated by a withering temptation, John Wesley wrote to her, "Christ is yours; and He is wiser and stronger than all the powers of hell. Hang upon Him . . . lean on Him with the whole weight of your soul" (1960:5:87). Her spiritual coach would not let her give up.

Advocate. As a spiritual friend, the mentor offers support and affirmation for the mentee's honest search for identity and meaning even when friends, family or the pastor may not understand.

Sponsor. Some churches appoint sponsors for youth. The sponsor-mentor is to be guide, friend, colearner and the one who leads the juvenile into full participation in the church.

Guarantor. Teens and young adults need "guarantors" who incarnate Christian adulthood in ways that encourage young people to grow. They guarantee that adulthood is a good place to be. The faith mentor communicates to the observing young person that authentic faith in God makes the future worthwhile.

Mediator. One of the basic Protestant principles is the priesthood of all believers. That means ordinary Christians can become priests to one another.

A faith mentor can mediate love, grace, self-knowledge and discernment of the will of God as well as acceptance, assurance and a sense of direction in life. A faith mentor can also mediate between a painful past and a promise-filled future (Tracy et al. 2000:168). The faith mentor as mediator brings the mentee's personal story into contact with the Bible, the Christian tradition and the church (Tracy et al. 1994:187).

Faith mentoring, as the term is used here, is primarily a journeyman-apprentice relationship. A faith mentor may fill any or all of the seven aforementioned roles and functions. The nature and gifts of the mentor and mentee and the life situation in which the relationship develops more or less shape the opportunities to serve as coach, guarantor, mediator and so on. Beyond the "nursing mother/spiritual father" relationship of faith mentoring, the mutual spiritual guidance of twin souls (to use Wesley's term) produces situations in which mature Christians also can serve each other in the seven roles and functions cited above.

INDICATORS OF MATURE SPIRITUALITY

The ideal spirituality is characterized, in the Wesleyan-holiness vision, by Christlikeness in relationship to God, neighbor and creation. Perilous it is to judge that in others. But a pastor might look for balance among several indirect indicators.

Practice of personal spiritual disciplines. Prayer is an essential discipline. In Wesleyan circles, a day without prayer is a boast against God. In *The Wesleyan-Holiness Way to Spiritual Formation* (Tracy 2003) the practice of prayer includes adoration, praise, thanksgiving, confession, intercession and petition (lessons 11-12).

Bible study is a core constituent of Wesleyan-holiness spirituality. "The Scripture, . . . the Old and New Testament is a most solid and precious system of divine truth. . . . It is the fountain of heavenly wisdom, which they who are able to taste, prefer to all the writings of men, however wise, or learned, or holy" (Wesley 1981:preface).

The Wesleyan-Holiness Way to Spiritual Formation (Tracy 2003:lesson 14) cites these disciplines of abstinence: (1) fasting from food for the body in order to prepare a feast for the soul, (2) chastity, refraining from sexual excess or from sexual expression even in marriage to elevate the spiritual over the physical, (3) solitude, fasting from convivial company in order to be alone, (4) silence, going beyond solitude to make time for listening, (5) simplicity, requiring that we "disentangle ourselves from too many commitments, relieve ourselves of debts and obligations that keep us anxious and burdened" (Steele 1990:93), and (6) secrecy, refraining from making our good deeds and qualities known (Willard 1988:172).

One reason we know so much about the spirituality of the Wesleyan movement is that John Wesley taught his people to keep a regular journal. The *Reflecting God Journal* (Tracy 2002) states that a regular time "to reflect and write can help bring integration to the flashing forces that fragment thought, befuddle hearts, clutter agendas, and reduce you and me to flustered ineffectiveness."

The spiritual disciplines of community. Nothing in the Wesleyan-holiness vision, certainly no private spiritual discipline, takes the place of corporate worship. Worship is not primarily about you and your bundle of felt needs, wishes, desires, good intentions, or a desire to escape dull or threatening realities of life through a swooning spiritual experience. "Worship is not about performance! The worship leaders are not there to keep us amused and entertained; they are not performers fishing for double encores. They are to guide us in offering a sacrifice of worship to God" (Tracy 2003:lesson 15). Worship is about God. We worship God because of who he is.

Though preaching—the sacrament of the Word—takes precedence over the sacrament of the Table, both the Lord's Supper and baptism are important in Wesleyan spirituality. Wesleyans celebrate two sacraments: baptism, the sacrament of initiation, and the Lord's Supper, the sacrament of sanctification. Proper practice of these sacraments would be an indirect indication of mature spirituality.

Avoidance of classes, prayer groups, Bible studies and the like would not be seen as a healthy sign. Wesleyans agree with Luciano de Crescenzo: "We are, each of us, angels with only one wing, and we can only fly embracing each other" (quoted in Tracy et al. 2000:127). George Whitefield, the famous evangelist who preached to more throngs than John Wesley, looked back on his career dolefully toward the end. "Brother Wesley acted wisely," he said. "The souls that were awakened under his ministry he joined in class, and thus preserved the fruits of his labor. This I neglected, and my people are a rope of sand" (quoted in Tracy et al. 1994:139).

One of the problems with evangelical spirituality is that Christians have no one to talk to. That makes the Wesleyan tradition of soul friends and faith mentors a precious resource. Wesleyan spirituality is not made for hermits, monks or ascetics. Not only was it designed to avoid such spiritual systems, it was designed in defiance of them. Wesley taught that the sanctified coal miner is every bit as holy as the ascetic fighting demons in the desert.

The spiritual disciplines of service. Some traditions publish spiritual manuals with hardly a hint at service as a spiritual discipline. But in the Wesleyan tradition, service is as much a spiritual discipline as prayer. Maxie Dunnam put it this way: "A spirituality that does not lead to active ministry becomes an indulgent preoccupation with self, and therefore grieves the Holy Spirit and violates the presence of the indwelling Christ" (1982:55). He was echoing the words of John Wesley: "We do not acknowledge him to have one grain of faith, who is not continually doing good, who is not willing to 'spend and be spent' in doing all good . . . to all men" (1978:8:271).

COMPARISON WITH PSYCHOTHERAPY AND PASTORAL COUNSELING

One of the most obvious contrasts between spiritual direction (as practiced in the Wesleyan-holiness movement) and psychotherapy has to do with the levels of education and professional expertise required and expected of the practitioners. Psychotherapists are highly trained professionals. The Wesleyan-holiness spiritual guide is usually the lay leader of a small group of friends committed to helping each other grow in Christlikeness.

Another contrast is seen in the typical focus of encounters. The psychotherapist is concerned with discovering, analyzing, interpreting and healing the inner self. The faith mentor, spiritual friend or covenant group leader cares more about growth in grace and movements of the Holy Spirit. There is, however, great wariness among the Wesleyan-holiness people about letting a "director" declare what the Spirit is saying, lest the "director" mistake his or her own impulses for the prompting of the Spirit.

The way a practitioner comes to a position of leadership highlights another contrast. Psychotherapists frame a diploma, hang a shingle and perhaps put an ad in the paper. The faith mentor or spiritual friend never advertises, hangs no shingle, and may or may not have a diploma worth mounting in a Wal-Mart frame. Rather, they are pressed into service because their integrity, holiness, wisdom and religious experience have been found worthy of trust by the family of faith. Spiritual guides in the Wesleyan-holiness movement are almost never paid; psychotherapists are almost always paid—at least they mail a bill.

One contrast lies in the area of compassion and empathy. The faith mentor will freely express compassion and empathy. Even interpersonal and existential psychotherapists seem to work hard to police feelings of empathy and compassion. Willard Gaylin declares, "The therapist is to guard against . . . compassion and empathy. . . . The therapist who indulges . . . compassion is not doing her duty. . . . The therapeutic alliance demands control of benevolent emotions" (2000:214).

Contrasts in practice reflect contrasts in theoretical foundations. An informed Wesleyan-holiness spiritual guide will stand on the devotional classics (Augustine's *Confessions,* Thomas à Kempis's *The Imitation of Christ* and the like), more recent venerable works arising within Wesleyan-Arminian ranks (Hannah Whitall Smith, *The Christian's Secret of a Happy Life;* E. Stanley Jones, *Mastery,* etc.), as well as contemporary titles. Psychotherapy may turn to Freud, Jung, Rank, Wundt, Horney, Skinner, and a covey of contemporary writers from Albert Ellis to Dr. Phil.

Pastoral counseling receives less of the pastor's attention and workweek than it did twenty-five years ago. Fewer than 5 percent of Wesleyan-holiness churches have a paid counselor on staff. The typical church has fewer than two hundred members, and budget realities make a counselor the last hired and the first fired. Further, the pastor who reserves an afternoon or two a week for professional counseling is rare.

Clinical training is a factor. While the Wesleyan-holiness pastor usually has more psychological training than church members who serve as faith mentors and covenant group leaders, he or she has considerably less clinical education than a psychotherapist. A study of one Wesleyan-holiness denomination revealed that only 7 percent of pastors hold doctorates, 45 percent hold master's degrees and many serve with a bachelor's degree or less education. Few package themselves as clinical specialists (Crow 2001:5).

One contrast between psychotherapy and pastoral counseling pertains to the presenting problem. The psychotherapist typically receives clients who are battling longstanding neuroses or abnormalities that produce personal or social dysfunctions. A long series of sessions exploring primal drives and exhuming painful memories in search of insight and healing will likely follow. The typical counseling encounter for the Wesleyan-holiness pastor is a "crisis counseling" situation sparked by job loss, death, divorce, crisis pregnancy, domestic violence or another urgent need. Such an existential crisis may prompt the parishioner to consult his spiritual guide, but more than likely it produces an unscheduled knock on the pastor's door. The pastoral counselor is not vitally concerned with "suppressed instinctual strivings or internalized . . . shards of forgotten traumatic memories" (Yalom 2002:xvii). Rather, helping the counselee survive an existential collision is the goal. Typically, the pastor will engage the parishioner-in-crisis in one to three sessions. Then the pastoral counselor may refer the member in crisis to a covenant group leader or a faith mentor for longer-term spiritual guidance.

Sometimes the crisis that brings a counselee to the pastor is guilt and shame over sins past and present. One veteran of forty-three years of pastoral service said that only teen-parent problems produce more counseling sessions. Different ways of dealing with guilt and shame point to yet another contrast among spiritual direction, pastoral counseling and psychotherapy. Though all practice "unconditional positive regard," psychotherapists—especially environmental determinists—regard the client as a victim of sickness and will often "normalize" the client's behavior. The psychiatrist will likely find a physical source for the symptom, thus making it billable to insurance companies that threaten to reduce psychiatrists to pharmacologists. The spiritual director and the pastoral counselor, however, take sin seriously and guide the counselee toward self-examination, confession, repentance and grace.

Pastoral counseling and spiritual direction in the Wesleyan-holiness movement share a common foundation in the Bible and theology. Wesleyan-holiness people embrace these identifying markers: Christian, Protestant, Arminian, Wesleyan and Holiness. Classic Christian teachings about God, humankind, sin and salvation—particularly the Wesleyan doctrines of justification and sanctification—frame the backdrop for practice.

As Wesleyan-holiness pastoral counselor and spiritual guides look at the psychological literature, they find some affinity and transferable concepts in the work of interpersonal and existential writers such as Karen Horney, Carl Rogers, Harry Stack Sullivan, Erich Fromm and Rollo May. The developmental work of Jean Piaget, Lawrence Kohlberg and Methodist James Fowler is also respected. Wesleyan-holiness practitioners, however, show considerable resistance to psychoanalytic and behavioral theorists who make the human being a passive lump on which environment acts. They know that no one is impervious to environment, but they conduct their work in the conviction that both life and Scripture present human beings as free and responsible. Environment does not have the last vote.

The pastoral counselor in the Wesleyan-holiness movement falls squarely between the spiritual director and the psychotherapist when it comes to education and clinical training. He or she is involved in both the care and cure of souls. Happy is the pastor who sees both the spiritual guide and the Christian psychotherapist as allies. More blessed still is the pastor who knows how to use this alliance.

WHEN THE SPIRITUAL GUIDE USES A MENTAL HEALTH PROFESSIONAL

In Wesleyan-holiness circles, pastors are regularly trained to refer parishioners or counselees to mental health professionals—Christian ones if available—when they see that the counselee has problems beyond the typical pastor's ability to solve. If, for example, the counselee seems on the brink of violence toward self or family, or exhibits extreme schizoid or paranoid behavior, or if the pastor thinks the disorder may spring from chemical imbalance, the pastor usually does not hesitate to refer to a mental health professional. Most pastors have a list at hand. Few have time for repeated and lengthy counseling sessions.

The hectic schedule of pastors often shoves them toward referring a counselee to the mental health professional too quickly. In doing this, the pastor forfeits a valuable tool for healing and wholeness that the clinical practitioner does not have: the church. The resources of worship, nurture, fellowship, face-to-face groups, faith mentors, soul friends—all these help make the church a healing community.

Table 6.2. Spiritual Direction, Psychotherapy and Pastoral Counseling

Dimension	Spiritual Direction	Psychotherapy	Pastoral Counseling
Presenting Problem	Hunger to know more of God; yearning for a deeper spiritual life; thirst for holiness, wholeness and Christlikeness Spiritual failure, sin, guilt, shame, "poverty of spirit"	Anxiety, fear, aimlessness, low self-esteem, alienation, depression, antisocial behavior, addiction	Existential crises: death, divorce, abuse, addiction, etc. Guilt, shame, anxiety
Goals	Transformation by the grace of God in Christ, wholeness, holiness, Christlikeness	Integration, becoming fully human, self-acceptance, self-actualization	Survival of life's jolts, coping with crisis; submission of sin, guilt, and shame, to the grace of God in Christ
Procedure	Guidance toward the transforming moments of saving and sanctifying grace; guidance for the lifelong journey of spiritual formation; sharing one's spiritual journey with a covenant group, twin soul, faith mentor	One-on-one counseling sessions exploring past and present problems Group therapy	Talking things over with the pastor; pastor really "listens" and verbalizes support Praying together: invocation of the presence and promises of God
Resources	Personal spiritual disciplines: prayer, Bible study Spiritual disciplines of community: worship, sacraments, face-to-face groups, fellowship and service Inner resource of the *imago Dei*; wisdom of the spiritual guide; guidance of the Spirit	Insights, experience, education and skill of the counselor Inner resources of the human personality; insights from the counselee's past and present experiences	Worldview of the Bible and Christian faith Congregational resources: worship, nurture, faith mentors, covenant groups Wisdom, discernment and spiritual experience of the pastor Christian literature on coping with the human condition Power and guidance of the Holy Spirit of Christ

In the Wesleyan worldview the threshold to the deeper spiritual life, to holiness, to Christlikeness for the born-again believer is entire consecration, that is, complete and loving submission to God. That being the case, perhaps it is fitting to close with this prayer transcribed by Steven J. Harper (1981:2:355) from John Wesley's personal prayer journal.

> O Lord Jesus,
> I give thee my body,
> my soul,
> my substance
> my fame,
> my friends,
> my liberty, and my life:
> dispose of me and all that is mine
> as it seems best to thee.
> I am now not mine, but thine:
> therefore claim me as thy right,
> keep me as thy charge, and love me as thy child.
> Fight for me when I am assaulted,
> heal me when I am wounded,
> and revive me when I am destroyed.
> Amen.

SUMMARY

Though the term "spiritual direction" is not a common part of the vocabulary of Wesleyan-holiness people, the goals of spiritual direction form the core of their spiritual quest. The goal of spiritual guidance is sanctification, holiness and Christlikeness. Avoiding "direction" for fear of spiritual abuse, Wesleyan-holiness people seek to help each other toward Christian perfection by way of face-to-face groups, spiritual companioning and faith mentoring. These structures and practices are rooted in the Wesleyan revival of eighteenth-century England and the American holiness movement of the nineteenth century.

Pastoral counseling in this movement usually takes the form of crisis counseling. The pastor often refers counselees to faith mentors or covenant groups. Wesleyan-holiness pastors and spiritual guides are not nearly as highly trained in clinical procedures as psychotherapists, and few package themselves as counselors. They do regularly refer parishioners to Christian psychotherapists.

Though the spiritual guide, the counseling pastor and the Christian psychotherapist are strategic allies, there is little to inspire the idea that classical spiritual direction will soon flourish in this faith family.

REFERENCES

Book of common prayer, The. 1979. New York: Church Hymnal Corporation.

Crow, K. 2001. Clergy preparation and church/college relationships. Typescript, Church of the Nazarene, Clergy Services.

Dunnam, Maxie. 1982. *Alive in Christ: The dynamic process of spiritual formation.* Nashville: Abingdon.

Dunning, H. Ray. 1988. *Grace, faith and holiness: A Wesleyan systematic theology.* Kansas City, Mo.: Beacon Hill.

Gaylin, Willard. 2000. *Talk is not enough.* New York: Little, Brown.

Harper, Steven J. 1985. John Wesley: Spiritual guide. *Wesleyan Theological Journal* 20:91-96.

Henderson, David Michael. 1980. John Wesley's instructional groups. Ann Arbor, Mich.: University Microfilms International, UMI 8029228.

Matthaei, Sondra H. 1991. Faith-mentoring in the faith community. Ph.D. diss., Claremont School of Theology.

Steele, Les L. 1990. *On the way: A practical theology of Christian formation.* Grand Rapids, Mich.: Baker.

Tracy, Wesley D. 1988. John Wesley, spiritual director: Spiritual guidance in Wesley's letters. *Wesleyan Theological Journal* 23:148-62.

———. 1991. John Wesley: Preacher of holiness. *Herald of Holiness* 80:24-25, 32.

———. 1993. The Nazarenes: Those radical optimists. *Herald of Holiness* 82:4-6.

———. 2002. *The reflecting God journal.* Kansas City, Mo.: Beacon Hill.

———. 2003. *The Wesleyan-Holiness way to spiritual formation.* Kansas City, Mo.: Church of the Nazarene Clergy Services (CD-ROM).

Tracy, Wesley D., Gary Cockerill, Donald Demaray and Steven H. Harper. 2000. *Reflecting God.* Kansas City, Mo.: Beacon Hill/Christian Holiness Partnership.

Tracy, Wesley D., E. Dee Freeborn, Janine Tartaglia and Morris A. Weigelt. 1994. *The Upward call: Spiritual formation and the holy life.* Kansas City, Mo.: Beacon Hill.

Tracy, Wesley D., and Stan Ingersol. 1998. *Here we stand.* Kansas City, Mo.: Beacon Hill.

Weigelt, Morris A., and E. Dee Freeborn. 2001. *Living the Lord's prayer: Design for spiritual formation.* Kansas City, Mo.: Beacon Hill.

Wesley, John. 1981. *Expository notes on the New Testament.* Vol. 1. Kansas City, Mo.: Beacon Hill.

———. 1978. *The works of John Wesley.* 3rd ed. Vols. 5-6, 8, 11. Ed. Thomas Jackson. Kansas City, Mo.: Beacon Hill.

———. 1960. *The letters of the Rev. John Wesley, A.M.* Vols. 2-3, 5-8. Ed. John Telford. London: Epworth.

Willard, Dallas. 1988. *The Spirit of the disciplines: Understanding how God changes lives.* San Francisco: HarperSanFrancisco.

———. 2000. *The divine conspiracy.* San Francisco: HarperSanFrancisco.

Yalom, Irvin D. 2002. *The gift of therapy.* New York: HarperCollins.

BEST WESLEYAN-HOLINESS BOOKS ON SPIRITUAL FORMATION

CLASSICS

Chambers, Oswald. *My Utmost for His Highest.* This book is the best devotional treatment of the sanctified life available today. First published in 1935, it has gone through many editions. One of the most recent, though not dated, is published by Barbour, Urichsville, Ohio.

Smith, Hannah Whitall. 1888. *The Christian's secret of a happy life.* New York: Fleming H. Revell.

Wesley, John. 1872. *A plain account of Christian perfection.* See *The Works of John Wesley*, 3rd ed., ed. Thomas Jackson, reprint, Kansas City: Beacon Hill, 1978.

CONTEMPORARY WORKS

The Reflecting God materials are intended to be a comprehensive set of spiritual formation resources in the Wesleyan-holiness tradition. These items are published by the Nazarene Publishing House/Beacon Hill Press of Kansas City under the auspices of the Christian Holiness Partnership (CHP).

Reflecting God Study Bible. 1999.

Tracy, Wesley, Gary Cockerill, Donald Demaray and Steven Harper. 2000. *Reflecting God.*

Tracy, Wesley. 2000. *Reflecting God* Leader's Guide.

———. 2000. *Reflecting God* Workbook.

———. 2002. *Reflecting God* Journal.

Tracy, Wesley D., Morris A. Weigelt, E. Dee Freeborn and Janine Tartaglia. 1994. *The Upward Call: Spiritual Formation and the Holy Life.* Kansas City, Mo.: Beacon Hill. Spanish edition available. This book gives more direct attention to matters relating to spiritual direction and guidance than the *Reflecting God* books.

Weigelt, Morris A., and E. Dee Freeborn. 2001. *Living the Lord's Prayer: Design for Spiritual Formation.* Kansas City, Mo.: Beacon Hill. This book is the fruit of eighteen years of team-teaching spiritual formation at Nazarene Theological Seminary by the authors.

COLLECTIONS

Exploring Christian Holiness. 1983-1985. 3 vols. Kansas City, Mo.: Beacon Hill.

Vol. 1, *The Biblical Foundations,* W. T. Purkiser

Vol. 2, *The Historical Development,* Paul M. Bassett and William M. Greathouse

Vol. 3, *Theological Formulation,* Willard H. Taylor

Great Holiness Classics, 6 vols. Kansas City, Mo.: Beacon Hill, various dates and editors.

Holiness Teaching—New Testament Times to Wesley

The Wesley Century

Leading Wesleyan Thinkers

The 19th-Century Holiness Movement

Holiness Preachers and Preaching

Holiness Teaching Today.

7

SPIRITUAL DIRECTION IN THE
SOCIAL JUSTICE TRADITION

Jerry A. Gladson

Hᴏw may spiritual formation, with emphasis on the individual, spiritual direction and the shaping of the spiritual life, and the ministry of social justice, with its stress on the community, be balanced in a religious tradition? I will attempt to answer that question from my perspective as a minister within the United Church of Christ, one of the major denominations in the United States that embodies a strong social justice tradition. The United Church of Christ will be our test case.

This denomination has approximately 1.2 million members in over six thousand churches. Four churches of historic importance constitute the United Church of Christ: the Congregational Church, the Christian Church, the Evangelical Synod and the Reformed Church. The first two were merged into the Congregational Churches in 1931 and were joined by the by-then-merged Evangelical and Reformed Church in 1957. Each faith community brought into the new denomination a "hidden" history (Zikmund 1984) in which seeds of social justice and piety were preserved. Representing a bold alternative to the divisions in modern Protestant life, the United Church of Christ has attempted to model an ecumenical healing of the scandalous ruptures in the Christian fabric. Through its four antecedent bodies, the United Church of Christ embraces elements of the whole Protestant expression of Christian faith.

To sharpen the denomination's focus on social justice, the United Church of Christ statement of faith, adopted in 1959 and partially quoted here in its doxological form, calls for "resist[ing] the powers of evil," which are understood in political as well as spiritual form. The statement continues in the Book of Worship (1986:514):

> You [God] promise to all who trust you
> forgiveness of sins and fullness of grace,
> courage in the struggle for justice and peace,
> your presence in trial and rejoicing . . .

While it accepts the Bible "as the authoritative witness to the Word of God," the ecumenical creeds and the confessions of the Reformation, the United Church of Christ does not impose any doctrine or form of worship on its members. It receives the historic creeds and confessions as testimonies but not tests of the faith (United Church of Christ 2001a). Thus while this statement of faith is not regarded as binding on congregations or individuals, it does accurately represent the faith, concern and focus of the uniting groups (Mead 1995).

Social service and justice have deep roots in the United Church of Christ and form a large piece of the fabric of its contemporary life. A brief examination of the September 2001 *United Church News,* the denomination's national newsletter, and the church's website will show something of this emphasis. The lead article in *United Church News* portrays a teen project in New York designed to bring together minorities and majorities by learning scuba diving. By learning together, the teens come to develop trust in others of a different culture (Comrie 2001). The Florida Conference of the United Church of Christ presented a resolution, subsequently voted by the United Church of Christ General Synod in Kansas City, Missouri, July 2001, calling for a boycott of Taco Bell because the restaurant purchases tomatoes from the Florida-based SixL company, which pays immigrant pickers a substandard wage (Golder 2001). The Southeast Conference, headquartered in Atlanta, Georgia, continued fund-raising efforts toward the "Adopt-A-Minefield" program, an endeavor to rid Third World nations of minefields (Kershner 2001).

These are not issues in which one finds many other Protestant churches involved. Spearheading such social justice activities is the denomination's Justice and Witness Ministries, one of the formally recognized "Ministries" in the United Church of Christ. This Ministry seeks to empower individuals and congregations to advocate justice in communities and in the world. A survey of its website on November 29, 2001 (United Church of Christ 2001a), yields thirty "weekly alerts," that is, calls to action regarding issues of social justice, essentially political in nature. The United Church of Christ aggressively speaks out on public policy, even when it is unpopular.

Norman Jackson, former conference minister of the Hawaii Conference, links the gospel with serving the "hungry, the sick, and victims of wars, disasters, and the globalized economy." The church's mission aims at "undermining the demonic dominant cultural status quo; challenging unjust structures; combating . . . governmental policies designed to serve the wealthy and the powerful" (Jackson 2000:31).

As admirable as this emphasis is, what place does such denominational life give to spiritual formation and direction, disciplines that stress individual spirituality and fellowship with God? How does the United Church of Christ address the balance between spiritual formation, with its emphasis on the individual, spiritual direction, and its shaping of spiritual life, and the ministry of social justice, with its accentuation of the community?

DEFINITION OF SPIRITUAL DIRECTION

Spirituality is rooted in the word *spirit,* which in Hebrew *(ruah),* Greek *(pneuma)* and Latin *(spiritus)* refers to "breath" or the spiritual life force. Spirituality embraces passion and inspiration that come from within and connect us with the world. It includes the fundamental forces of life, that which motivates love, concern and passion. It does not constitute a separate category, as **Gerald** May (2001) points out, but rather is a part of all emotions, connections, work and everything existentially meaningful to human beings. Nor is spirituality something ethereal. Rather, it is quite ordinary and natural. Everyone has spiritual needs, in my opinion, whether acknowledged or not. Spirituality, as Rudolf Otto (1923) observed in his classic analysis, is a nonreducible experience somehow inherent in the human psyche in every culture.

Spirituality, moreover, constitutes the living core of every great religion. One could even say that religion is really about the cultivation, in some way, of this living core. Traditionally, spiritually has been expressed in three principal ways: knowing, acting and feeling. Accordingly, God is conceived as ultimate Truth, Goodness and Beauty. Analogous to the Hindu idea of the three ways as yogas, disciplines or paths (Weightman 1984), these might be thought of as the Way of the True, the Way of the Good and the Way of the Beautiful (May 2001).

The Way of the True appeals to those whose interest lies in philosophy, theology and psychology, all ways of knowing. For those whose interest takes them in the direction of helping the poor and the sick and creating a more just society, there is the Way of the Good. Passion, empathy and intimacy, or the affective experience, form the Way of the Beautiful (May 2001). Spiritual formation may be seen as drawing from all three ways. It has to do with cultivation of the spiritual, usually in intentional disciplines, such as prayer, meditation and loving service.

Spiritual *direction* guides spiritual formation and is grounded in two basic assumptions: (1) one's relationship with God (the vertical dimension) is primary, and (2) one's relationship with God is bound up inextricably with one's relationship with others and the entire created order (the horizontal dimension; Jones 1999). This interpretation of spiritual direction and spiritual formation, widely accepted in the United Church of Christ, understands social justice as a way the horizontal dimension of spiritual formation may be realized.

HISTORY OF SPIRITUAL DIRECTION IN THE UNITED CHURCH OF CHRIST

Given that religion must inevitably have redemptive social consequences, and that spiritual development is a necessary prerequisite for these social consequences to emerge, how has the United Church of Christ historically brought them together?

The United Church of Christ champions social justice, identifying with the rights of the marginalized, women, victims of AIDS and racial minorities. It maintains a very open stance on ordination and seeks to bring racial minorities "into the mainstream of life both in the church and in society." For the United Church of Christ, to profess the gospel inevitably means the liberation of human beings from both spiritual and physical bondage (Rosten 1975). The gospel and social justice, "justice and shalom in all human relationships and social structures" (Foster 1998), are inextricably linked.

As of this writing, the United Church of Christ has no formally institutionalized program of spiritual direction. In large part this is attributable to the nature of United Church of Christ polity, which is congregational and thus precludes the superimposing of universal programs on individual parishes. Programming in the United Church of Christ tends to develop at the grassroots level. When it is developed at a national or synodal level, it may only be recommended to other organizations within the denomination.

Throughout the first three decades of the denomination's history (1960-1990), little formal attention was given to spiritual formation. The emphasis during this period largely fell on social justice issues. Throughout the struggle for civil rights, women's rights and the inclusion of marginalized populations in mainstream American life, and its own struggle to carve out an identity, the United Church of Christ had its hands full. But beginning in the late 1980s and 1990s, in part as a counterbalance to the denomination's strong emphasis on social justice, but also as a response to cultural thirst for spirituality, interest in spirituality has moved into greater prominence. Signs of this interest are everywhere.

The Evangelism Ministry Team, a component of the Local Church Ministries of the United Church of Christ, has adopted as its mission the development of resources and training for church members and leaders in "evangelism, increased worship attendance, membership growth, and *spiritual development*" (United Church of Christ 2001d, emphasis added). The Twenty-second General Synod (1999) adopted a resolution that directly links spiritual formation and social justice, calling for spiritual formation to help persons "discover the movement of God in their lives through prayer, bible [sic] study, spiritual friendships," to assist them in being "in solidarity with one another as crucial issues are addressed such as ending patterns of emotional and spiritual isolation, confronting racism, sexism . . .

and violence," and in service to the church and its ministries of social justice (United Church of Christ 2001c).

Representing pastoral interest, in response to the terrorist attack on the World Trade Center on September 11, 2001, the Reverend James Todhunter of the Silver Spring Christ Congregational United Church of Christ (Maryland), linked spiritual formation and social justice. The "only true and lasting way to combat evil is through spiritual means . . . through prayer and love," he pointed out. Spiritual disciplines such as prayer lead one toward peacemaking and a rejection of vengeance. He urged his congregation to do something tangible for the victims of the World Trade Center disaster, one of whom was a member of Christ Congregational (Todhunter 2001).

The United Church of Christ has long taken the lead among Protestants in the full acceptance of all gender orientations within its membership. Instead of focusing exclusively on homosexuality, however, it seeks to encompass sexuality as a whole. To further this end, the denomination has developed resources for persons of all gender orientations intended to provide "avenues for spiritual growth, prophetic visions and action for justice" (United Church of Christ 2001b). Melanie Morrison (2000), realizing how far short the church falls in these efforts, calls on the denomination to welcome all wounded by shame, homophobia and fear-based images of God and points to the deep remediation found in God's grace, faith and justice.

These are representative examples in the contemporary United Church of Christ, where church leaders presently see the need to develop a spirituality capable of sustaining ministries of social justice.

At the local level, interest in both spirituality and social justice is burgeoning. First Community Church, United Church of Christ and Christian Church (Disciples of Christ), in Columbus, Ohio, operates a Spiritual Guidance Center, directed by Richard Wood Sr., who is a graduate of the Shalem Institute and the Harvard University Spirit/Mind/Body Institute. In Winston-Salem, North Carolina, Prodigals Community utilizes spiritual formation as a key component in its program for recovery from drug addiction (Starling-Melvin 2001).

First Congregational Church, United Church of Christ, in Berkeley, California, directs the Durant House and the Lloyd Center for Pastoral Counseling and Spiritual Direction, with Kathy Kunst as director, and is affiliated with San Francisco Theological Seminary in San Anselmo. "Spiritual direction," the Lloyd Center indicates (Durant House 2001), "is the art of Christian listening carried out in the context of a trusting one-to-one relationship." Insights from pastoral counseling, theology, psychology and yoga are integrated at the center, with the goal of "health and wholeness."

After nearly fifty years of existence, the United Church of Christ is recognizing and fostering the relationship between its historic interest in social justice and the rapidly developing practice of the disciplines of spirituality. "The church requires spiritual discipline rooted in scripture and prayer," observes Frederick Trost, a United Church of Christ administrator. "Prayer and deed are related" (2000:80).

THE PROCESS OF AUTHENTIC TRANSFORMATION

In keeping with Reformation tradition, the United Church of Christ does not see spiritual "perfection" as arising in the present state. Sanctification is regarded as the first indication of the goal of redemption. "Never perfected, always harassed by the sin it represents, it nevertheless is a hint of the final Things to Come" (Fackre and Fackre, 1991:138). What happens in the present life, according to Roger Shinn (1990), is the experience of divine forgiveness, empowerment in the struggle for justice, peace, an abiding sense of the divine presence and, in the end, eternal life. These elements appear in the denomination's Statement of Faith:

> You promise to all who trust you
> forgiveness of sins and fullness of grace,
> courage in the struggle for justice and peace,
> your presence in trial and rejoicing,
> and eternal life in your realm which has no end. (Book of Worship 1986:514)

Coming to humanity in Christ, God offers grace. "We are saved by grace, by God's amazing grace," writes Shinn (1990:100). This forgiveness is at the heart of the gospel and remains with humanity even in the struggle for justice.

God offers courage in this struggle, a divine empowerment to live out the command of Jesus to serve humanity. In this service, God grants spiritual peace. "Our prayers for peace will not be for some divine intervention that will end war apart from our acts; they will include prayers for courage and wisdom in the struggle for peace" (Shinn 1990:103).

Through it all—and here is where formal spiritual formation may provide a foundation—there is a sense of the divine presence. The precariousness of human existence makes all of life a risk. "When we ask God's presence, whether in trial or rejoicing, God will be there," affirms Shinn (1990:107). "Indeed, God will be there, whether or not we ask."

Finally, there is eternal life. The God of creation is the God at humanity's final destination. Although conceptions of what this mean vary in the United Church of Christ, the church teaches that "destiny is in the care of the eternal God, whose steadfast love is not defeated by our sin and our death" (Shinn 1990:109).

ROLE OF THE SPIRITUAL DIRECTOR

Spiritual direction, which helps shape spiritual formation, requires someone to lead, or give direction. This is the spiritual director or "spiritual friend," who, according to Alan Jones, is "someone who listens to us lovingly and accurately and, by the gift of caring attention, reveals to us God's open heart" (1999:ix, 4). It involves presence and attentiveness, "holy listening," to individuals who seek the wholeness of God (Guenther 1992:1-2). Similar to good teaching, it is a kind of midwifery of the soul (Guenther 1992). Spiritual direction, or "spiritual mentoring," as Keith Anderson and Randy Reese prefer (1999:36), is a mutual relationship entered into with another in obedience to the revelation of God in Christ. Such a relationship can exist either formally or informally. The formal variety manifests itself in an agreement between a mentor and a mentee/mentoree, directee or protégé (Anderson and Reese 1999), to confer on a regular basis and to be guided by a mutual pact of consent. Informally, spiritual direction may be obtained whenever spiritually prudent people offer guidance to those who seek it. It may even take place through the writing of spiritually discerning authors (Jones 1999). Whatever the type, "the true director . . . [is] the Holy Spirit" (Jones 1999:10). "The Paraclete, the Holy Spirit, whom the Father will send in my name, that one will teach you all things and remind you of all that I have said to you" (Jn 14:26, my translation). For Jones, the principal desire in spiritual direction is for "simple companionship" or spiritual friendship (1999:11). What is important in the relationship is not simply self-affirmation but being honest about oneself and willing to be scrutinized because one knows one is loved (Jones 1999).

Thomas Merton captures the essence of spiritual direction in these words: "The whole purpose of spiritual direction is to penetrate beneath the surface of a man's life, to get behind the facade of conventional gestures and attitudes which he presents to the world, and to bring out his inner spiritual freedom, his inmost truth, which is what we call the likeness of Christ in his soul" (1960:16).

Because it draws on the imaginative powers of the mind, spiritual direction offers a new perspective. It offers a sensitivity to what is, to the actual conditions of life viewed in the light of God, and thus naturally leads to the contemplative disciplines. And finally, if one is willing to pay the price of brokenness, it leads to spiritual growth (Jones 1999). Even though Jones and other writers mentioned here write from other traditions, there is nothing to suggest the understanding of spiritual direction would be different in the United Church of Christ.

INDICATORS OF MATURE SPIRITUALITY

No one individual speaks for the entire United Church of Christ. So it is impossible to identify precisely how mature spirituality might be interpreted through the entire denomination. An example of one United Church of Christ theologian's interpretation of mature spirituality may be seen in Howard Clinebell (1965), who works in the field of pastoral counseling. Clinebell suggests these tests of a mentally healthy religion:

1. Does it build bridges or barriers between people?

2. Does it foster healthy or unhealthy dependency relationships?

3. Does it move from a sense of guilt to forgiveness?

4. Does it increase or lessen enjoyment of life?

5. Does it handle sexuality in constructive or repressive ways?

6. Does it lead to an acceptance or denial of reality?

7. Does it emphasize love or fear?

8. Does it strengthen or weaken self-esteem?

In an ideal healthy religious community, individuation, community and concern for the larger world are in balance, and thus spiritual formation, even if informally pursued, and social justice are congruent. There is a healthy, life-affirming interaction among them. When any one of these three—individuation, community or concern for the other—is neglected, suppressed or becomes pathological, the religious system becomes unhealthy.

Comparison with Psychotherapy and Pastoral Counseling

Although spiritual direction is not psychotherapy or pastoral counseling (Guenther 1992; Bakke 2000), the dividing line between traditional psychotherapy and spiritual direction appears to be somewhat fluid. On the side of psychology there is a growing awareness of the significance of spirituality and its role in personal well-being and meaningfulness, and on the side of spiritual direction, a growing sense of the insights into the human psyche offered by psychological analysis. Jones is tempted to speak of some of kind of convergence, "the possibilities for a marriage between the best of the insights of depth psychology and those of the Christian spiritual tradition" (1999:38).

> The doctrine of justification by faith alone, for example, has taken on a healing dynamism for me. The more I know about the workings of my labyrinthine psyche, the more I am convinced of my need of a savior! And my need for the Savior brings me into a fellowship of pilgrims who offer companionship along the way. (Jones 1999:44)

Jones thinks both worlds, the psychotherapeutic and the spiritual, are subsumed in the spiritual, since the greater, the spiritual, contains the lesser, the psychological (Jones 1999).

Another psychotherapist, also trained as a religious scholar, who has seen this unity is Thomas Moore. His book *The Re-enchantment of Everyday Life* explores the integral connection between humanity, the spiritual and the created world. Referring to the lessons to be learned by considering the created world, Moore notes that contemplation shows "our lives would not be divided from the nature that is our substance and our guide" (1996:33).

Table 7.1. **Comparison of Spiritual Direction, Psychotherapy and Pastoral Counseling**

Dimension	Spiritual Direction	Psychotherapy	Pastoral Counseling
Presenting Problem	Spiritual issues	Relational or personal problem	Relational, personal or spiritual problems
Goals	Experience of the divine presence leading to justice and well-being in all human relationships and social structures	Personal wholeness or homoeostasis and social harmony	Personal wholeness, social and spiritual well-being
Procedure	Individual or group counseling and prayer	Individual counseling or group counseling	Individual counseling
Resources	Prayer, confession, spiritual disciplines, worship, faith	Therapeutic theory and practice, medication referral	Therapeutic theory and practice, spiritual disciplines

There are, of course, distinctions between spiritual direction and traditional psychotherapy, as table 7.1 indicates, but much more common ground is developing between these disciplines than has been previously the case. Indeed, religious experience itself is now recognized "as a phenomenon that exceeds all possibility of complete understanding" and thus a fruitful field of study on the part of both religion and psychology (Burris 2001:91). Spiritual development offers an appropriate place where the coming together of these realms can prove effective.

As in the case of psychotherapy, the difference between spiritual direction and pastoral counseling has become less distinct. In response to growing specialization, Donald Browning (1985) distinguishes between pastoral care, which includes a whole range of pastoral interactions such as home and hospital visitation, pastoral counseling, in-depth personal intervention by the pastoral counselor, and the more specialized pastoral psychotherapy, carried out in a more specialized setting with more specialized goals.

Pastoral counseling, as ancient as the Christian community itself but in its modern form influenced by the insights of Freudian psychology, has through the pioneering work of Anton Boisen (1936) and Seward Hilter (1949) and the further adaptation of the client-centered approach of Carl Rogers (1942), come into its own as a field of study and practice (Hulme 1956). Typically, practitioners of specialized pastoral counseling received their training in Clinical Pastoral Education (C.P.E.) programs, where learning concentrates on "living human documents," rather than in traditional psychological graduate schools. Interestingly, the orientation is often more nondirectional and psychological than religious or spiritual.

Experienced pastoral counselors will say, however, that more and more clients are now requesting spiritual direction in sessions (Miller and Jackson 1995). This demand reflects the realization that most human difficulties are really mixtures of "conflicted human freedom" and "moral and religious discernment" (Browning 1985:6). C. W. Brister contends that in contrast to psychotherapists, who look to the inner healing forces of life, the pastoral counselor relies upon the power of God present in life itself (1964).

So the lines between pastoral counseling and spiritual direction are increasingly hard to draw, despite the heavier psychological orientation of the former. For this reason William Miller and Kathleen Jackson (1995) insist that the pastoral counselor and the spiritual director not "see these as separate roles" (1995:9). Pastoral counseling, they suggest, may be understood as a process of removing barriers that obstruct a person's natural journey of spiritual growth toward God. Thus its goals parallel those of spiritual direction.

WHEN A SPIRITUAL DIRECTOR MAKES REFERRALS

Since the United Church of Christ utilizes cultural resources, including scientific ideas and research, theological scholarship, and medical knowledge, a spiritual director within the denomination would have no trouble referring a mentee to a professional psychologist or counselor where necessary. The United Church spiritual director recognizes the complex factors shaping personality, attitudes and behavior. He or she would not think that spiritual resources alone could resolve issues that may need more in-depth therapy and medication. When the fine line between spiritual issues and mental or personality problems is crossed, the United Church spiritual director would make a referral.

SPIRITUAL DIRECTION AND SOCIAL JUSTICE

Considered theologically, there is no real conflict between spiritual direction and social justice. Contemplative spirituality, according to May, should not be associated exclusively with silence and stillness (2001). The simplest definition of contemplation, he insists, is "presence to what is." The Christian lives and moves in God (Acts 17:28). In the words of Brother Lawrence, it is "the loving gaze which

---

HELPFUL LITERATURE ON SPIRITUAL DIRECTION
AND THE UNITED CHURCH OF CHRIST

The United Church of Christ, ecumenical to the core, seeks to define Christian faith in a way that does not preclude the authenticity of other religious traditions and welcomes them into dialogue on spirituality.

Drawing on global interest in spirituality (May 2001), the denomination accepts insights regarding spiritual formation and direction from all the major religious traditions, as emphasis on yoga in the programs at the Lloyd Center demonstrates. Pilgrim Press, the denominational publishing house, has issued several volumes containing daily spiritual readings drawn from the Islamic, Hindu, Buddhist, Jewish, Taoist and Confucian traditions as well as Christianity: Joan C. Borton, *Deep in the Familiar: Four Life Rhythms* (Cleveland, Ohio: Pilgrim, 2001). Perhaps in the future someone may write a definitive assessment of the approaches to spirituality, spiritual formation and spiritual direction in the denomination, but that has yet to happen. We must be content at present with the random literature available.

---

finds God everywhere" (quoted in May 2001:3). If this definition is accepted, contemplation takes cognizance of all reality, not only one's inner experience but the external needs of the world as well. This does not lead the contemplative person merely to try to balance contemplation and action, but rather to understand contemplation "in action, undergirding and embracing everything" (May 2001:4).

Contemplation grounds spirituality in the real world. It opens the person to the divine movements that penetrate the whole of life, and it actually becomes true contemplation when God "takes over and carries us beyond ourselves" (May 2001:4). May summarizes this concept of spirituality:

> The Christian contemplative approach always winds up putting primary emphasis on God's initiative and action in life. . . . We must *receive* the truth that will set us free, *be guided* in the good actions that truly serve our neighbors and world, and *be given* an appreciation of the beauty within and around us. Only as this happens, only as we let God lead the divine dance, can we more fully participate in God's loving presence in and for the world. (2001:5)

Alan Jones similarly finds a core relationship between social justice and spiritual direction. Spiritual direction fosters acceptance of "God's wild generosity," that God loves everyone "without exception." Such generosity enrages many religious people, because they find such incredible love intolerable. By emphasizing participation in the inclusivity of divine love, spiritual direction leads to "inner disarmament," the "dismantling of the arsenal of destruction we amass inside ourselves."

When these destructive tendencies are dismantled, the tendency to act out the violence implicit within them is also defused (Jones 1999:ix). Spiritual direction leads to a less violent world and thus to greater justice among all peoples.

Thus spiritual direction and social justice are linked. Service, often recognized as a spiritual discipline, becomes a "sacrament" of the divine presence and thus conveys spiritual development. Through deeds of loving service God is expressed or proclaimed. Henri Nouwen (1994) tells of a contemplative monk, Father Bruno, who came to L'Arche Daybreak community in Toronto, where Nouwen served as pastor, to spend a few months. He was asked to live in one of the homes and take care of Adam, a man almost totally handicapped. Adam could not speak or recognize individual people and could communicate only by hand signs. He needed total care. Over three months Bruno came to love Adam. When he left L'Arche, he described his experience:

> As abbot I have given many talks about the spiritual life and tried to live it myself. . . . I always knew that I had to become empty for God, gradually letting go of thoughts, emotions, feelings, and passions that prevented that deep communion I desired. When I met Adam, I met a man who, while considered by the world as profoundly disabled, was chosen by God to be the bearer of a profound grace of God's presence. (quoted in Nouwen 1994:84)

Here the ministry of "presence," often examined in the literature of pastoral psychology, becomes the channel of spiritual grace not only toward others but also to the one serving. Service becomes a two-way mediation of grace, an incarnational event. Nouwen observes that ministry is first a receiving of God's blessing from those whom one serves, so that in service to the poor and disabled one "can see the face of Jesus" (Nouwen 1994:83).

Spirituality includes social concern, because there can be no "total" gospel without it. The incarnation represents an enfleshing of the divine, so the Christian cannot rightfully ignore the material order. "The Word became flesh and lived among us" (Jn 1:14 NRSV). God's love for humanity encompasses what humanity considers the deserving as well as the undeserving. Elton Trueblood, speaking from the Quaker tradition, which has consistently sought to link spiritual development and social service, decries any form of spirituality that has "no redemptive social consequences" (1970:85). Linking the community, the individual, spiritual development and social action, John Donne puts it this way: "I am involved in mankind" (1959:109). Thomas Merton considers social action to be peculiarly Christian because it "discovers religion in politics, religion in work, religion in social programs for better wages." It is especially christocentric, "because God became man, because every man is potentially Christ, because Christ is our brother, and because we have no right to let our brother live in want, or in degradation, or in any form of squalor whether physical or spiritual" (1966:69). An inner religion without an outward expression in service is a truncated religion.

Once we see the unity between spiritual formation, the function of spiritual guidance in directing that formation, and the love of God it fosters within the individual soul that is to be directed in loving service toward the world, it is easy to grasp why the United Church of Christ, with its strong, persistent interest in social justice, would be interested in this connection.

SUMMARY

The United Church of Christ is one of the leading voices of social justice in Christianity. Its pulpits, newsletters and publications continually prick the conscience about applying the love of Christ to social challenges. During the first two or three decades of its existence, interest in social justice, in the view of observers, seemed to eclipse the more spiritual and pietistic aspects of Christian life, which seemed for the most part to lie hidden in the legacies of the denominations that merged to form the United Church of Christ in 1957. Evelyn Underhill's warning that if a "purely social interpretation of religion be allowed to continue unchecked, the result can only be an impoverishment of our spiritual life" (1962:69), seemed in danger of being realized.

With a newfound, burgeoning interest in spirituality in society since the 1990s, however, the United Church of Christ found itself compelled to tap into its latent traditions of spirituality and to reflect more carefully on the relationship between spirituality and social justice. Its ecumenical interests meant it would seek to incorporate insights from religious traditions other than Christianity, a kind of "deep ecumenism."

Thus today the denomination, both at the national level and at the local level through individual programs, is now starting to link spirituality, spiritual formation and spiritual direction with social justice ministry. The outcome of this nascent connection is yet to be realized, but there are signs of a more holistic emphasis on social justice and spirituality throughout the denomination. This cannot but be welcomed by all. The United Church of Christ, long a leader in social justice, may yet provide a notable model of the coalescence of spiritual formation and social conscience.

REFERENCES

Anderson, Keith, and Randy Reese. 1999. *Spiritual mentoring: A guide for seeking and giving direction.* Downers Grove, Ill.: InterVarsity Press.

Bakke, Jeannette A. 2000. *Holy invitations: exploring spiritual direction.* Grand Rapids, Mich.: Baker.

Boisen, Anton. 1936. *The exploration of the inner world.* N.p.: Willet and Clark.

Boisvert, Donald L. 2001. *Out on holy ground: Meditations on gay men's spirituality.* Cleveland, Ohio: Pilgrim.

Book of worship: United Church of Christ. 1986. New York: United Church of Christ Office for Church Life and Leadership.

Borton, Joan Cannon. 2001. *Deep in the familiar: Four life rhythms.* Cleveland, Ohio: Pilgrim.

Brister, C. W. 1964. *Pastoral care in the church.* New York: Harper & Row.

Browning, Donald. 1985. Introduction to pastoral counseling. In *Clinical handbook of pastoral counseling,* ed. R. Wicks, R. Parsons and D. Capps, pp. 5-13. New York: Paulist.

Burris, J. P. 2001. Of historians of religions, religious historians, and agnostic anthropologists: Tacit assumptions about religion in the human sciences. *Bulletin of the Council of Societies for the Study of Religion* 30, no. 4:87-92.

Church Office of Communication. 1975. What is the United Church of Christ? in *Religions of America: Ferment and faith in an age of crisis,* ed. Leo Rosten. New York: Simon and Schuster.

Clinebell, Howard. 1965. *Mental health through Christian community.* Nashville: Abingdon.

Comrie, M. M. 2001. Diving for God: How "scuba ministry" changes the lives of youth. *United Church News,* national ed., September, p. A1.

Donne, John. 1959. *Devotions upon emergent occasions.* Ann Arbor: University of Michigan Press.

Durant House. 2001. Durant House. Available at <www.duranthouse.org>.

Fackre, Dorothy, and Gabriel Fackre. 1991. *Christian basics: A primer for pilgrims.* Grand Rapids, Mich.: Eerdmans.

Foster, Richard. 1998. *Streams of living water.* San Francisco: HarperCollins.

Golder, W. E. 2001. Synod urges Taco Bell boycott. *United Church News,* national ed., September, p. A9.

Guenther, Margaret. 1992. *Holy listening: The art of spiritual direction.* Boston: Cowley.

Gunneman, Louis. 1977. *The shaping of the United Church of Christ: An essay in the history of American Christianity.* New York: Pilgrim.

Hiltner, Seward. 1949. *Pastoral counseling.* Nashville: Abingdon.

Horton, Douglas. 1962. *The United Church Of Christ: Its origins, organization and role in the world today.* New York: Thomas Nelson and Sons.

Hulme, William. 1956. *Counseling and theology.* Philadelphia: Muhlenberg.

Jackson, N. 2000. Our Christendom church. *Prism* 15, no. 1:21-35.

Johnson, Daniel J., and Charles Hambrick-Stowe. 1990. Theological tradition of Congregationalism. In *Theology and identity: Traditions, movements and polity in the United Church of Christ,* ed. Daniel Johnson and Charles Hambrick-Stowe, pp. 15-25. New York: Pilgrim.

Jones, Alan. 1999. *Exploring spiritual direction.* Boston: Cowley.

Kershner, T. 2001. Southeast Conference churches "adopt-a-minefield." *United Church News,* national ed., September, p. A8.

May, Gerald. 2001. *Contemplative spiritual formation: An introduction.* Available at <www.shalem.org/spirform.html>.

Meade, Frank S. 1995. *Handbook of denominations.* Rev. ed. Samuel S. Hill. Nashville: Abingdon.

Merton, Thomas. 1966. *Conjectures of a guilty bystander.* Garden City, N.Y.: Doubleday.

Miller, William R., and Kathleen A. Jackson. 1993. *Practical psychology for pastors.* 2nd ed. Englewood Cliffs, N.J.: Prentice-Hall.

Moore, Thomas. 1996. *The re-enchantment of everyday life.* New York: HarperCollins.

Morrison, Melanie. 2000. *The grace of coming home: Spirituality, sexuality and the struggle for justice.* New York: Pilgrim.

Nouwen, Henri. 1994. *Here and now: Living in the Spirit.* New York: Crossroad.

Olmstead, Clifton E. 1960. *History of religion in the United States.* Englewood Cliffs, N.J.: Prentice-Hall.

Otto, Rudolf. 1923. *The idea of the holy.* Trans. John W. Harvey. New York: Oxford University Press.

Rogers, Carl. 1942. *Counseling and Psychotherapy.* Boston: Houghton Mifflin.

Shinn, Roger Lincoln. 1990. *Confessing our faith: An interpretation of the statement of faith of the United Church of Christ.* New York: Pilgrim.

Starling-Melvin, G. 2001. Building a better world: Volunteerism and the UCC. *United Church News,* June, p. 1.

Todhunter, James A. 2001. Terror and faith. Available at <www.ucc.org/911/sermons.htm>.

Trost, F. R. 2000. Spiritual formation and reformation. *Prism* 15, no. 1:73-86.

Trueblood, Elton D. 1970. *The new man for our time.* New York: Harper & Row.

Underhill, Evelyn. 1962. Life of the Spirit and social order. In *The Evelyn Underhill reader,* ed. T. Kepler, pp. 68-71. Nashville: Abingdon.

United Church of Christ. 2001a. About us. Available at <ucc.org/aboutus/index.html>.

———. 2001b. Human sexuality. Available at <www.ucc.org/justice/sexuality.html>.

———. 2001c. Justice ministries. Available at <www.ucc.org/justice/index.html>.

———. 2001d. Local church ministries. Available at <www.ucc.org/ministries/index.html>.

———. 2001e. Resolution: "Men's" ministry in the United Church of Christ. Available at <www.ucc.org/mens/resolution.html>.

———. 2001f. Welcome to the United Church of Christ. Available at <ucc.org/aboutus/index.html>.

Weightman, S. 1984. Hinduism. In *A handbook of living religions,* ed. John R. Hinnells, pp. 191-236. New York: Viking.

Zikmund, B., ed. 1984. *Hidden histories in the United Church of Christ.* New York: United Church Press.

8

SPIRITUAL DIRECTION IN THE PENTECOSTAL/CHARISMATIC TRADITION

Oliver McMahan

Pentecostals and charismatics are known for their emphasis on the work of the Holy Spirit within the life of the believer. Historically, Pentecostals and charismatics have a relatively young tradition. The Pentecostal movement began at the beginning of the twentieth century. Early Pentecostals usually lived on the poorer side of town, in rural hamlets and various impoverished pockets of the world. Since their modern beginning, Pentecostals have continued to develop as a stream of spirituality within the landscape of Christianity. Charismatics, breaking out within various denominations and independent groups, have been a more recent movement with boundaries that are still in formation.[1]

As fellowships, churches, church groups, movements and denominations, Pentecostals and charismatics focus much of their activity within the worship setting of the church. Spirituality is frequently defined within the context of a church ser-

---

[1]While there are many similarities between Pentecostals and charismatics, there are a number of differences, particularly in history, religious practice and constituencies. Historically, Pentecostals began at the dawn of the twentieth century, while charismatics began in the late 1960s and early 1970s. Pentecostals quickly formed independent groups which eventually became international denominations. Charismatics began within mainline denominations, and many have continued in those denominations. Other charismatics have formed independent churches, autonomous and congregational in polity and practice, avoiding the creation of denominations. Still other charismatic groups like the Vineyard movement have formed denominational fellowships. The religious practice of Pentecostals ranges from formal worship to open, unstructured worship. Charismatics generally have been very open and spontaneous in their worship services. Pentecosals have tended to hold more conservative beliefs about dress, entertainment and theology. Charismatics have been more open and willing to change their practices and beliefs. Finally, the constituents of Pentecostal churches have been among the more impoverished of society, while charismatics have been marked by greater affluence. These are broad distinctions that have tended to change over time. However, Pentecostals and charismatics are knit together in their emphasis on the work of the Holy Spirit.

vice, more than a devotional closet. Both private and public spirituality within Christendom as a whole has taken many forms. The work of the Spirit with its demonstration of gifts in a worship service is often emphasized more than the Spirit's work within each individual believer.

Spirituality for Pentecostals and charismatics centers on a continual quest to re-capture a person's original reception of the Spirit. This backward look for a fresh move of the Spirit sets up a dual consciousness that at times is helpful but at other times may be a form of denial. Particularly among Pentecostals who have a multi-generational heritage, references to the Spirit may be in the past tense more than in the flow of the present. Pentecostals may feel that worship was better in the re-vival days of the early movement. They may hold the perception that people were more fervent in their worship and there were more miracles in that earlier time.

The Spirit of God sends believers in all traditions on a remarkable journey. At its very origin, spirituality is a powerful experience, giving birth to a lifetime jour-ney with God. The beginning of one's spiritual journey is like the headwaters of a stream. The headwaters are the source. At the swirl of these beginning headwaters the new believer first tastes of the spiritual waters that will fill, carry and guide him or her on this remarkable pilgrimage. For Pentecostals and charismatics, the initial experience of the baptism of the Spirit is a headwaters experience. Also, there are subsequent experiences of the Spirit that mark fresh beginnings.

The believer testifies of these first experiences as initial believing, recalling the purifying power of God or telling others about first coming into an awareness of the work of the Spirit. These experiences are "firsts" not only in sequence but also in their power to revive the flow of God's Spirit in our lives. They may include re-demptive experiences of God's grace at crisis moments of our finitude, when the world caves in on us. In tragedy the Spirit of God forms a wall of mercy that holds back the deluge of the world and supports us through the floods.

For many believers, drinking of the Spirit is a reminder of the gospel message. However, for others, including Pentecostals and charismatics, the goal of spiritu-ality becomes reviving rather than building on the past. Before one revival ends in some Pentecostal and charismatic fellowships, the next one is being planned. Some fellowships even call themselves "revival centers," desiring a constant state of renewal. Descriptions of spirituality are more rehearsals of the past than cele-brations of the present. Preoccupation with the beginnings and renewals of the work of the Spirit leads to special therapeutic issues for Pentecostals and charis-matics, which will be discussed later in this chapter.

DEFINITION OF SPIRITUAL DIRECTION: Marking the Headwaters

The search for renewal has taken charismatics and Pentecostals from Tulsa to Toronto, from Pensacola to Azusa and back to the local church. From revivals to renewal conferences, study pamphlets to cassettes and back to the prayer closet, Pentecostals and charismatics have sought to experience the freshness of the Spirit. For some, "spiritual direction" means getting directions to the location of a revival meeting.

Though the search has taken them to different places, there are a few common elements that mark their experience. These elements are not exclusively Pentecostal or charismatic. They are and have been experienced by other believers in various traditions of Christendom (Burgess and McGee 1988).

"Spirit baptism" and the "filling of the Spirit" are expressions used by Pentecostals and charismatics to describe an experience that usually includes the recipient's speaking in unknown tongues. Traditional Pentecostals believe speaking in unknown tongues is the initial evidence of the baptism of the Holy Spirit. Biblical references for both Pentecostals and charismatics concerning the experience of unknown tongues include Acts 2, Acts 10 and 1 Corinthians 12-14. The person speaks in a language that is unknown to her or him. The language may not be traceable to any known language. At exceptional times, some have spoken a language not known to them but identifiable as another known language. The language may be identified as a "language of heaven" (1 Cor 13:1), and whether similar to an earthly language or heavenly, the full meaning of what is spoken is known only by God (1 Cor 14:1-3).

Spirit baptism is also marked by a sense of being overwhelmed emotionally and at times physically. Persons may experience a flood of emotions. They may react physically, waving their arms, running or jumping. Pentecostals and charismatics draw on descriptions such as that found in Acts 2:15, in which the disciples are described at Pentecost as appearing to be drunk. Accompanying physical effects include those mentioned earlier as well as swooning, laughing and crying. Recipients report a heightened awareness of the Holy Spirit. Some report a loss of awareness of their surroundings. Pentecostals and charismatics refer to Scriptures such as Psalm 16:8-9, used by Peter on the day of Pentecost (Acts 2:25-26), as an explanation of their experiences. In the psalm David speaks of an experience of the Holy Spirit in which he felt God was face to face with him. As a result, David says, he spoke with a "glad tongue."

Charismatics and Pentecostals describe "yielding" or "surrendering" to the Spirit as an important part of the process of spirituality. Yielding to the Spirit is part of many aspects of Christian spirituality, including initial believing, exercising faith, pursuing holiness and many other dimensions of the believer's life. Pentecostals and charismatics describe yielding to the Spirit as part of participation in corporate worship. A person may yield to the Spirit and exercise a gift of the Spirit in that setting. Yielding to the Spirit is also described as what a person does in order to carry out special directions in fulfilling God's will. It also is part of opening oneself up to ecstatic laughter, swooning and other experiences in the Spirit.

The spiritual experience of Pentecostals and charismatics, like that of all believers, naturally leads to a desire for more. Having drawn from the flow of living water, they want to stay in the flow. But more does not necessarily mean farther or deeper. Rather, at times to charismatics and Pentecostals it means more of the same. Drifting downstream in the journey of Christianity, they desire to go back to the refreshing source. Their perception is that recaptured initial experiences of the Spirit are purer, fresher and more enriching. At times genuine spiritual renewal is experienced. At other times a place, a time, an experience or even personal power is actually what is most desired. In any case, having drawn from the origins of Christian experience and the believer's life in the Spirit, Pentecostals and charismatics want more from the source (Land 1993; Moore 1991).

HISTORY: Spiritual Mothers, Fathers and Gifted Leaders

Within the Pentecostal/charismatic movement, the history of spiritual direction has involved hearing the testimonies of spiritual siblings, parents and leaders. The qualifications of such directors are informal and nonacademic. The movement at times has steered away from requiring formal education, seeking only that a spiritual director has been to the headwaters of initial Spirit baptism and renewal.

A Pentecostal or charismatic may be moved more to follow a gifted leader with a word of the Spirit for the moment than to give allegiance to a creed or a director's lifetime of knowledge. As a result, spiritual direction has been very immediate and gratifying but has sometimes lacked depth and the continuity of lessons learned from others. Exceptions have come in the context of the familial bond of the Spirit. When a person's knowledge and wisdom was accepted, it was because of the common blood of spiritual experience that was shared.

Two forms of spiritual direction among Pentecostals and charismatics have been the oral traditions of prophecy and testimony (Ellington 2000). In church services, prayer meetings and small groups, spiritual directors have been like oracles speaking in these two nontraditional forms. Manifestations have included practices described in 1 Corinthians 12—14, such as public tongues speaking, interpretation of tongues uttered in groups, the word of wisdom and the word of knowledge. Gifted leaders have provided episodic leadership, but there have also been spiritual fathers and mothers who have been followed with familial loyalty (Synan 1971; Burgess and McGee 1988).

Some of the gifted leaders serving as spiritual directors have been evangelists. Evangelists gained attention as they drew people into a renewal of initial believing and experience. By means of tent meetings, evangelists have given spiritual direction to Pentecostal/charismatic followers. Included among these evangelists would be spiritual leaders whose ministries emphasize healing. Especially during worship services, even today, devotees listen loyally to the spiritual direction given by evangelists. Attendees may be singled out in the service, even brought to the front of the church auditorium to openly receive spiritual direction.

Another form of spiritual direction among Pentecostals and charismatics has been spiritual deliverance. Based on scriptural texts such as Ephesians 6, trouble and despair are interpreted in spiritual terms. Individuals come to special meetings or prayer services for deliverance, sensing that spiritual forces bind them. Through prayer, exhortation, the recitation of Scripture and other means, directors intercede for the spiritual deliverance of those in need. One name sometimes used to identify these spiritual directors is "prayer warrior." At times evangelists or pastors are sought out for such spiritual deliverance.

Psychotherapists and pastoral counselors also work as spiritual directors within the Pentecostal/charismatic tradition. That model at various times has included elements of the prophetic and the charismata. This has meant that directors minister with an immediate sense of God speaking to the individual and community of faith as part of therapy. Usually such directors are gifted individuals within the church they serve (Land 1993).

The Pentecostal/charismatic model of spirituality communicates the sense that anyone within the community of believers can claim to have been to the very source, God himself, for spiritual direction at any moment.

THE PROCESS OF AUTHENTIC TRANSFORMATION:
Drinking from the Headwaters

Authentic transformation for Pentecostals and charismatics means changed lives. Such change occurs at different levels, at different times and in different ways. Pentecostals have held two dominant views of transformation, evidenced in separate but perhaps complementary theologies of sanctification. One group of Pentecostals, including the Church of God (Cleveland, Tennessee) and the International Pentecostal Holiness Church, has taught that sanctification occurs instantaneously in a person's life. Another group of Pentecostals, including the Assemblies of God, has taught that sanctification occurs as a process over time. These two groups have in recent years tended to merge their views in a combined view in which sanctification and transformation are spontaneous in their beginning but are lived out and grow over the course of time.

One important element of the process of transformation for Pentecostals and charismatics is the experience of Spirit baptism. The experience often comes in the context of a worship service. The music and order of service set an atmosphere of surrender to the presence and work of the Holy Spirit. Pentecostals and charismatics believe they are personally experiencing the Pentecost event as it occurred in the lives of the believers in Acts 2. They do not experience what sounded like wind and looked like tongues of fire. They do experience glossolalia (speaking in other tongues), peace, joy and other manifestations of spirituality.

Many Pentecostals and charismatics are new converts to Christian faith. Often their family of origin is unchurched (Burgess and McGee 1988). The headwaters of spiritual experience may have been sought initially, but the cares and difficulties of life have now brought them into unfamiliar waters, with little recourse but to pursue uncharted waters. Faith develops as the waters of human encounter and grief take them downstream into tragedy and arouse spiritual questions. The questions are about things unfamiliar: why a disease is not healed, a loved one remains unemployed or a wayward son or daughter continually rebels against God. Growth occurs but leaves such questions unanswered. As a result, spiritual transformation is frequently resisted (Hayford 2001; Maachia 1998; Moore 1995; Gernert 2000).

Eventually, after initial surprise and even resistance to new paths of spiritual depth, denial gives way to discovery. Gradually, through a critical step of engagement, Pentecostals and charismatics begin to navigate these unfamiliar waters. Engagement involves integration of new truth and experience that appears contradictory to previous experience. A critical compass during this time of engagement has been spiritual guides—more commonly referred to as "prayer partners," "intercessors" or "more mature believers." *Guides* seems a more fitting term than *directors,* since the latter suggests a defined path laid out by someone else, whereas *guide* allows room for a personalized process of spiritual formation (Del Colle 2000). But regardless of the title or particular identity, within the family of Pentecostals and charismatics, spiritual guidance generally occurs during times of grief and struggle.

THE ROLE OF THE DIRECTOR: All in the Family

The role of the spiritual director (a term that is very rarely used) begins with being perceived as a member of the spiritual family of faith. Guidance is readily sought from a pastoral counselor or psychotherapist who is functioning as a member of the spiritual community or family. The professional who is not part of a client's community of faith may find it difficult to establish such trust (Parker 1996). It is even more difficult if the spiritual guide is not perceived as being part of any community of faith. Given these potential difficulties, developing a sense of trust and faith within the context of the counseling hour is vital. The counselor-client relationship becomes spiritual community for the Pentecostal/charismatic. The pastoral counselor or psychotherapist as spiritual guide/director assumes the role of a fellow member of the family of faith.

With a relationship of trust established, the pastoral counselor or psychotherapist can—under certain circumstances—function at times in a role similar to that of a spiritual director or guide (Moon 1996). Ongoing spiritual guidance is crucial. The client may resist growth. There may be a desire for only episodic experiences of Spirit baptism rather than sustained experiences of spiritual growth. The struggle is between personal freedom and structure. The spiritual director must embrace the tension, willing to work with the client's frequent desire for spiritual renewal while helping the client to sustain longer processes of growth. A spiritual director may be engaging, much like a persistent family member. But the pastoral counselor or psychotherapist will also be objective like any ethical professional, giving the Pentecostal/charismatic the freedom to which he or she is accustomed.

INDICATORS OF MATURE SPIRITUALITY:
Struggling to Remain Near the Source

Maturity from the Pentecostal/charismatic perspective is not easily defined, at least using traditional definitions of maturity. Stages and frameworks for achieving maturity may be resisted or reshaped by Pentecostals and charismatics because of their preference for initial experience, unattached to structured definitions of spiritual experience.

The boundaries of spiritual development have been defined by both mainstream and Pentecostal/charismatic writers (Foster 1978, 1998; Hayford 2001; Tan and Gregg 1997; Malony 1977; Batson and Ventis 1982). Traditional virtues have been identified as meditation, prayer, fasting, study, simplicity, solitude, submission, service, confession, worship, guidance and celebration (Foster 1978; Baker 1995). Pentecostal/charismatic authors have identified these and other critical virtues of spiritual formation, such as community/group critical reflection, yielding and confession, witness, solitude and silence, committing oneself to hear God's voice and live in the power of one's baptism (C. Johns 1993; Johns and Johns 1992; Tan and Gregg 1997; Hayford 2001; Boom 1996; McMahan 2000).

All of these are authentic and real. However, Pentecostals and charismatics, because of a tendency to resist structure, may emphasize the process of spiritual formation itself, unattached to practices that they see as attempting to confine the work of the Spirit to a step, a principle or a guideline. Therefore one of their indicators of spiritual maturity is to be continually searching, paddling upstream, looking for an experience of God. For the spiritual director, this calls for openness to a quest for an experience of God rather than a lesson about or direction toward God (Yang 1996; McMahan 1997).

Despite the Pentecostal/charismatic propensity to subjectivism, spiritual maturity in this tradition is also marked by the ability to be part of the family of the community of faith. Even though Pentecostals and charismatics cherish the individual nature of their experience of God, they respect and embrace those whom they perceive as being a part of their family of faith. A characteristic of spiritual maturity is being able to continue seeking experiences of God while remaining with the community of faith and sharing one's experience with others.

Another mark of spirituality according to Pentecostals and charismatics is charismatic giftedness. Persons with special supernatural abilities are often considered spiritually mature. These individuals are seen as having been to the renewing sources of spiritual maturity and having experienced enough closeness to God to bear gifts that come from those experiences. This perception is not without problems, because charismata are not necessarily the same as spiritual maturity. Giftedness needs to be grounded in an ongoing demonstration of the fruit of the Spirit (Ingram 1996). Giftedness is enormously valuable for service and ministry, but a gifted person may still be spiritually immature (Gilbert and Brock 1985; Vining 1992, 1995a; Decker 1996).

All believers share in the fruit of the Spirit. For Pentecostals and charismatics, the fruit of the Spirit has been and can continue to be a means of defining spirituality and maturity. Especially appealing for them is the fact that the fruit reflects the presence of the Holy Spirit in a person's life. Further, the fruit of the Spirit is seen in the believer's daily life rather than just the church worship service.

Psychotherapists, spiritual directors and pastoral counselors must deal with Pentecostals and charismatics who mark their spiritual journey with miraculous milestones. Certainly, charismata and gifts are a reality of the church and faith. Therefore psychotherapists, spiritual directors and pastoral counselors can be effective with Pentecostals and charismatics by being open to spiritual giftedness and the streams that flow from them (McMahan 1995). This includes openness to the work of the Spirit in the life of the client and their own life. At the same time, they have to model mature and ethical behavior, even when spiritual gifts are not apparent (McMahan 1995, 1997).

Another mark of spiritual maturity for charismatics and Pentecostals is ministry to the spiritual community, including noncharismatics. Pentecostals and charismatics seek fulfillment of their spiritual experience through ministry to all believers and the evangelization of nonbelievers. They desire spiritual growth in others as well as themselves. There have been times in Pentecostal history when they have seen themselves as an exclusive group (Synan 1971; Burgess and McGee 1988); charismatics, however, have generally been inclusive as a movement (Burgess and McGee 1988). Indeed, openness toward all believers is now seen by both as a mark of spiritual maturity.

Some Pentecostals and charismatics see openness to those outside the community of faith as a mark of maturity. Though Pentecostals and charismatics treasure the bond of spiritual community, they are empathic to suffering, regardless of a person's religious orientation (Burgess and McGee 1988). They are caring regardless of culture (Yang 1996). Many Pentecostals and charismatics are advocates of social justice, no doubt because they have at times been marginalized (Land 1992; Cox 1992, 1995). In this sense, psychotherapists, spiritual directors and pastoral counselors may observe adaptability and social sensitivity in their Pentecostal or charismatic clients (Yang 1996; Yong 1999).

Contrast to Psychotherapy and Pastoral Counseling: Discovering the Breadth of the Stream

The distinctives of Pentecostal/charismatic spiritual maturity carry several implications for psychotherapists and pastoral counselors. Psychotherapists, spiritual directors and pastoral counselors working with Pentecostals and charismatics would do well to foster a bond of community and mutuality during the counseling hour. They must be careful of dual role relationships and ethical violations yet be ready to move into the role of spiritual "kin," born of the Spirit, rather than assuming a rigid distance.

Besides legitimacy based on relationship, recognition of the value and challenges of seeking the renewal of Spirit baptism is important. Psychotherapists, spiritual directors and pastoral counselors desire to see growth and maturity occur, and Pentecostals and charismatics are already seeking growth. They are motivated to grow, to experience more of God. What they need is someone to assist with defining and clarifying the integration of life and spirituality. The spiritual director can merge spiritual direction with therapy in the pursuit of client growth and welfare (McMahan 1995).

Psychotherapists, spiritual directors and pastoral counselors can use the fact that the Pentecostal/charismatic may want to return to familiar beginnings, the places where they first knew the Lord, where they first encountered the power of God's might, and to other benchmarks of their spirituality. The Pentecostal or charismatic can be overly consumed with a quest to simply relive the past rather than look at it introspectively (Burgess and McGee 1988). Reflection and integration may be less desirable to them than putting on a proven perception. Spiritual direction would facilitate discernment and insight. Traditional psychotherapy might be limited to memory and history, while a spiritual guide could probe and reflect on basic assumptions about one's spiritual past that may have changed. A pastoral counselor would facilitate both discernment and critical analysis of a client's past. The headwaters kind of experience may change, and it may be necessary to do spiritual reflection about that experience as well as probe other aspects of one's past.

HELPFUL BOOKS ON SPIRITUAL DIRECTION
FROM THE PENTECOSTAL/CHARISMATIC TRADITION

A very helpful two-volume set on the history, theology, theories and techniques of psychotherapy and pastoral counseling used by Pentecostals and charismatics is Marvin G. Gilbert and Raymond T. Brock, *The Holy Spirit and Counseling: Theology and Theory,* 2 vols. (Peabody, Mass.: Hendrickson, 1985, 1989). Though written in the 1980s, these books still provide valuable resource information regarding the formative concepts and approaches used by Pentecostals and charismatics in therapy.

Insights into the dynamics of Pentecostal spiritual formation are provided in four volumes:

Hayford, Jack. 2001. *Living the spirit-formed life: Growing in the 10 principles of Spirit-filled discipleship.* Ventura, Calif.: Regal.

Land, S. J. 1993. *Pentecostal Spirituality: A passion for the kingdom.* Sheffield, U.K.: Sheffield Academic.

McMahan, Oliver. 2000. *Deepening discipleship.* Cleveland, Tenn.: Pathway.

Tan, Siang-Yang, and Douglas H. Gregg. 1997. *Disciplines of the Holy Spirit: How to connect to the Spirit's power and presence.* Grand Rapids, Mich.: Zondervan.

These books offer information about spiritual disciplines practiced by Pentecostals and charismatics historically and globally, currently and throughout much of their young history.

Soul care providers also do well to recognize the propensity of some Pentecostals and charismatics to overspiritualize and emotionally interpret their personal problems. Pentecostal and charismatic psychotherapists and pastoral counselors have endeavored to bring a balance to this tendency (Gilbert and Brock 1985, 1989; Dobbins 1995). They have integrated traditional psychotherapeutic methods such as cognitive, behavioral, systemic and contextual approaches to correct overspiritualizing and emotionalizing (McMahan 1995). Also, Christian spiritual disciplines have been formalized into psychotherapeutic techniques in approaches such as intensive prayer counseling.

Pentecostals and charismatics may resist encouragement to rest in harbors of reflection. They may be suspicious of anything that departs from immediate experience. Spiritual directors may have to use immediate, sensory and awareness methods rather than automatically and clinically requiring an in-depth look at a person's past (McMahan 1995; Gilbert and Brock 1985, 1988).

Psychotherapists, spiritual directors and pastoral counselors may also find it helpful to identify which life circumstances may be moving the Pentecostal or charismatic further downstream. Embracing the grief, living in the midst of tragedy and feeling the pain of life may be the spiritual agenda. What is the comfort level of the client? How can the spiritual dimensions of these life experiences be recognized? Whom can the client trust when life itself becomes untrustworthy? Some psychotherapeutic approaches embrace such spiritual paradox, while others deny it. Psychotherapists, spiritual directors and pastoral counselors working with Pentecostals and charismatics may do well to use interventions involving spiritual paradox, as they may be the key that takes the client deeper and further. They can help clients learn from pain as they experience God in the midst of suffering rather than just trying to quickly sweep it out of the conscious mind.

At the transition points where Pentecostals or charismatics encounter questions that upset their spiritual identity, psychotherapists, spiritual directors and pastoral counselors can assist with identifying possible stages or transitions. The client may be in the rough waters of spiritual change. During this time the structure of the clinical process may have to be paradoxical or crisis-oriented rather than just cognitive or behavioral.

Pentecostals and charismatics may need to be pointed away from their individual selves toward an experience of community with others. While traditional therapy emphasizes the private hour between the clinician and counselee, that privatization may further fuel an already too personalized quest for spiritual direction. The spiritual guide may direct the client to other helpers, both lay and professional, who can create the community the client needs (Tan 1991). Lay counseling or participation in the therapeutic process is a departure from the clinical or medical model used by some clinicians, but it may be very effective for Pentecostals and charismatics.

There are other times when the community itself is the problem the client is encountering in developing his or her spirituality. In these cases the spiritual director may opt for more traditional approaches, using the one-on-one client-therapist relationship as a time of healing from community dysfunction or even abuse. Clients may experience frustration with their mental illness because they participate in a faith community that demonstrates little capacity for dealing with persistent life and health questions. The spiritual director can provide a sense of community, addressing the client's relational issues. The spiritual director may even serve as an advocate in helping the client identify another community of faith to join. Such advocacy, of course, differs from traditional psychotherapy approaches that remain within the confines of the professional office or facility.

Pastoral counselors in the Pentecostal/charismatic tradition have been characterized in different ways. They have primarily done counseling informally. When a member of a church has a need, a pastor or staff member may set up an appointment or may counsel the individual immediately. Pastoral counseling is usually done by pastors with little if any formal training in counseling. The counsel given emphasizes the Word of God, theology and morality. Spiritual direction is given in the context of the triad of Word, theology and morality. Spirituality, listening to God and maturing one's faith are generally reserved for worship. Counseling is seen as crisis intervention and endeavors to stabilize the person. Spiritual growth is a byproduct rather than focus of counseling.

Pastoral counseling has often been seen by Pentecostals and charismatics as episodic and reactive rather than an enduring process. It is often viewed as a response to the negatives of one's life. Spiritual formation, listening to God and developing spiritual companionship have not been generally addressed within the context of counseling, but rather within corporate worship. In this sense, pastoral counseling by Pentecostals and charismatics has been more need-based, even psychotherapeutically oriented, than a process of spiritual formation.

Pastoral counseling for spiritual direction is developing, however, among pastors in the Pentecostal/charismatic tradition who are comfortable with their call to be spiritual mentors and companions in one-on-one or small group settings as well as in congregational meetings. Some pastors remain uncomfortable with it, because spiritual direction within the context of pastoral counseling calls for greater vulnerability and spiritual dialogue, qualities not always required in larger corporate settings.

Table 8.1 conveys some of the differences between psychotherapy and spiritual direction from the Pentecostal/charismatic perspective.

REFERRALS TO MENTAL HEALTH PROFESSIONALS: A Question Come of Age

Pentecostals and charismatics are becoming more and more open to mental health referrals. Exceptions are found among conservative Pentecostals, who see referrals as a departure from their search for the spiritual experience and believe psychology is a threat to their doctrinal purity. Exceptions are also found among charismatics who feel that referrals are unnecessary in light of their faith. Still, the pressures and pain of life have gradually confronted Pentecostals and charismatics with the need for professional assistance.

Referrals can enhance the spiritual journey of Pentecostals and charismatics if managed from the harbor of community. Referral becomes part of the spiritual growth of the client when made by a spiritual guide who maintains community with the client. The referral becomes part of the river of spirituality. The psychological aspects of the referral become transformed: they remain psychological but are framed by the relationship forged between the spiritual director, the client and the Spirit. In the communion of the Spirit, the spiritual director monitors the referral, and the client follows a new stream of both psychological and spiritual depth.

Table 8.1. Comparison of Spiritual Direction, Psychotherapy and Pastoral Counseling

Dimension	Spiritual Direction	Psychotherapy	Pastoral Counseling
Presenting Problem	Reconciling unresolved past tragedies with relationship with God	Relief of pain and emotional stress brought on by crisis events	Coping with immediate crisis and maintaining a relationship with God and the church
Goals	Assist directee in experiencing the reality of God's presence and arriving at a sense of peace with issues of theodicy	Assist the client with understanding the grief process; also, assist with life transitions resulting from crisis events	Continue to function on personal, family and church levels, addressing issues like forgiveness and reconciliation, coping with crisis
Procedure	Prayer, instruction, worship in the Spirit including silence, glossolalia, singing and celebration; also, reading Scriptures that speak of persons who endured tragedy, e.g., Job	Reviewing the incident(s) of crisis, drawing on emotional responses, cognitive questions and options the client may have tried, using face-to-face therapy, homework and readings about similar crises experiences	Immediate crisis intervention, brief counseling with individual, family and others, addressing issues from ecclesial, social, theological and moral perspectives
Resources	Scripture stories and testimonies of individuals who were spiritual but experienced crises; members of the client's spiritual community who have experienced tragedy	Literature with instructions for coping with change, especially recovering from critical crisis incidents; medical assistance with adjustments and responses to crises	Church, community, tradition, doctrine, corporate worship

In the referral process the Pentecostal and charismatic client is asked to maintain spiritual vitality and experience in the midst of confrontation with psychological need. The referral is the fulfillment of spiritual disciplines such as submission and grace. The spiritual director leads in the referral process, expanding the faith and the experience of the Pentecostal and charismatic, discovering with the client ways the Spirit moves even beyond experiences like initial Spirit baptism and subsequent renewals of those beginnings.

SUMMARY

Charismatics and Pentecostals have had a relatively brief history and tradition. In just over one hundred years for Pentecostals and only a few decades for charismatics, a number of characteristics have emerged. Charismatics and Pentecostals have sought renewal but may, in their desire to return to initial spiritual experiences of believing and Spirit baptism, have missed opportunities for reflection. Their spiritual directors have been diverse but usually part of the community of believers. The close community has seemed like a family as much as a spiritual movement. Spiritual directors and counselors who seek to serve them do well to understand their history and motivations.

REFERENCES

Baker, R. O. 1995. Pentecostal Bible reading: Toward a model of reading for the formation of Christian affections. *Journal of Pentecostal Theology* 7:34-48.

Batson, C. Daniel, and W. Larry Ventis. 1982. *The religious experience: A social-psychological perspective.* New York: Oxford University Press.

Bergin, A. E. 1980. Psychotherapy and religious values. *Journal of Consulting and Clinical Psychology* 48:95-105.

Boone, R. J. 1996. Community and worship: The key components of Pentecostal Christian formation. *Journal of Pentecostal Theology* 8:129-42.

Burgess, Stanley M., and Gary B. McGee, eds. 1988. *Dictionary of Pentecostal and charismatic movements.* Grand Rapids, Mich.: Zondervan.

Cartledge, M. J. 1998. Interpreting charismatic experience: Hypnosis, altered states of consciousness and the Holy Spirit? *Journal of Pentecostal Theology* 13:117-32.

Collins, Gary R. 1998. *The soul search: A spiritual journey to authentic intimacy with God.* Nashville: Thomas Nelson.

Cox, H. 1994. Review of *Pentecostal spirituality: A passion for the kingdom* by Steven J. Land. *Journal of Pentecostal Theology* 5:3-12.

———. 1995. *Fire from heaven.* Reading, Mass.: Addison-Wesley.

Cross, T. L. 1993. Toward a theology of the Word and the Spirit: A review of J. Rodman Williams's renewal theology. *Journal of Pentecostal Theology* 3:113-35.

Daffe, Jerald. 1995. *In the face of evil: You can find faith.* Cleveland, Tenn.: Pathway.

Decker, E. E. 1996. Hearing the voice of God. In *Soul care: A Pentecostal-charismatic perspective,* ed. John K. Vining and E. E. Decker, pp. 88-100. New York: Cummings and Hathaway.

Del Colle, R. 2000. Postmodernism and the Pentecostal-charismatic experience. *Journal of Pentecostal Theology* 17:97-116.

Dobbins, R. 1995. What makes counseling Pentecostal. In *Soul care: A Pentecostal-charismatic perspective,* ed. John K. Vining and E. E. Decker, pp. 15-23. New York: Cummings and Hathaway.

Ellington, S. A. 2000. The costly loss of testimony. *Journal of Pentecostal Theology* 16:48-59.

Ellis, A. 1980. Psychotherapy and atheistic values: A response to A. E. Bergin's "Psychotherapy and religious values." *Journal of Consulting and Clinical Psychology* 48:635-39.

Foster, Richard. 1978. *Celebration of discipline: The path to spiritual growth.* New York: Harper & Row.

———. 1998. *Streams of living water: Celebrating the great traditions of Christian faith.* London: Fount.

Gernert, M. O. 2000. Pentecost confronts abuse. *Journal of Pentecostal Theology* 17:117-30.

Gilbert, Marvin G., and Raymond T. Brock. 1985. *The Holy Spirit and counseling: Theology and theory.* Vol. 1. Peabody, Mass.: Hendrickson.

———. 1989. *The Holy Spirit and counseling: Theology and theory.* Vol. 2. Peabody, Mass.: Hendrickson.

Han, S. E. 1999. A response to Dongsoo Kim. *Journal of Pentecostal Theology* 15:141-43.

———. 2000. "Compassion" as a Christian emotion in the culture of Han: A constructive theological analysis and reflection. In *Collection of Faculty Articles.* 3rd ed. Ed. Sang Ehil Han, pp. 11-37. Seoul: Han Young Theological University Press.

Hayford, Jack. 2001. *Living the Spirit-formed life: Growing in the 10 principles of Spirit-filled discipleship.* Ventura, Calif.: Regal.

Henderson, D. Michael. 1997. *John Wesley's class meeting: A model for making disciples.* Nappanee, Ind.: Evangel.

Ingram, J. A. 1996. Psychological aspects of the filling of the Holy Spirit: A preliminary model of post-redemptive personality functioning. *Journal of Psychology and Theology* 24:104-13.

Johns, J. D., and C. B. Johns. 1992. Yielding to the Spirit: A Pentecostal approach to group Bible study. *Journal of Pentecostal Theology* 1:109-34.

Johns, Cheryl Bridges. 1993. *Pentecostal formation: A pedagogy among the oppressed.* Sheffield, U.K.: Sheffield Academic Press.

Johns, J. D. 1995. Pentecostalism and the postmodern worldview. *Journal of Pentecostal Theology* 7:73-96.

Johnson, Ben Campbell. 1988. *Pastoral spirituality: A focus for ministry.* Philadelphia: Westminster Press.

Kelly, Eugene W., Jr. 1995. *Spirituality and religion in counseling and psychotherapy: Diversity in theory and practice.* Alexandria, Va.: American Counseling Association.

Kim, D. 1999. The healing of "Han" in Korean Pentecostalism. *Journal of Pentecostal Theology* 15:123-39.

Knight, H. H., III. 1993. God's faithfulness and God's freedom: A comparison of contemporary theologies of healing. *Journal of Pentecostal Theology* 2:65-89.

Koenig, Harold George, Michael E. McCullough and David B. Larson. 2001. *Handbook of religion and health.* Oxford: Oxford University Press.

Kydd, R. A. N. 1993. Jesus, saints and relics: Approaching the early church through healing. *Journal of Pentecostal Theology* 2:91-104.

Land, S. J. 1992. A passion for the kingdom: Revisioning Pentecost spirituality. *Journal of Pentecostal Theology* 1:19-46.

————. 1993. *Pentecostal spirituality: A passion for the kingdom.* Sheffield, U.K.: Sheffield Academic Press.

Law, William, ed. 1985. *The heart of true spirituality: John Wesley's own choice.* Grand Rapids, Mich.: Zondervan.

Macchia, F. D. 1998. Groans too deep for words: Towards a theology of tongues as initial evidence. *Asian Journal of Pentecostal Studies* 1:149-73.

Matthew, T. K. 1996. Ministering between miracles: A Pentecostal perspective of pastoral care. In *Soul care: A Pentecostal-charismatic perspective,* ed. John K. Vining and Edward Decker, pp. 129-39. New York: Cummings and Hathaway.

————. 1997. Pentecostal pastoral care in historical perspective: From first covenant to third wave. In *The Spirit of the Lord is upon me: Essential papers on Spirit-filled caregiving,* ed. John K. Vining, pp. 3-25. New York: Cummings and Hathaway.

McMahan, Oliver. 1995. *Scriptural counseling: A God-centered method.* Cleveland, Tenn.: Pathway.

————. 1997. The identity of the Holy Spirit and resulting implications for counseling. In *The Spirit of the Lord is upon me: Essential papers on Spirit-filled caregiving,* ed. John K. Vining, pp. 85-100. New York: Cummings and Hathaway.

————. 2000. *Deepening discipleship.* Cleveland, Tenn.: Pathway.

Miller, A. 1996. Pentecostalism as a social movement: Beyond the theory of deprivation. *Journal of Pentecostal Theology* 9:97-114.

Miller, William R. 1999. *Integrating spirituality into treatment: Resources for practitioners.* Washington, D.C.: American Psychological Association.

Moltmann, Jürgen. 1996. A Pentecostal theology of life. *Journal of Pentecostal Theology* 9:3-15.

Moon, Gary W. 1996. *Homesick for Eden: Confession about the journey of a soul.* Ann Arbor, Mich.: Servant.

Moore, R. D. 1991. The threat of fragmentation in the family of God. Paper presented at Leadership and Doctrinal Integrity: In-Service Training for State Overseers, Church of God Theological Seminary, Cleveland, Tenn.

————. 1995. Deuteronomy and the fire of God: A critical charismatic interpretation. *Journal of Pentecostal Theology* 7:11-33.

Neuman, H. T. 1996. Paul's appeal to the experience of the Spirit in Galatians 3:1-5: Christian existence as defined by the cross and effected by the Spirit. *Journal of Pentecostal Theology* 9:53-69.

Parker, Stephen E. 1996. *Led by the Spirit: Toward a practical theology of Pentecostal discernment and decision making.* Sheffield, U.K.: Sheffield Academic Press.

Pemberton, Larry D. 1985. *Called to care.* Cleveland, Tenn.: Pathway.

Randour, Mary Lou. 1993. *Exploring sacred landscapes: Religious and spiritual experiences in psychotherapy.* New York: Columbia University Press.

Richards, P. Scott, and Allen E. Bergin. 1997. *A spiritual strategy for counseling and psychotherapy.* Washington, D.C.: American Psychological Association.

————. 1999. *Handbook of psychotherapy and religious diversity.* Washington, D.C.: American Psychological Association.

Shafranske, Edward. 1996. *Religion and the clinical practice of psychology.* Washington, D.C.: American Psychological Association.

Shaull, Richard, and Waldo Cesar. 2000. *Pentecostalism and the future of the Christian churches.* Grand Rapids, Mich.: Eerdmans.

Spener, Philipp Jakob. 1964. *Pia desideria.* Philadelphia: Fortress.

Synan, Vinson. 1971. *The holiness-Pentecostal movement in the United States.* Grand Rapids, Mich.: Eerdmans.

―――. 2000. A healer in the house? A historical perspective on healing in the Pentecostal/charismatic tradition. *Asian Journal of Pentecostal Studies* 3:189-201.

Tan, Siang-Yang. 1991. *Lay counseling: Equipping Christians for a helping ministry.* Grand Rapids, Mich.: Zondervan.

Tan, Siang-Yang, and Douglas H. Gregg. 1997. *Disciplines of the Holy Spirit: How to connect to the Spirit's power and presence.* Grand Rapids, Mich.: Zondervan.

Therron, J. P. 1999. Towards a practical theological theory for the healing ministry in Pentecostal churches. *Journal of Pentecostal Theology* 14:49-64.

Thomas, J. C. 1993. The devil, disease and deliverance: James 5:14-16. *Journal of Pentecostal Theology* 2:25-50.

―――. 1994. Women, Pentecostals and the Bible: An experiment in Pentecostal hermeneutics. *Journal of Pentecostal Theology* 5:41-56.

―――. 1998. *The devil, disease and deliverance: Origins of illness in New Testament thought.* Sheffield, U.K.: Sheffield Academic Press.

Van Kaam, Adrian L. 1995. *Transcendence therapy: Formative spirituality.* Vol. 7. New York: Crossroad.

Vining, John K. 1992. *Caring and curing: A proven process for health and healing.* Columbus, Ga.: Brentwood Christian.

―――. 1995a. *Spirit-centered counseling.* New York: Cummings and Hathaway.

―――, ed. 1995b. *Pentecostal caregivers: Anointed to heal.* New York: Cummings and Hathaway.

―――, ed. 1997. *The Spirit of the Lord is upon me: Essential papers on Spirit-filled caregiving.* New York: Cummings and Hathaway.

Vining, John K., and E. E. Decker, eds. 1996. *Soul care: A Pentecostal-charismatic perspective.* New York: Cummings and Hathaway.

Wesley, John. 1952. *A plain account of Christian perfection.* Westminster, U.K.: Epworth.

Yang, H. 1996. *Cross-cultural counseling: A Christ centered approach and application.* Cleveland, Tenn.: Pathway.

Yong, A. 1999. "Not knowing where the wind blows . . ." On envisioning a Pentecostal-charismatic theology of religions. *Journal of Pentecostal Theology* 14:81-112.

PART TWO

THE THREE
MAJOR VOICES
OF SOUL CARE

9

SPIRITUAL DIRECTION
AND PSYCHOTHERAPY

Conceptual Issues

Len Sperry

Believing that spirituality is vital for growth and essential for dealing with life's problems, many individuals are pursuing a journey of spiritual growth. Pursuing this journey typically involves a commitment to engage in spiritual practices such as prayer and meditation. As a result of this pursuit, some are finding their lives are more centered and fulfilling, while others find themselves trapped in old feelings, attitudes and habits that appear to undo their progress. Even those who have made progress on the journey often encounter spiritual and psychological roadblocks to growth.

But fewer are approaching the institutional church for help with these concerns. Why is this? Presumably because of spiritual homelessness, the experience of no longer feeling at home in one's religious tradition or with ministry personnel (Steere 1997). Jean Stairs, describes this phenomenon thus: "The world is crying our for the church to be more the like the church, to represent the space and place where holiness, meaning, and God can be found, experienced, understood, and reimagined" (2000:3). Because of the extent of spiritual homelessness, it should not be surprising that many are turning to psychotherapy rather than to ministers for spiritual advice. And many who are already in psychotherapy expect that therapy will focus on their spiritual concerns (Westfeld 2001).

These observations raise a number of questions. Are spiritual concerns appropriate and proper for psychotherapy? Shouldn't these individuals be seeking spiritual direction or pastoral counseling instead? Can psychotherapy become more receptive to these spiritual concerns? If so, how?

This chapter attempts to address these questions. It begins by differentiating psychotherapy from spiritual direction and pastoral counseling. While pastoral counseling will be briefly described in relation to psychotherapy, this chapter primarily compares and contrasts spiritual direction and psychotherapy. Since a major point of commonality between spiritual direction and psychotherapy is core functions, eight such functions in spiritual direction are compared with similar functions in psychotherapy. Next, the discussion turns to ways of integrating the spiritual direction functions into the practice of psychotherapy. Finally, three perspectives and two strategies for integrating the spiritual direction functions are discussed.

SPIRITUAL DIRECTION, PASTORAL COUNSELING AND
SPIRITUALLY ORIENTED PSYCHOTHERAPY

Like spiritual direction, pastoral counseling and spiritually oriented psychotherapy can and do address spiritual concerns and issues. Beyond this commonality, the three modalities differ with regard to type of clientele served, goals and purposes, the nature of the relationship with the professional, and the type of interventions used. Brief descriptions of the practice of spiritual direction, pastoral counseling and spiritually oriented psychotherapy are provided in this section. Each of the three modalities will be discussed in terms of likely clientele, goals, type of relationship and preferred interventions. Also included is a description of the training and professional organizations supporting each modality.

Spiritual direction. Spiritual direction is also known as spiritual guidance, spiritual friendship and spiritual companionship. There are various ways of defining spiritual direction in the Christian tradition. Definitions span the gamut from "Spiritual direction is the application of theology to the life of prayer" (Thornton 1984:1) to "Spiritual direction, or the cure of souls, is a seeking after the leading of the Holy Spirit in a given psychological and spiritual situation" (Leech 1977:34). It is noteworthy that two themes, "life of prayer" and "seeking after the leading of the Holy Spirit," are reflected in many descriptions of spiritual direction.

The clientele that may be most responsive to spiritual direction are relatively healthy spiritual seekers. Nevertheless, spiritual direction is quite inclusive, and many writers contend that spiritual direction is appropriate for most Christians. However, some would limit spiritual direction to those who possess a moderate degree of psychological health and well-being (May 1992).

Unlike psychotherapy and pastoral counseling, which focus more on symptom reduction or problem resolution, spiritual direction focuses principally on the development and maintenance of spiritual health and well-being. The basic goal of spiritual direction is to develop the directee's relationship with God. Because prayer is critical to this relationship, the directee's prayer life is a major consideration. This includes both discursive and meditative or centering prayer.

Spiritual direction involves a trained director who guides or companions another person—often called a "directee"—listening to that person's life story with sensitivity to the movement of God in the directee's daily life. The relationship that develops in spiritual direction differs from the type of relationship established in psychotherapy and pastoral counseling. For one, the relationship in Christian spiritual direction is triadic, involving the director, the directee and the Holy Spirit. For another, the relationship between directee and director is primarily a mutual collaboration.

Interventions in spiritual direction include instruction in prayer and prescription of rituals and other spiritual practices. When indicated, spiritual directors may refer directees with psychological problems for concurrent psychotherapy or suspend spiritual direction until a course of therapy is completed (Culligan 1983). Whether one professional can effectively and appropriately provide both spiritual direction and psychotherapy or pastoral counseling is a matter of considerable debate (May 1992).

What training and level of certification are required of spiritual directors? Currently there are no set educational and experience requirements or certification for the practice of spiritual direction. Some contend that spiritual direction is a vocation rather than a profession, a special calling for which formal coursework and supervision are not essential. Others contend that specialized training in various areas of theology and psychology are helpful and essential. There are a number of formal training institutes and programs in spiritual direction, such as Shalem Institute and the Institute for Psychospiritual Health, but there is no universally recognized certification or licensure for spiritual directors. As a specialty, spiritual direction is now in a stage of expansion and professionalization. Spiritual Directors International is an ecumenical professional organization for spiritual directors and claims a worldwide membership of thirty-five hundred. It has begun publishing its own professional journal, *Presence,* and has ratified a set of ethical standards and guidelines for the practice of spiritual direction (Lescher 1997).

Pastoral counseling. Currently two forms of pastoral counseling are practiced: a brief, time-limited form that is problem-solving or solution-focused, and a long-term form that is often psychoanalytically oriented and focuses on personality change (Stone 1999). Clergy and other ministry personnel who have some training in pastoral care and counseling provide most of the short-term pastoral counseling. However, persons with formal supervised training in counseling and psychotherapy and who are certified and/or licensed can practice what is called pastoral psychotherapy. Pastoral psychotherapy is variously defined but tends to involve longer-term therapy and in some instances is difficult to distinguish from general psychotherapy (Wise 1983).

While in the past *pastoral care* and *pastoral counseling* were often used synonymously, today they are distinguished. *Pastoral care* refers to pastoral communication that helps and nurtures persons and interpersonal relationships in supportive ministries such as visitation of the sick. This may involve the use of counseling skills, but in a briefer and less therapeutically complex manner than in pastoral counseling. In a sense, pastoral care is a form of precounseling that takes place outside a formal counseling context. Pastoral counseling is a more structured and complex form of pastoral communication that starts after an articulated request for help and is carried out in a formal counseling context. Specific arrangements for sessions, times and fees are mutually negotiated in pastoral counseling.

Clientele of pastoral counseling are persons struggling with life transitions, emotional or relational crises, guilt, abuse, addictions, or low self-esteem. Pastoral counseling is well suited for such crises and concerns and is a distinctive form of counseling that draws on religious and spiritual resources as well as psychological understanding for healing and growth.

The primary goals of pastoral counseling are symptom relief, problem resolution and restoration of psychological health. Personality change is not usually a goal of pastoral counseling. However, as in secular psychotherapy, personality change is typically a goal of pastoral psychotherapy.

The relationship that develops between client and pastoral counselor varies. It some instances the pastoral counselor takes the expert role and offers interpretations or advice. In other instances the relationship is one of mutual collaboration, the relationship style commonplace in spiritual direction.

Treatment interventions usually include active listening and other problem-solving or solution-focused counseling methods. They may also include advice on religious or spiritual matters, such as forgiveness. Unlike spiritual direction, pastoral counseling typically does not draw on the resources of the client's faith community for healing, growth or integration. Pastoral counselors are likely to refer clients with certain issues for psychotherapy.

Like spiritual direction, pastoral counseling is currently in the process of becoming a recognized profession. This means that issues of training, certification and professional identity are central concerns. An increasing number of pastoral counselors are licensed to practice, usually in one of the mental health specialties, such as licensed professional counselor, and certification is available from the American Association of Pastoral Counselors. This professional organization represents three thousand pastoral counselors and is actively exploring ways of incorporating a focus on spiritual concerns and spiritual direction methods into the practice of pastoral counseling. While some are wary of extending the scope of pastoral counseling, citing major differences in epistemological perspectives and praxis between the two fields, others are supporting this extension (Galindo 1998). Needless to say, the identity of pastoral counseling is significantly affected by such forces as managed behavioral healthcare and the increasing numbers of spiritual directors and mental health counselors who compete for many of the same clients as pastoral counselors (Stone 1999).

Spiritually oriented psychotherapy. This field encompasses a variety of psychotherapeutic approaches that are sensitive to the spiritual dimension. Such approaches range from non-Christian transpersonal psychotherapies (Cortright 1997; Karasu 2000) to theistic (Richards and Bergin 1999) and various Christian approaches (Propst 1996; Steere 1997; Sperry 1998, 2001; Benner 2002). Despite considerable variability among the approaches, some general observations about typical clientele, goals and purposes, the nature of the relationship with the professional, and the type of interventions used in spiritually oriented psychotherapy are possible.

Persons seeking spiritually oriented psychotherapy range from relatively healthy spiritual seekers to disordered clients presenting with symptomatic distress or impairment in one or more areas of life functioning.

The goals of treatment vary according to client presentation and need. They may include help with spiritual emergencies, the process of spiritual growth, increased psychological well-being, self-fulfillment or individuation, or the reduction of symptomatic distress and the restoration of baseline functioning.

The therapeutic relationship typically involves mutual collaboration. Those practicing spiritually oriented psychotherapy presumably will demonstrate respect for the client's spiritual values and concerns.

Various psychotherapeutic interventions are used, depending on client need and indication. If indicated, referral for a psychiatric evaluation for medication or hospitalization may occur. Spiritual interventions are also involved. These include spiritual practices such as prayer and meditation and, when indicated, collaboration with or referral to clergy or a chaplain.

Spiritual counseling may take an approach similar to but distinct from traditionally practiced psychotherapy and spiritual direction (Sperry 1998). In this approach the clinician functions as psychotherapist and spiritual guide simultaneously. Spiritual counseling addresses a wide range of psychological and spiritual concerns of clients. It is based on a composite developmental and pathology model of health and well-being, and it views growth in a holistic fashion, including the psychological, moral, somatic and spiritual dimensions. Because of its holistic focus, a comprehensive assessment is made of the client's overall health, psychological strengths and defenses, and moral and spiritual development. Spiritual considerations include relationship with God, God-image or representation, prayer life and spiritual practices, as well as involvement in a faith community and the type and level of support it provides. The goal is to promote the process of transformation in all dimensions. Various psychotherapeutic and spiritual modalities, including spiritual disciplines such as prayer and meditation, are used to achieve this goal.

Unlike data on membership in professional spiritual direction and pastoral counseling organizations, there are no firm estimates on the number of professionals practicing spiritually oriented psychotherapy. There are approximately 500,000 practicing psychotherapists (psychologists, social workers, psychiatrists, marital and family therapists, mental health counselors, etc.) in the United States. If even a small percentage of these psychotherapists chose to practice some form of spiritually sensitive psychotherapy, there would be considerably more such psychotherapists available than there are available spiritual directors.

The phenomenon of "spiritual homelessness" may restrain some people from seeking spiritual guidance from spiritual directors with institutional church ties. Even if pastors were to wholeheartedly embrace the role of spiritual counselor (Stairs 2000), it is unlikely that they could be expected to deal adequately with complex psychospiritual issues.

This means that persons seeking spiritual advice are likely to have greater access to spiritually sensitive psychotherapists than to spiritual directors, and they can expect that psychotherapists who are sensitive to spiritual issues will have more specialized training in dealing with complex psychological problems that have spiritual aspects than most spiritual directors. Because of this, spiritually sensitive psychotherapists have a distinct advantage over spiritual directors without formal training in psychotherapy. This factor cannot be underplayed for clients who have experienced early life traumas, have a substance or drug abuse history, or are struggling with significant stressors and conflicts and who are seeking spiritual advice. Thus it does not seem unreasonable to conclude that psychotherapists sensitive to the spiritual dimension, with adequate training,[1] could reasonably address the spiritual concerns of their clients.

But how can the practice of psychotherapy become more receptive and effective in dealing with spiritual issues and concerns? I propose that psychotherapy can become more receptive and effective by incorporating some or all of the functions of spiritual direction.

---

[1]The ethical considerations regarding training and experience to extend the scope of one's practice are an important matter that will not be addressed here due to space limitations.

THE FUNCTIONS OF SPIRITUAL DIRECTION

There are various functions performed by or involving the spiritual director and the directee. Eight such functions, some of which have their counterparts in psychotherapy, are described in this section. Table 9.1 lists them.

Table 9.1. Functions of Spiritual Direction and Psychotherapy

Functions of Spiritual Direction	Functions of Psychotherapy
Spiritual assessment	Initial psychological evaluation
Differentiating spiritual experience from psychopathology	Differential diagnosis
Triadic relationship	Dyadic therapeutic alliance
Advisement	Therapeutic interventions: interpretation, cognitive restructuring, etc.
Discernment	Mutual collaboration
Spiritual resistance	Psychological resistance
Transference and countertransference	Transference and countertransference

Spiritual assessment. The purpose of the spiritual assessment is to understand a client's spiritual experiences, orientation and beliefs. Even though spiritual experience is the core dynamic in spiritual direction, a person's beliefs may impact his or her experience of God. For that reason the spiritual assessment deals with both experiences and beliefs. A useful beginning question is "Can you tell me a little about your religious beliefs and feelings?" (May 1992:204). This can be followed up with questions that elicit the client's specific experience of God, prayer and so on. Some spiritual directors conduct a formal spiritual history as part of this assessment. It might include the directee's religious upbringing, their images of God, their basic values and beliefs, their involvement in a spiritual community, and the place of prayer and other spiritual practices in their life. The concomitant of the spiritual assessment in traditional psychotherapy is the initial intake evaluation, in which the client is queried about the presenting problem, past history of symptoms and treatments, social and developmental history, sexual and work history, health status and the like.

At the outset of spiritual direction, some directors inform the directee that an evaluation of the relationship with the director and progress in spiritual direction is usually made after about six months (Edwards 2001). Several questions might be discussed at that time:

- How is grace manifesting itself in the relationship?

- Do the ways the director reflects, questions, prays and maintains silence assist or hinder the directee's connection with God?

- Does it feel appropriate and right to continue the direction relationship? (Edwards 2001:121)

Differentiating spiritual experience from psychopathology. Some unusual and troubling spiritual experiences can arise during the spiritual journey, and clinicians need to be able to differentiate such experiences from major psychopathology. *Spiritual emergency* is a term for the way the self becomes disorganized and overwhelmed by an infusion of spiritual energies that it is unable to integrate. The term was coined by Stanislav Grof and Christina Grof (1989) to identify the psychological difficulties encountered by Americans who engaged in Eastern meditative practices in the 1960s. New realms of spiritual experiences can appear suddenly and dramatically, leading to immense confusion, anxiety and sometimes impaired functioning. Persons with no obvious personal vulnerability or family history of mental illness may wonder if they are experiencing psychosis or psychotic symptoms. Not surprisingly, mystical experiences such as visions have been misdiagnosed as psychosis, just as "dark night" experiences have been misdiagnosed as depressive disorder.

A phenomenon known as "the awakening of kundalini" may be the unusual spiritual experience reported most often by spiritual seekers exploring Eastern practices (Grof and Grof 1989: 15). Energy residing in the body's energy centers or chakras is activated by meditation or other spiritual practices. The energy flow may be gentle or overwhelmingly intense and can result in visions, widening of consciousness, clairvoyant perception, or frightening involuntary spasms, jerking or repetitive movements. Since it tends to be misdiagnosed as mania, anxiety disorder or conversion disorder, it is essential that clinicians are aware of its manifestations. The function of differentiating spiritual experiences from psychopathology in spiritual direction is akin to the function of differential diagnosis in psychotherapy and psychiatry.

Transformation. Transformation, perhaps the central issue and goal of spiritual direction (Gratton 1992), is the process of undergoing a radical change of mind and heart, a dying to the false self and a continually assenting to one's true self, which reflects the image and likeness of God. Transformation is a lifelong process.

In comparison, the goal or goals of psychotherapy are more circumscribed. They may be limited to symptom resolution or increased functioning, or they extend to personality change.

Fostering the relationship between God and the directee. Coming under spiritual direction is one means of developing one's relationship with God. Essentially, spiritual direction is a relationship among three persons: God, the directee and the director. The relationship between the directee and the director can be instrumental "for the development of the relationship of the directee and God, but the latter relationship exists prior to and is independent of the former. Directors do not create relationships between God and their directees; they try to foster such relationships" (Barry and Connolly 1982:29).

While there are some obvious similarities between the establishment of a therapeutic alliance between client and psychotherapist in psychotherapy and fostering the relationship in spiritual direction, there is an obvious difference.

Advisement. In pursuit of the goal of transformation, a spiritual director focuses on advising the directee about the life of prayer and the use of spiritual practices (Edwards 2001). Advice and instruction on prayer and meditation are key methods of spiritual direction. Typically such advice arises out of questions and concerns brought up by the advisee. Given the context of mutual collaboration, advisement comes in the guise of suggestions rather than firm directives.

The closest analogues to advisement in psychotherapy are clinical interventions such as interpretation, cognitive restructuring, "homework" and, of course, advice-giving. Spiritual practices are commonly discussed and prescribed in spiritually oriented psychotherapies.

Discernment. Discernment is the function of spiritual direction concerned with "seeking after the leading of the Holy Spirit." In the past, directors typically discerned "spirits" and major life decisions for their directees (Thornton 1984; Conroy 1995). Tilden Edwards notes that discernment in the "Roman Catholic, Anglican and mainstream Protestant church practice of spiritual direction today . . . has shifted from the director to the directee, or to a kind of mutual discernment between them" (2001:68). Now directors "listen with the directee for what God's Spirit seems to be up to, asking probing questions, perhaps offering suggestions, and above all providing a supportive, prayerful presence for deep listening. They see themselves as co-discerners with the directee" (ibid.:69).

There is no direct analogue in psychotherapy to the process of discernment in spiritual direction. Mutual collaboration in making decisions about treatment is tangentially related but does not, of course, involve the key element of seeking the Spirit's leading. Clinical case formulation is an even more distant analogue.

Dealing with resistance. Three forms of resistance in spiritual direction have been noted: resistance to spiritual experience, resistance to the spiritual director or to spiritual direction, and the director's resistance to directees or their religious experience (Ruffing 2000).

The first form of resistance involves avoidance of religious or spiritual experience itself. Since spiritual direction primarily involves the directee's relationship with God, this form of resistance involves the directee's movement away from God's inbreaking in her life because of fear. This fear might be of the intensity of God's presence, a perceived threat to her self-image, some change in her prayer experience or an unpleasant consequence she anticipates. According to Ruffing (2000), resistance to prayer is probably most common: the directee may have difficulty establishing a regular discipline of prayer or experience unpleasant memories or feelings while engaging in meditation. The form of resistance in directees "depends on their psychological makeup and the particular psychological defenses they habitually employ in other areas of their lives" (ibid.:41).

The second form involves resistance to the spiritual director or to spiritual direction. It may develop in response to the director's ineptitude, lack of attentiveness, judgmental attitude or abusiveness. The director's timing or manner of questioning or reflecting the directee's concern may be off on a particular day, or the overall chemistry between the two may underlie the resistance. The result is that directees become averse to sharing their intimate experiences of and response to God, fearing they will be controlled, misunderstood or judged by the director. Such resistance to spiritual direction is the most common reason for premature terminations.

Janet K. Ruffing contends that resistance in spiritual direction is far less likely to be related to the director's skill than is resistance in psychotherapy, which more often reflects the therapist's skill. Resistance in spiritual direction, she says, is more frequently related to the directee's avoidance of spiritual disciplines. This "avoidance has nothing to do with the director's skill or presence. Rather, these directees avoid the qualitative commitment to spiritual growth that ongoing spiritual direction facilitates. Some directees slow down their own process by withdrawing from spiritual direction" (Ruffing 2000:45).

The third form involves the director's avoidance of something in the spiritual direction process. Dreading dealing with an issue that must be confronted, the director may forget the appointment or arrive late; or the director may be discouraged at the directee's lack of progress. Avoidance of the "directee's religious experience comprises an even more serious form of resistance" (Ruffing 2000:47). Perhaps the director is experiencing a "dark night" and the directee wants to share highly positive experiences, or maybe the director is frightened by or unsure how to respond to the directee's mystical experience or imagery. Sometimes such resistance is part of the director's countertransference.

Dealing with transference and countertransference. Does transference occur in spiritual direction, and if so, how? Transference is an unconscious projection of the directee's positive or negative expectations onto the director. Since spiritual direction tends to be scheduled monthly, whereas dynamically oriented psychotherapy may be timed twice weekly, directors may assume that because spiritual direction is less intensive, transference is unlikely to develop. Because spiritual direction focuses primarily on the directee's relationship with God rather than with the director, directors may seldom need to engage transference directly. Nevertheless, transference does occur in spiritual direction, and the director may not be sufficiently trained to recognize and deal with it.

Any directee "is susceptible to bringing unresolved emotional conflicts to the spiritual direction relationship and reenacting them in this new setting" (Ruffing 2000:158-59). "When the relationship between the director and direction—instead of the directee's relationship with God—becomes the focus . . . the entire process of spiritual direction can become sidetracked" (ibid.:162).

Ruffing describes four transferences that may happen in spiritual direction:

1. The directee idealizes the director, who is perceived as embodying spiritual qualities to which the directee aspires.

2. The directee develops an erotic attraction to the director based on their soul friendship.

3. The directee symbolically views the director as representing God.

4. The directee forms an institutional transference to the director—that is, identifies the director with a particular religious denomination or institution. (ibid.:169-79)

It shouldn't be surprising that countertransference also occurs in spiritual direction, since countertransference is elicited by the directee and is reciprocal. Director resistances in spiritual direction are part of his or her countertransference.

Needless to say, managing transference and countertransference in spiritual direction requires considerable skill. Those practicing spiritual direction who also have formal training in psychotherapy presumably have an advantage in dealing with such transferences. Through supervision and psychological consultation, directors with less training and experience can learn to manage transference and their own reactions to directees.

INTEGRATING SPIRITUAL DIRECTION FUNCTIONS IN PSYCHOTHERAPY

Integrating spiritual direction functions into the process of psychotherapy may seem rather straightforward and uncomplicated. On first reflection it would seem no different from adding a relapse prevention component to cognitive-behaviorally oriented psychotherapy. If spiritually oriented psychotherapy involved only the addition or incorporation of a spiritual assessment and spiritually oriented therapeutic interventions or spiritual practices and disciplines, it would probably present few difficulties or challenges. However, incorporating the spiritual direction functions requires some major changes in the therapeutic process. These changes involve not just different types of interventions but differences in relationship, focus and stance. Not only is the working relationship in spiritual direction triadic instead of dyadic as in psychotherapy, the spiritual director is a companion or fellow traveler on the same spiritual journey as the directee. Spiritual direction's focus on prayer and the directee's ongoing relationship with God is considerably different from the psychotherapeutic focus on symptoms, problems or personality change.

Even more different is the stance or disposition of the director from that of the therapist. The therapist's stance is supportive and analytic—particularly in dynamically oriented psychotherapies—and operates in a mode of reflection, clarification, confrontation and interpretation, with the goal of curing the individual, "restoring efficient functioning and increasing well-being" (May 1992:209). The spiritual director's stance involves quietly waiting and listening for the movement of the Spirit in pursuit of the goal of healing the individual, "increasing love" (ibid.:210). The director's stance is closer to the "being" end of the being-doing continuum, whereas the therapist's stance is toward the "doing" end. The tempo in direction is more relaxed and essentially free of utilization review provisions so prevalent today in psychotherapy—that is, the need to fulfill specific therapeutic objectives within a given number of authorized sessions.

Beyond these relationship, focus and stance differences is the basic question whether spiritual direction functions *should* be incorporated within psychotherapy. Three different perspectives or points of view on this question deserve careful consideration: the positive perspective, the negative perspective and the negotiated perspective.

The *positive perspective* endorses the incorporation of many or all of the spiritual direction functions. This perspective is advocated by practitioners and supporters of various spiritually oriented psychotherapies. Transpersonal psychotherapies, in particular, are based on a belief that the therapeutic relationship is the ideal context for dealing with both spiritual and psychological dimensions, whether simultaneously or sequentially (Cortright 1997). Training, prescribing and advising about meditation, among other spiritual practices, in the context of psychotherapy has been normative for most transpersonal psychotherapies over the past four decades. While many transpersonal approaches are not overtly Christian in orientation, they appear to have successfully and effectively combined many spiritual direction functions along with psychotherapy functions within the work of the spiritually oriented psychotherapist. While the clients may also be involved with a meditation teacher or group, many, if not all, of the spiritual direction functions are performed by their psychotherapist.

The *negative perspective* is championed by Gerald May, who is both a psychiatrist and a spiritual director. He has definite opinions about the roles and functions of spiritual direction and psychotherapy, and he refrains from combining the two

roles or functions in his practice. Presumably he would not favor spiritually oriented psychotherapies combining functions and roles of psychotherapy and spiritual direction. While he believes that psychotherapists must be sensitive to the
spiritual domain in their work, he contends that it "is inappropriate to make spirituality the *primary agenda* of a psychotherapeutic consultation" (2000:202). Only
when the psychotherapist is "a gifted spiritual director—and if a clear discernment
has been made with the person as to the rightness of the relationship," and only
on a temporary basis, would he sanction a helper's taking on both roles.

May supports this position with the following reasons. First, he insists that it is
"an unwise economy of time and emphasis" (ibid.:207), noting that clients want
to use their session time to deal with their problems and difficulties, leaving little
time for spiritual direction functions.

> When you're trying to be spiritual director at the same time, you have to make sure
> you allow enough time to deal with how prayer is going, what kind of subtle move-
> ments and invitations might be happening, the nuances of discernment. Too often
> these spiritual guidance questions are ignored completely or left for the last few min-
> utes of the hour. (ibid.)

Second, he believes that it is difficult for both client and helper to shift back
and forth between the more analytic process of psychotherapy and the very reflective stance and pace of spiritual direction. "You and the client somehow have to
shift your attitudes away from problem-solving toward more prayerful openness,
and that is not always easy" (ibid.).

While the value of the positive position is its advocacy of the spiritual dimension in psychotherapy, the value of the negative position is its recognition of logis-
tical problems that can arise in a nonnuanced approach to spiritually oriented psychotherapy. The *negotiated perspective* bridges these two perspectives, recognizing
and respecting the subtle and not so subtle differences between spiritual direction
and psychotherapy sensitive to the spiritual dimension. In the negotiated perspective, the same helper provides both spiritual direction and psychotherapy functions but in a planned, negotiated manner. This perspective recognizes and ac-
commodates for the problems and challenges noted by May.

Here is how the functions and roles might be negotiated. If a client in weekly
psychotherapy wants and needs to focus on spiritual issues, treatment can be
planned so that one session a month focus specifically on these while the other
three sessions of the month focus on therapy. While similar issues may be discussed in both types of sessions, the intent and emphasis of each is clear and defined. Since spiritual direction sessions in the Christian tradition are typically
scheduled monthly, the negotiated perspective provides a proper and effective format for combining the two sets of functions and roles. In my own professional ex-

perience, this has been the most appropriate format for practicing Christian spiritually oriented psychotherapy.

STRATEGIES FOR INTEGRATING THE SPIRITUAL DIRECTION FUNCTIONS

While spiritual direction and psychotherapy share some commonalities, they are far from being interchangeable. This poses a number of challenges for those desiring to integrate the two. Nevertheless, integrating spiritual direction functions into psychotherapy does not have to be an all-or-nothing proposition: either integrate all eight functions or don't incorporate any functions. At least two integration strategies are possible.

Strategy 1. In this strategy all eight functions, or most of them, are incorporated into the psychotherapy process. Psychotherapists who are likely to use this strategy typically have participated in their own spiritual direction with an experienced director. They also experience a strong desire and feel called to offer spiritual direction. Moreover, they have clients who want spiritual direction provided in the context of their psychotherapy. Finally, they have been able to arrange scheduling and fees so that the spiritual direction functions can be sequenced with the psychotherapy functions. For example, for a client who is seen weekly, the therapist may schedule one session a month devoted principally to spiritual direction concerns while the other sessions that month are devoted primarily to psychotherapeutic concerns.

Strategy 2. In this strategy only two or three of the spiritual direction functions are incorporated into psychotherapy. Many psychotherapists are interested in providing psychotherapy that is sensitive to spiritual issues but cannot easily incorporate more than a couple of spiritual direction functions in their therapy. The two spiritual direction functions that are most easily incorporated are spiritual assessment and advisement.

Spiritual assessment is essential for a therapist who endeavors to offer spiritually sensitive psychotherapy. Even a brief assessment can reveal the client's current spiritual practices, image of God, and past and present religious and spiritual concerns. Based on this assessment, the therapist, in collaboration with the client, can choose to focus therapeutically on a issue that has spiritual meaning, refer the client to a minister or other spiritual guide, or consider a spiritual practice.

Advisement may involve the therapist's prescribing and monitoring certain spiritual practices, offering advice and feedback in the process. Spiritual practices are focused activities that foster spiritual qualities and can result in a balanced and disciplined lifestyle. Whether used as an intervention within a treatment session or prescribed as an intersession activity, spiritual practices can be a powerful adjunct to the treatment process. Commonly used spiritual practices include meditation, fasting, reading sacred writings, healing prayer, forgiveness, moral instruction and service. Spiritually oriented interventions include spiritually focused cognitive restructuring and guided imagery strategies. Several other spiritual practices and interventions have been described (Richard and Bergin 1997; Miller 1999; Sperry 2001).

CONCLUDING COMMENT

A fascinating trend has been noted in the past few years: clients are seeking to deal with spiritual issues and concerns in the context of psychotherapy. This phenomenon has increased interest in the spiritually oriented psychotherapies, and not surprisingly, psychotherapists with an interest in the spiritual dimension are considering how they might respond to the need.

Four questions were posed at the beginning of this chapter. The first and second asked whether it is appropriate for psychotherapy to deal with spiritual concerns that traditionally have been the focus of spiritual direction. It was concluded that spiritual concerns can be appropriately dealt with in psychotherapy, and that because of accessibility and competence, spiritually sensitive psychotherapists will increasingly be called upon to provide such services. While it is unlikely that spiritually oriented psychotherapy will or should replace spiritual direction, it is a useful and sometimes necessary adjunct.

The third and fourth questions concerned the receptivity and effectiveness of psychotherapy in dealing with spiritual concerns. It was proposed that psychotherapy increases its receptivity by incorporating some or all of the functions of spiritual direction. Some ways of incorporating these functions were suggested, as well as certain cautions.

There is reason to believe that this trend will not be short-lived. Needless to say, the impact it is having on the practice of psychotherapy is heartening to professionals with a faith perspective. For many it portends a challenging way of extending the scope of their practice in line with their beliefs and values.

REFERENCES

Barry, William, and William Connolly. 1982. *The practice of spiritual direction.* New York: Seabury.

Benner, David G. 2002. *Sacred companions: The gift of spiritual friendship and direction.* Downers Grove, Ill.: InterVarsity Press.

Conroy, Maureen. 1995. *Looking into the well: Supervision of spiritual directors.* Chicago: Loyola University Press.

Cortright, Brant. 1977. *Psychotherapy and spirit: Theory and practice in transpersonal psychotherapy.* Albany: State University of New York Press.

Culligan, Kevin. 1983. The counseling ministry and spiritual direction. In *Pastoral counsel-*

ing, ed. Barry K. Estadt, pp. 37-49. Englewood Cliffs, N.J.: Prentice-Hall.

Edwards, Tilden. 1980. *Spiritual friend: Reclaiming the gift of spiritual direction.* New York: Paulist.

————. 2001. *Spiritual director, spiritual companion: Guide to tending the soul.* New York: Paulist.

Galindo, Israel. 1997. Spiritual direction and pastoral counseling. *Journal of Pastoral Care* 51:395-402.

Gratton, Carolyn. 1992. *The art of spiritual guidance.* New York: Crossroad.

Grof, Stanislav, and Christina Grof, eds. 1989. *Spiritual emergency: When personal transformation becomes a crisis.* pp. 1-26. New York: Tarcher/Putnam.

Karasu, T. 1999. Spiritual psychotherapy. *American Journal of Psychotherapy* 53:143-62.

Leech, Kenneth. 1977. *Soul friend: The practice of Christian spirituality.* San Francisco: Harper & Row.

Lescher, B. 1997. The professionalization of spiritual direction: Promise and peril. *Listening* 32:81-90.

May, Gerald. 1992. *Care of mind, care of soul: A psychiatrist explores spiritual direction.* San Francisco: HarperCollins.

Miller, William R., ed. 1999. *Integrating spirituality into treatment: Resources for practitioners.* Washington, D.C.: American Psychological Association.

Propst, L. Rebecca. 1996. Cognitive-behavioral therapy and the religious person. In *Religion and the clinical practice of psychology,* ed. Edward P. Shafranske, pp. 391-408. Washington, D.C.: American Psychological Association.

Richards, P. Scott, and Allen Bergin. 1997. *A spiritual strategy for counseling and psychotherapy.* Washington, D.C.: American Psychological Association.

Rose, Elizabeth, John Westfeld and Timothy Ansley. 2001. Spiritual issues in counseling: Clients' beliefs and preferences. *Journal of Counseling Psychology* 48:61-71.

Ruffing, Janet K. 2000. *Spiritual direction: Beyond the beginnings.* New York: Paulist.

Sperry, Len. 1998. Spiritual counseling and the process of conversion. *Journal of Christian Healing* 20:37-54.

————. 2001. *Spirituality in clinical practice: Incorporating the spiritual dimension in psychotherapy and counseling.* New York: Brunner/Routeledge.

Stairs, Jean. 2000. *Listening for the soul: Pastoral care and spiritual direction.* Minneapolis: Fortress.

Steere, Douglas. 1997. *Spiritual presence in psychotherapy: A guide for caregivers.* New York: Brunner/Mazel.

Stone, H. 1999. Pastoral counseling and the changing times. *Journal of Pastoral Care* 53:119-27.

Thornton, Martin. 1984. *Spiritual direction.* New York: Cowley.

Wise, Caroll A. 1983. *Pastoral psychotherapy: Theory and practice.* New York: Jason Aronson.

10

SPIRITUAL DIRECTION AND PSYCHOTHERAPY

Ethical Issues

Siang-Yang Tan

Integrating spirituality and religion into psychotherapy (Tan 1996b, 1999c, 2001b) has become a significant area of interest and emphasis in the mental health field in general (e.g., Akhtar and Parens 2001; Becvar 1997; Canda and Furman 1999; Cornett 1998; Cortright 1977; Fukuyama and Sevig 1999; Genia 1995; Griffith and Griffith 2001; Kelly 1995; Lovinger 1984, 1990; G. Miller 2003; W. R. Miller 1999; Nielsen, Johnson and Ellis 2001; Richards and Bergin 1997, 2000, 2004; Shafranske 1996; Sperry 2001; Steere 1997; Walsh 1999; West 2000), as well as in Christian counseling in particular (e.g., Anderson, Zuehlke and Zuehlke 2000; Benner 1988, 1998; McMinn 1996).[1] A more specific focus that is receiving greater attention recently is integrating *spiritual direction* into psychotherapy and counseling (e.g., see Benner 1998). These recent developments are part of a larger movement in the mental health and health arenas emphasizing the significant relationship, often positive, between religion and health (e.g., see Koenig 1998, 1999; Koenig and Cohen 2002; Koenig, McCullough and Larson 2001; Larson, Swyers and McCullough 1998; Plante and Sherman 2001; also see Francis and Kaldor 2002; Mills 2002), although there are critics of this movement (e.g., see Sloan and Bagiella 2002).

Literature on spiritual direction itself has mushroomed especially in recent years. Keith Anderson and Randy Reese (1999) reviewed contemporary definitions

---

[1]This chapter is an expanded version of the William C. Bier Award (Division 36, Psychology of Religion) address presented by the author at the 110th Annual Convention of the American Psychological Association, Chicago, August 23, 2002.

of spiritual mentoring or spiritual direction by William Barry and William Connolly (1982), Marie Coombs and Francis Nemeck (1984), Tilden Edwards (1980), Richard Foster (1988), Margaret Guenther (1992), Alan Jones (1982), Jean Laplace (1988), Kenneth Leech (1977), Thomas Merton (1960) and Eugene Peterson (1989). They also recommended a bibliography for spiritual mentoring or direction that further included Joseph Allen (1994), Carolyn Gratton (1992), Irene Hausherr (1990) and Morton Kelsey (1983)—also see Thomas Dubay (1993). Since then several other significant books on spiritual direction have been published (e.g., Benner 2002; Rosage 1999; Ruffing 2000; Stairs 2000; also see Benner 2003; Crabb 1997, 1999; Moon 1997a), including a more comprehensive text covering twelve biblical and practical approaches to spiritual formation (Boa 2001).

A well-known definition of Christian spiritual direction is the following, by Barry and Connolly:

> We define Christian spiritual direction, then, as help given by one Christian to another which enables that person to pay attention to God's personal communication to him or her, to respond to this personally communicating God, to grow in intimacy with this God, and to live out the consequences of the relationship. (1982:8)

David G. Benner has defined spiritual direction as a "prayer process in which a person seeking help in cultivating a deeper personal relationship with God meets another for prayer and conversation that is focused on increasing awareness of God in the midst of life experiences and facilitating surrender to God's will" (2002:94). He clarified that spiritual direction is not new, is not authoritarian, is not giving advice, is not discipling, is not preaching, is not moral guidance, is not teaching and is not counseling, although it shares several features with counseling or psychotherapy. Spiritual direction differs from counseling in at least three major ways, according to Benner: (1) counseling is problem-centered, whereas spiritual direction is Spirit-centered; (2) counselors seek to be empathic to the inner experience of those seeking help from them, whereas spiritual directors make their empathic focus not so much on the directee as on the Spirit of God; and (3) counselors engage in note taking and record keeping, whereas spiritual directors usually do not (also see Moon 1994).

William West compared psychotherapy and spiritual direction as follows (2000, see 127):

1. *Features of psychotherapy and counseling:* helping and supportive relationship in a professional or agency context; one-to-one or group; client has emotional or psychological distress; clinic or office based; can be seen as helping client adjust to society; focus on emotional and mental dimensions; aims to strengthen client's autonomy; and often formal hourly sessions over weeks, months, or years.

2. *Features of spiritual direction:* helping and supportive relationship in a faith context; one-to-one or group; client may not have a crisis; based in a community of
   faith; helps clients lead a life of faith; focus on spiritual issues such as prayer life,
   religious experiences, and relationship with God; aims to self-surrender to the
   will of God; sometimes informal, periodic, and intensive (e.g., retreats).

In spiritual direction thus defined, it is not uncommon for the spiritual director
and directee to practice spiritual disciplines such as prayer, Scripture meditation
and silence during the time of spiritual direction. This can also take place in Christian counseling and psychotherapy where appropriate (Tan 1996a, 1996b, 1998;
also see Eck 2002; Hall and Hall 1997; Willard 1996). Gary Moon, Dale Willis,
Judy Bailey and John Kwasny (1993) found that consistent with previous research,
the spiritual guidance techniques most frequently used (out of a list of twenty) by
Christian psychotherapists, pastoral counselors and spiritual directors were spiritual history, discernment, forgiveness, solitude or silence, intercessory prayer and
teaching from Scripture. An earlier study by Marilyn Ganje-Fling and Patricia Mc-
Carthy (1991) showed that spiritual directors were more likely than psychotherapists to incorporate techniques and topics from the other discipline into their
practice, although significant overlap between the two disciplines was also suggested by the results obtained.

Interestingly, Benner has changed his earlier view of Christian psychotherapy
and spiritual direction as being so different in role demands and focus that they
cannot be integrated or combined (see Benner 1988; also see May 1992). His current view is that they can be combined, although we have little experience or few
models for doing such integration. He described two examples of combining spiritual direction and psychotherapy: Bernard Tyrell's Christotherapy (1982) and
Benner's own intervention, called an intensive soul care retreat (Benner 1998). In
both these examples, psychotherapeutic techniques as well as spiritual exercises
or spiritual direction are employed. Integrating spiritual direction into psychotherapy, especially Christian psychotherapy, can therefore be an important part of
professional integration (Tan 2001b), or what M. Elizabeth Hall and Todd Hall
have called "integration in the therapy room" (1997:86). However, it is essential
to practice such integration in an ethical and helpful way. The present article
therefore focuses on ethical issues and guidelines for integrating spiritual direction into psychotherapy.

ETHICAL ISSUES

Books have been published on legal (Levicoff 1991; Ohlschlager and Mosgofian
1992) and ethical (Sanders 1997; also see Tjeltveit 1999) issues pertinent to
Christian counseling and psychotherapy. Here I will explore ethical issues and

guidelines that are more specific to the integrating of spiritual direction into psychotherapy.

It should first be pointed out that Christian counseling or psychotherapy often aims at the ultimate goal of facilitating the spiritual growth of clients, not just the alleviation of symptoms and resolution of problems. Spiritual direction, including the use of spiritual disciplines and other religious resources, is therefore often seen as an integral part of Christian counseling. Spiritual direction, pastoral counseling and Christian psychotherapy can be viewed as greatly overlapping though not synonymous areas of people helping. Rodger Bufford summarized the following distinctives of Christian counseling: "The counselor has a deep faith; counsels with excellence; holds a Christian world view; is guided by Christian values in choosing the means, goals, and motivations of counseling; actively seeks the presence and work of God; and actively utilizes spiritual interventions and resources within ethical guidelines" (1997:120). Christian counselors and psychotherapists, however, differ as to how explicitly they integrate spiritual direction, including the use of spiritual disciplines, directly into the therapy session. While some have advocated more explicit integration in clinical practice where appropriate (see Tan 1996a, 1996b, 1998, 1999b, 1999c; Tan and Dong 2001), others have suggested caution but not censure (e.g., McMinn and McRay 1997).

A degree of caution is appropriate, given the dangers of abusing or misusing spiritual direction in psychotherapy. P. Scott Richards and Allen Bergin devoted an entire chapter to ethical issues and guidelines in their well-known text on a spiritual strategy for counseling and psychotherapy (1997), published by the American Psychological Association. They covered the following potentially difficult ethical questions and challenges: dual relationships (religious and professional), displacing or usurping religious authority, imposing religious values on clients, violating work-setting (church-state) boundaries and practicing outside the boundaries of professional competence. Two other significant concerns they raised regarding the use of spiritual interventions in psychotherapy are becoming enmeshed in superstition and trivializing the sacred or numinous (1997:143-69).

Elsewhere I summarized the following potential pitfalls or dangers of religious psychotherapy, which are also relevant to integrating spiritual direction into psychotherapy:

1. imposing the therapist's religious beliefs or values on the client, thus reducing the client's freedom to choose

2. failing to provide sufficient information regarding therapy to the client

3. violating the therapeutic contract by focusing mainly or only on religious goals rather than therapeutic goals, and thus obtaining third-party reimbursement in-

appropriately (however, sometimes it is difficult to clearly differentiate between spiritual and therapeutic goals, because they tend to overlap for religious clients)

4. lacking competence as a therapist in the area of converting client values ethically or conducting religious psychotherapy appropriately

5. arguing over doctrinal issues rather than clarifying them

6. misusing or abusing spiritual resources like prayer and the Scriptures, thus avoiding dealing with painful issues in therapy

7. blurring important boundaries or parameters necessary for maintaining the therapeutic relationship

8. assuming ecclesiastical authority and performing ecclesiastical functions inappropriately, when referral to church leaders may be warranted

9. applying only religious interventions to problems that may require medication or other medical or psychological treatments (Tan 1994:390)

A particular ethical concern raised by Mark McMinn and Barrett McRay has to do with charging fees and receiving third-party reimbursement for spiritual interventions in psychotherapy (also see Tjeltveit 1986):

> More generally, the fee for service practices of most psychologists introduce a number of challenges when using spiritual disciplines as part of psychotherapy. Is it legitimate to charge for work that has historically been given away as part of pastoral care? What information should be given to insurance companies who pay part of the client's bill? Is spiritual development a legitimate goal of psychotherapy in an era where time-limited interventions are increasingly the standard of care? These are troubling matters that warrant careful consideration in the years ahead. (McMinn and McRay 1997:108)

McMinn and McRay underscored the need to empirically demonstrate the efficacy of spiritual interventions or methodologies, especially given the recent emphasis on using empirically supported therapies, which have most recently grown to a list of 108 for adults and 37 for children (Chambless and Ollendick 2001; Tan 2001a). However, this emphasis on empirically supported therapies has also been critiqued (see Tan 2001a, 2002), with Larry Beutler (2000) in particular proposing going beyond empirically supported treatments to empirically informed principles of treatment selection (also see Beutler, Clarkin and Bongar 2000; Beutler and Harwood 2000). John Norcross (2002) has emphasized the need to pay greater attention to empirically supported therapeutic relationships (ESRs) or psychotherapy relationships that work (see Tan 2003).

The ethical issues just reviewed are not exhaustive, but they include the major potential pitfalls inherent in any religious or spiritual approach to psychotherapy, including the integration of spiritual direction. These ethical dangers can be minimized or avoided by following a number of ethical guidelines for the practice of religious psychotherapy that incorporates spiritual direction.

ETHICAL GUIDELINES

Richards and Bergin have provided a long list of ethical recommendations or guidelines for dealing with the five major ethical issues they raised for psychotherapists who follow a theistic spiritual strategy in their practice (see 1997:143-69).

Therapist-religious leader/associate *dual relationships should be avoided* (Richards and Bergin 1997:147-48). If a therapist concludes after careful review that a dual relationship may be in a client's best interest, the therapist should consult with a supervisor or professional colleagues to see if they agree before entering into such a relationship. If agreement is found, the therapist should clearly define and explain the limits and risks of the dual relationship to the client. Frequent consultation should be sought by the therapist, and the dual relationship should be terminated and an appropriate referral made if it is believed that the client is being harmed by it. Careful documentation should be kept.

Given the danger of displacing or usurping religious authority, Richards and Bergin recommend ethical guidelines for *collaborating with religious authorities* (1997:151-53): Therapists should determine clients' religious or denominational tradition, if any, and whether they see their religious leaders as possible sources of support or help. If the client agrees, therapists should obtain their written informed consent to contact, consult and cooperate with their religious leaders. Therapists should be clear, respectful and courteous in communicating with the client's religious leaders and should thank them for their assistance.

Prior to using spiritual interventions (including spiritual direction or spiritual guidance techniques), therapists should make explicit to their client that they have no ecclesiastical authority over the client and they cannot act or speak officially for the client's religious leaders or institution. Therapists should not perform ecclesiastical functions limited to their clients' religious leaders (e.g., hearing confessions and absolving or pardoning sins). Therapists should explain where their therapeutic role overlaps with that of their client's pastor(s). Therapists should make sure the client feels it is appropriate for them to use a particular spiritual intervention, such as religious imagery and prayer, *before* using it. Therapists should not put down or ridicule their client's religious leaders and should let clients know that they generally see religious leaders and communities as potential sources of support and assistance (also see Brantley and Brantley 2001; McRay et al. 2001).

To avoid the danger of therapists imposing their religious values on clients, Richards and Bergin (1997) give guidelines for *respecting client values* (1997:158-59). Therapists should respect their clients' right to have religious convictions that are different from their own. Therapists should not attempt to convert or proselytize clients to their own religious faith or denomination. Therapists should not arrogantly condemn their clients' behaviors or choices that run counter to their own convictions or beliefs, but they can engage in open exploration and discussion of the spiritual and moral aspects and consequences of a client's value choices and behaviors if the client wants to do so. When value conflicts occur between therapist and client, the therapist can express his or her own views while preserving the client's right to have different values. They should consider whether their disagreement in values could negatively affect therapy and whether referral to another therapist may be warranted. Therapists should include spiritual and religious goals and interventions (including spiritual direction and other spiritual guidance techniques) only when proper informed consent is obtained from a client who has clearly expressed interest in pursuing such goals and participating in such interventions, after an explicit and brief description has been provided.

Richards and Bergin include the following guidelines for *respecting church-state boundaries* (1997:162-63): Therapists in civic settings must follow policies and laws regarding the separation of church and state in such settings. Therapists in civic and other settings should not employ spiritual interventions to impose a specific religious tradition on clients but should always work within a client's value system (as far as possible). Therapists in civic settings should get written consent from both client and supervisor prior to using spiritual or religious interventions, and when conducting therapy with children and adolescents they should obtain written parental permission. Therapists working in public schools or other civic settings with children and adolescents as clients are advised not to engage in spiritual interventions such as praying with clients, using Scripture with them or giving out religious literature.

To address the danger of practicing outside the boundaries of competence, Richards and Bergin, following APA ethical guidelines, make the following recommendations for *education and training standards* for professional psychotherapists wanting to use a theistic spiritual strategy (1997:166). Therapists should be trained in foundational multicultural counseling attitudes and skills (also see Sue and Sue 2003; Tan 1999a; Tan and Dong 2000). Therapists should read relevant and helpful scholarly articles and books on spiritual issues in counseling and psychotherapy, as well as on the psychology and sociology of religion. Therapists should attend at least one workshop or course on religion and mental health and spiritual issues in psychotherapy and should take a class or read one or two good books on world religions. Therapists should obtain specific knowledge of religions and spiritual traditions that they often encounter in therapy (for a helpful book, see Richards and Bergin 2000). Therapists should seek supervision or consultation when they first see a client from a particular religious tradition, especially with issues the therapist has not dealt with before, or when they first start using spiritual interventions—or new, untried ones—in their therapeutic work.

Richards and Bergin have thus provided a comprehensive, conservative and cautious list of ethical guidelines for conducting spiritually oriented psychotherapy. Their guidelines apply well to the integration of spiritual direction into psychotherapy.

Gary Moon also reviews a number of guidelines and considerations for the ethical use of spiritual interventions in psychotherapy, including spiritual direction and spiritual disciplines (1997b:287). He summarizes several ethical guidelines from P. Scott Richards and Richard Potts (1995): Use spiritual interventions only when led or prompted by the Spirit to do so. Prior to using such interventions, make sure that there is first a relationship of trust with the client. Informed consent from the client should be obtained, and the client's religious beliefs should be assessed, before any spiritual interventions are initiated. Work within the client's level of spirituality and value system. Spiritual interventions should be used sparingly and carefully. Spiritual interventions may be less effective with severely disturbed clients, and therefore referral may be warranted in such situations. Use spiritual interventions cautiously if religion appears to be part of the client's problems.

Moon also summarizes the following ethical guidelines from my list (Tan 1994) based on Alan Nelson and William Wilson (1984): The client should share the therapist's basic religious or spiritual belief system; the client has asked for religious and spiritual input into psychotherapy and therefore has given informed consent; and there is a good reason for using a particular spiritual intervention—it is relevant to the clinical problem and is expected to ameliorate psychological distress. Finally, Moon mentions two ethical recommendations from Mark McMinn (1996): Guidelines for informed consent must be carefully followed, and it is safest for psychologists to use specific techniques, including spiritual interventions, that have received empirical support, preferably from two independent, double-blind studies.

Moon proceeded to offer twelve goals or recommendations for the formal training of psychotherapists to practice spiritually oriented psychotherapy, perhaps integrating spiritual direction (see 1997b:291-92):

1. Following Sorenson (1996), more theologians should be recruited as faculty members and journal contributors, so that we can have better applied theology.

2. Instructors should be willing to model interventions that come from religious/ Christian spirituality practices, and use competency-based training methods in training and supervising students.

3. Training programs should emphasize the methodology of the three disciplines

(psychology, theology, and spiritual formation)—statistics and research skills, hermeneutics, critical thinking, and honest introspection.

4. Courses and activities aimed at developing Christian character traits in students (through instruction and practice of the Christian disciplines) seem very appropriate.

5. Require a year of personal psychotherapy.

6. Require another year of spiritual direction.

7. Require a course on the history of classic pastoral care/counseling.

8. The church should be considered as a site for service delivery (not just as a source for client referrals).

9. Integration training programs should take seriously the need to include spiritual formation training for the students.

10. Much more empirical outcome research is needed (with well-controlled studies that meet the criteria for empirically supported therapies).

11. The ethics of providing services to people with diverse religious values and backgrounds must be covered with the students.

12. Finally, there should be much more discussion across the boundaries between psychotherapy, pastoral counseling, and spiritual direction, with an appreciation of the differences between them.

Other recommendations for training mental health professionals in spirituality in clinical practice are also available (Bowman 1998; W. R. Miller 1999; Tan 1993, 1999c; West 2000), including a model curriculum for the training of psychiatric residents (Larson, Lu and Swyers 1996).

Much more work needs to be done in the formal training of mental health professionals in the use of spiritual interventions in psychotherapy. It is important, however, to retain the goals of psychotherapy, the amelioration of symptoms and reduction of psychological distress, intact in therapeutic work. Spiritual direction aimed at spiritual growth and the development of one's relationship with God has a valid place in psychotherapy that is holistic and integrated. However, spiritual direction should not completely replace psychotherapy in the *therapy* session. If and when the goals of psychotherapy per se are achieved and only spiritual direction is desired, psychotherapy should be terminated. When a client wants only spiritual direction, a referral to a spiritual director or pastor may be appropriate. This can help the therapist avoid potential ethical problems related to charging fees and especially receiving third-party reimbursement for doing only spiritual direction without any reference to psychotherapeutic work or goals related to symptoms and psychological distress or problems (see McMinn and McRay 1997). It may be simpler to integrate spiritual direction, including the use of spiritual disciplines, into Christian lay counseling where fees are not charged (see Tan 1991, 1997).

However, if a client chooses with full informed consent to continue to see a Christian therapist for only spiritual direction (instead of accepting a referral to a pastor or spiritual director), after the goals of therapy have been achieved and symptoms substantially ameliorated, then the Christian therapist has a number of ethical options to select from:

- agree with the client to continue sessions for spiritual direction, with the client paying for the sessions without third-party payments

- provide services or sessions pro bono (free) to the client

- switch to a suggested donation arrangement with no third-party payments

Those in charge of formal training programs, especially at the doctoral level, may need to develop a more effective curriculum for training students in explicit integration of spiritual direction in the therapy room (Tan 1996a, 1996b, 1998, 1999b, 1999c; also see Eck 2002; Hall and Hall 1997). Moon et al. (1993) found that doctoral-level religious mental health practitioners were less likely to use explicit spiritual guidance techniques (e.g., prayer and quoting or teaching Scripture) than were master's-level practitioners. They also noted that such spiritual interventions were not often addressed in a course syllabus or given much formal lecture time. They therefore suggested that it may be time to develop specialized education and certification in religious counseling or psychotherapy. An attempt in this direction has been made by Moon and his colleagues at the Psychological Studies Institute in Atlanta, through the Institute of Clinical Theology (see Moon 1997b).

SPIRITUAL DIRECTION AND PASTORAL COUNSELING

Len Sperry (2003) has provided a helpful discussion and delineation of commonalities as well as differences among spiritual direction, pastoral counseling and spiritually oriented psychotherapy. He points out that presently there are two major forms of pastoral counseling: short-term pastoral counseling that is problem-solving or solution-focused, provided mainly by clergy and other ministry staff, and long-term pastoral psychotherapy that is often psychoanalytically oriented, provided by ministry staff and others with formal certification or licensure in counseling and psychotherapy (Stone 1999). Pastoral psychotherapy is difficult at times to differentiate from psychotherapy (Wise 1983).

As Sperry notes, the "primary goal of pastoral counseling is symptom relief, problem resolution, and restoration of psychological health. Personality change is not usually a goal of pastoral counseling. However, as in secular psychotherapy, personality change is typically a goal of pastoral psychotherapy" (2003:5). Pastoral counseling "is a unique form of counseling which uses religious and spiritual resources as well as psychological understanding for healing and growth" (ibid.), and as such it overlaps much with spiritually oriented counseling and psychotherapy. Incorporating spiritual direction and other spiritual resources into pastoral counseling, however, is relatively easy and already often practiced, since pastoral counseling is a spiritually based form of counseling (see Galindo 1997).

Clergy and other ministry staff who provide pastoral counseling informally and without fees will find some of the ethical issues and guidelines regarding integrating spiritual direction into psychotherapy and counseling not relevant or applicable. The issue of charging fees does not apply, and assuming ecclesiastical or clergy roles is actually appropriate in pastoral counseling done by pastors or clergy! However, licensed or certified pastoral counselors who charge fees will find many of the guidelines applicable.

Although spiritual direction can be more easily incorporated into pastoral counseling than into psychotherapy or counseling per se, it should be noted that spiritual direction is not identical to pastoral counseling that focuses on symptom alleviation and problem resolution.

SUMMARY

Integrating spiritual direction into psychotherapy is a valid and exciting undertaking. The field of spiritual direction has grown significantly in recent years, with a mushrooming literature and with new training programs at the certificate, master's and even doctoral levels being offered at various seminaries and universities. Formal training programs in the mental health professions, especially Christian doctoral-level programs, need to incorporate more comprehensive and effective training for integrating spiritual direction and spiritual disciplines into Christian psychotherapy. There are of course several ethical issues and dangers inherent in such integration, but following the guidelines and recommendations covered in this chapter will help therapists to minimize or avoid potential ethical problems and pitfalls.

Ultimately, integrating spiritual direction into psychotherapy from a biblical perspective requires dependence on the Holy Spirit (see Tan 1999b) and a prayer-filled life yielded to the lordship of Christ, including regular practice of the spiritual disciplines (Tan and Gregg 1997; also see Foster 1988; Willard 1988) on the part of the therapist (Tan 1987). The potential is great for deep blessing and greater wholeness and shalom for the client who freely chooses therapy that aims for psychological *and* spiritual growth as well as the reduction of psychological distress.

Elizabeth Rose, John Westefeld and Timothy Ansley (2001), in a study using actual clients (rather than potential clients as in previous analogue studies), found that clients believed religious concerns are appropriate for discussion in counseling and had a preference for discussing spiritual issues in therapy:

> Clearly, many clients, especially the highly spiritual, believe that religious and spiritual issues not only are acceptable and preferable for discussion in therapy but also are important therapeutic factors, central to the formation of worldview and personality and impacting human behavior. Psychologists who provide psychotherapeutic services need to be sensitive to clients' needs to address religious and spiritual issues; those who provide training to future counseling psychologists need to prepare students to deal with these issues; and researchers need to identify the therapeutic aspects of religion and spirituality in counseling. (Rose, Westefeld and Ansley 2001:69)

Integrating spirituality, including spiritual direction, into psychotherapy and counseling in an ethical and helpful way is desired by many clients. More and better training and research are needed before more definitive conclusions can be made regarding the efficacy of an integrated psychospiritual approach to psychotherapy (see McCullough 1999; Worthington, Kurusu, McCullough and Sandage 1996). A review of nine empirical studies of religiously accommodative Christian ($n = 6$) and Muslim ($n = 3$) psychotherapy concluded that there is some limited support for its efficacy, particularly with depressed clients (see Worthington and Sandage 2001). A later empirical outcome study of religious-cultural (Muslim) psychotherapy in the management of Muslim patients with generalized anxiety disorder also yielded positive results (Razali, Aminah and Khan 2002).

REFERENCES

Akhtar, Salman, and Henri Parens, eds. 2001. *Does God help? Developmental and clinical aspects of religious belief.* Northvale, N.J.: Jason Aronson.

Allen, Joseph J. 1994. *Inner way: Toward a rebirth of Eastern Christian spiritual direction.* Grand Rapids, Mich.: Eerdmans.

Anderson, Keith R., and Randy D. Reese. 1999. *Spiritual mentoring: A guide for seeking and giving direction.* Downers Grove, Ill.: InterVarsity Press.

Anderson, Neil T., Terry E. Zuehlke and Julianne S. Zuehlke. 2000. *Christ-centered therapy: The practical integration of theology and psychology.* Grand Rapids, Mich.: Zondervan.

Barry, William A., and William J. Connolly. 1982. *The practice of spiritual direction.* San Francisco: Harper & Row.

Becvar, Dorothy S. 1997. *Soul healing: A spiritual orientation in counseling and therapy.* New York: BasicBooks.

Benner, David G. 1988. *Psychotherapy and the spiritual quest.* Grand Rapids, Mich.: Baker.

———. 1998. *Care of souls: Revisioning Christian nurture and counsel.* Grand Rapids, Mich.: Baker.

————. 2002. *Sacred companions: The gift of spiritual friendship and direction.* Downers Grove, Ill.: InterVarsity Press.

————. 2003. *Surrender to love: Discerning the heart of Christian spirituality.* Downers Grove, Ill.: InterVarsity Press.

Beutler, Larry E. 2000. David and Goliath: When empirical and clinical standards of practice meet. *American Psychologist* 55:997-1007.

Beutler, Larry E., John F. Clarkin and Bruce Bongar. 2000. *Guidelines for the systematic treatment of the depressed patient.* New York: Oxford University Press.

Beutler, Larry E., and T. Mark Harwood. 2000. *Prescriptive psychotherapy: A practical guide to systematic treatment selection.* New York: Oxford University Press.

Boa, Kenneth. 2001. *Conformed to his image: Biblical and practical approaches to spiritual formation.* Grand Rapids, Mich.: Zondervan.

Bowman, Elizabeth S. 1998. Integrating religion into the education of mental health professionals. In *Handbook of religion and mental health,* ed. H. G. Koenig, pp. 367-78. San Diego, Calif.: Academic.

Brantley, Astra P., and Robert L. Brantley. 2001. Barriers and benefits to clergy-psychology collaboration. *Journal of Psychology and Christianity* 20:162-67.

Bufford, Rodger K. 1997. Consecrated counseling: Reflections on the distinctives of Christian counseling. *Journal of Psychology and Theology* 25:111-22.

Canda, Edward R., and Leola D. Furman. 1999. *Spiritual diversity in social work practice.* New York: Free Press.

Chambless, Dianne L., and Thomas H. Ollendick. 2001. Empirically supported psychological interventions: Controversies and evidence. *Annual Review of Psychology* 52:685-716.

Coombs, Marie T., and Francis K. Nemeck. 1984. *The way of spiritual direction.* Collegeville, Minn.: Liturgical.

Cornett, Carlton. 1998. *The soul of psychotherapy: Recapturing the spiritual dimension in the therapeutic encounter.* New York: Free Press.

Cortright, Brant. 1977. *Psychotherapy and spirit: Theory and practice in transpersonal psychotherapy.* Albany: State University of New York Press.

Crabb, Larry. 1997. *Connecting.* Nashville: Word.

————. 1999. *The safest place on earth.* Nashville: Word.

Dubay, Thomas. 1993. *Seeking spiritual direction.* Ann Arbor, Mich.: CHARIS.

Eck, Brian E. 2002. An exploration of the therapeutic use of spiritual disciplines in clinical practice. *Journal of Psychology and Christianity* 21:266-80.

Edwards, Tilden. 1980. *Spiritual friendship: Reclaiming the gift of spiritual direction.* New York: Paulist.

Foster, Richard J. 1988. *Celebration of discipline.* 2nd ed. San Francisco: Harper & Row.

Francis, Leslie J., and Peter Kaldor. 2002. The relationship between psychological well-being and Christian faith and practice in an Australian sample. *Journal for the Scientific Study of Religion* 41:179-84.

Fukuyama, Mary A., and Todd D. Sevig. 1999. *Integrating spirituality into multicultural counseling.* Thousand Oaks, Calif.: Sage.

Galindo, Israel. 1997. Spiritual direction and pastoral counseling. *Journal of Pastoral Care* 51:395-402.

Ganje-Fling, Marilyn A., and Patricia R. McCarthy. 1991. A comparative analysis of spiritual direction and psychotherapy. *Journal of Psychology and Theology* 19:103-17.

Genia, Vicky. 1995. *Counseling and psychotherapy of religious clients.* Westport, Conn.: Praeger.

Gratton, Carolyn. 1992. *The art of spiritual guidance.* New York: Crossroad.

Griffith, James L., and Melissa E. Griffith. 2001. *Encountering the sacred in psychotherapy.* New York: Guilford.

Guenther, Margaret. 1992. *Holy listening: The art of spiritual direction.* Cambridge, Mass.: Cowley.

Hall, M. Elizabeth L., and Todd W. Hall. 1997. Integration in the therapy room: An overview of the literature. *Journal of Psychology and Theology* 25:86-101.

Hausherr, Irene. 1990. *Spiritual direction in the early Christian East.* Kalamazoo, Mich.: Cistercian.

Jones, Alan W. 1982. *Exploring spiritual direction.* New York: Seabury.

Kelly, Eugene W. 1995. *Religion and spirituality in counseling and psychotherapy.* Alexandria, Va.: American Counseling Association.

Kelsey, Morton T. 1983. *Companions on the inner way: The art of spiritual guidance.* New York: Crossroad.

Koenig, Harold G., ed. 1998. *Handbook of religion and mental health.* San Diego, Calif.: Academic.

————. 1999. *The healing power of faith: Science explores medicine's last great frontier.* New York: Simon & Schuster.

Koenig, Harold G., and Harvey Jay Cohen, eds. 2002. *The link between religion and health: Psychoneuroimmunology and the faith factor.* New York: Oxford University Press.

Koenig, Harold G., Michael E. McCullough and David B. Larson. 2001. *Handbook of religion and health.* New York: Oxford University Press.

Laplace, Jean. 1988. *Preparing for spiritual direction.* 3rd ed. Chicago: Franciscan Herald.

Larson, David B., Francis G. Lu and James P. Swyers, eds. 1996. *Model curriculum for psychiatry residency training programs: Religion and spirituality in clinical practice.* Rockville, Md.: National Institute for Healthcare Research.

Larson, David B., James P. Swyers and Michael E. McCullough, eds. 1998. *Scientific research on spirituality and health.* Rockville, Md.: National Institute for Healthcare Research.

Leech, Kenneth. 1977. *Soul friend: The practice of Christian spirituality.* San Francisco: Harper & Row.

Levicoff, Steven. 1991. *Christian counseling and the law.* Chicago: Moody Press.

Lovinger, Robert J. 1984. *Working with religious issues in therapy.* Northvale, N.J.: Jason Aronson.

————. 1990. *Religion and counseling.* New York: Continuum.

May, Gerald G. 1992. *Care of mind, care of spirit: A psychiatrist explores spiritual direction.* Rev. ed. New York: HarperCollins.

McCullough, Michael E. 1999. Research on religion-accommodative counseling: Review and meta-analysis. *Journal of Counseling Psychology* 46:92-98.

McMinn, Mark R. 1996. *Psychology, theology and spirituality in Christian counseling.* Wheaton, Ill.: Tyndale House.

McMinn, Mark R., and Barrett W. McRay. 1997. Spiritual disciplines and the practice of integration: Possibilities and challenges for Christian psychologists. *Journal of Psychology and Theology* 25:102-10.

McRay, Barrett W., Mark R. McMinn, Karen Wrightsman, Todd Burnett and Shiu-Ting Ho. 2001. What evangelical pastors want to know about psychology. *Journal of Psychology and Theology* 29:99-105.

Merton, Thomas. 1960. *Spiritual direction and meditation.* Collegeville, Minn.: Liturgical.

Miller, Geri. 2003. *Incorporating Spirituality in Counseling and Psychotherapy.* New York: Wiley.

Miller, William R., ed. 1999. *Integrating spirituality into treatment: Resources for practitioners.* Washington, D.C.: American Psychological Association.

Mills, Paul J. 2002. Spirituality, religiousness and health: From research to clinical practice. *Annals of Behavioral Medicine* 24, no. 1:1-2.

Moon, Gary W. 1994. Spiritual directors and Christian counselors: Where do they overlap? *Christian Counseling Today* 2, no. 1:29-33.

———. 1997a. *Homesick for Eden.* Ann Arbor, Mich.: Vine.

———. 1997b. Training tomorrow's integrators in today's busy intersection: Better look four ways before crossing. *Journal of Psychology and Theology* 25:284-93.

Moon, Gary W., Dale E. Willis, Judy W. Bailey and John Kwasny. 1993. Self-reported use of Christian spiritual guidance techniques by Christian psychotherapists, pastoral counselors and spiritual directors. *Journal of Psychology and Christianity* 12:24-37.

Nelson, Alan A., and William P. Wilson. 1984. The ethics of sharing religious faith in psychotherapy. *Journal of Psychology and Theology* 12:15-23.

Nielsen, Stevan L., W. Brad Johnson and Albert Ellis. 2001. *Counseling and psychotherapy with religious persons. A rational-emotive behavior therapy approach.* Mahwah, N.J.: Lawrence Erlbaum Associates.

Norcross, John, ed. 2002. *Psychotherapy relationships that work.* New York: Oxford University Press.

Ohlschlager, George, and Peter Mosgofian. 1992. *Law for the Christian counselor.* Dallas: Word.

Peterson, Eugene H. 1989. *The contemplative pastor: Returning to the art of spiritual direction.* Grand Rapids, Mich.: Eerdmans.

Plante, Thomas G., and Allen C. Sherman, eds. 2001. *Faith and health: Psychological perspectives.* New York: Guilford.

Razali, S. M., K. Aminah and U. A. Khan. 2002. Religious-cultural psychotherapy in the management of anxiety patients. *Transcultural Psychiatry* 39:130-36.

Richards, P. Scott, and Allen E. Bergin. 1997. *A spiritual strategy for counseling and psychotherapy.* Washington, D.C.: American Psychological Association.

———, eds. 2000. *Handbook of psychotherapy and religious diversity.* Washington, D.C.: American Psychological Association.

———, eds. 2004. *Casebook for a spiritual strategy in counseling and psychotherapy.* Washington, D.C.: American Psychological Association.

Richards, P. Scott, and Richard W. Potts. 1995. Using spiritual interventions in psychotherapy: Practices, successes, failures and ethical concerns of Mormon psychotherapists. *Professional Psychology: Research and Practice* 26:163-70.

Rosage, David E. 1999. *Beginning spiritual direction.* Eugene, Ore.: Wipf and Stock.

Rose, Elizabeth M., John S. Westefeld and Timothy N. Ansley. 2001. Spiritual issues in counseling: Clients' beliefs and preferences. *Journal of Counseling Psychology* 48:61-71.

Ruffing, Janet K. 2000. *Spiritual direction: Beyond the beginnings.* New York: Paulist.

Sanders, Randolph K., ed. 1997. *Christian counseling ethics.* Downers Grove, Ill.: InterVarsity Press.

Shafranske, Edward P., ed. 1996. *Religion and the clinical practice of psychology.* Washington, D.C.: American Psychological Association.

Sloan, Richard P., and Emilia Bagiella. 2002. Claims about religious involvement and health outcomes. *Annals of Behavioral Medicine* 24, no. 1:14-21.

Sorenson, Randolph L. 1996. The tenth leper. *Journal of Psychology and Theology* 24:197-212.

Sperry, Len. 2001. *Spirituality in clinical practice: Incorporating the spiritual dimension in psychotherapy and counseling.* New York: Brunner/Routledge.

———. 2003. Integrating spiritual direction functions in the practice of psychotherapy. *Journal of Psychology and Theology* 31:3-13.

Stairs, Joan. 2000. *Listening for the soul: Pastoral care and spiritual direction.* Minneapolis: Fortress.

Steere, Douglas A. 1997. *Spiritual presence in psychotherapy: A guide for caregivers.* Bristol, Penn.: Brunner/Mazel.

Stone, Howard. 1999. Pastoral counseling and the changing times. *Journal of Pastoral Care* 53:119-27.

Sue, Derald Wing, and David Sue. 2003. *Counseling the culturally diverse: Theory and practice.* 4th ed. New York: Wiley.

Tan, Siang-Yang. 1987. Intrapersonal integration: The servant's spirituality. *Journal of Psychology and Christianity* 6, no. 1:34-39.

———. 1991. *Lay counseling: Equipping Christians for a helping ministry.* Grand Rapids, Mich.: Zondervan.

———. 1993. Training in professional psychology: Diversity includes religion. Paper presented at the National Councils of Schools of Professional Psychology (NCSPP) conference, "Clinical Training in Professional Psychology," La Jolla, Calif., January.

———. 1994. Ethical considerations in religious psychotherapy: Potential pitfalls and unique resources. *Journal of Psychology and Theology* 22:389-94.

———. 1996a. Practicing the presence of God: The work of Richard J. Foster and its applications to psychotherapeutic practice. *Journal of Psychology and Christianity* 15:17-28.

———. 1996b. Religion in clinical practice: Implicit and explicit integration. In *Religion and the clinical practice of psychology,* ed. E. P. Shafranske, pp. 365-87. Washington, D.C.: American Psychological Association.

———. 1997. The role of the psychologist in paraprofessional helping. *Professional Psychology: Research and Practice* 28:368-72.

———. 1998. The Spiritual disciplines and counseling. *Christian Counseling Today* 6, no. 2:8-9, 20-21.

———. 1999a. Cultural issues in Spirit-filled psychotherapy. *Journal of Psychology and Christianity* 18:164-76.

———. 1999b. Holy Spirit, role in counseling. In *Baker encyclopedia of psychology and counseling,* ed. David G. Benner and Peter C. Hill, 2nd ed., pp. 568-69. Grand Rapids, Mich.: Baker.

———. 1999c. Religion in psychological therapy. *Psychology of Religion Newsletter* 24, no. 3:1-7.

———. 2001a. Empirically supported treatments. *Journal of Psychology and Christianity* 20:282-86.

———. 2001b. Integration and beyond: Principled, professional and personal. *Journal of Psychology and Christianity* 20:18-28.

———. 2002. Empirically informed principles of treatment selection: Beyond empirically supported treatments. *Journal of Psychology and Christianity* 21:54-56.

———. 2003. Empirically supported therapy relationships: Psychotherapy relationships that work. *Journal of Psychology and Christianity* 22:64-67.

Tan, Siang-Yang, and Natalie J. Dong. 2000. Psychotherapy with members of Asian-American churches and spiritual traditions. In *Handbook of psychotherapy and religious diversity,* ed. P. Scott Richards and Allen E. Bergin, pp. 421-44. Washington, D.C.: American Psychological Association.

———. 2001. Spiritual interventions in healing and wholeness. In *Faith and health: Psychological perspectives,* ed. Thomas G. Plante and Allen C. Sherman, pp. 291-310. New York: Guilford.

Tan, Siang-Yang, and Douglas H. Gregg. 1997. *Disciplines of the Holy Spirit.* Grand Rapids, Mich.: Zondervan.

Tjeltveit, Alan C. 1986. The ethics of value conversion in psychotherapy: Appropriate and inappropriate therapist influence on client values. *Clinical Psychology Review* 6:515-37.

———. 1999. *Ethics and values in psychotherapy.* New York: Routledge.

Tyrell, Bernard J. 1982. *Christotherapy II.* New York: Paulist.

Walsh, Froma, ed. 1999. *Spiritual resources in family therapy.* New York: Guilford.

West, William. 2000. *Psychotherapy and spirituality: Crossing the line between therapy and religion.* London: Sage.

Willard, Dallas. 1988. *The Spirit of the disciplines.* San Francisco: Harper & Row.

———. 1996. Spirituality: Going beyond the limits. *Christian Counseling Today* 4, no. 1:16-20.

Wise, Carol. 1983. *Pastoral psychotherapy: Theory and practice.* Northvale, N.J.: Jason Aronson.

Worthington, Everett L., Jr., Taro A. Kurusu, Michael E. McCullough and Steven J. Sandage.
    1996. Empirical research on religion and psychotherapeutic processes and outcomes: A
    10-year review and research prospectus. *Psychological Bulletin* 119:448-87.
Worthington, Everett L., Jr., and Steven J. Sandage. 2001. Religion and spirituality. *Psycho-
    therapy* 38:473-78.

SPIRITUAL DIRECTION AND
PASTORAL COUNSELING

Israel Galindo

W hen faced with the common crises of our lives—whether these are marital, parental, familial, vocational, relational or "religious"—many people turn to pastoral counselors. These persons are, after all, trained in counseling and pastoral care, and we trust them to address the needs of the spirit. We are confident that trained counselors will be able to give us the advice we need to overcome the crises faced at one time or another. We have come to expect that our pastoral counselors will be adept and knowledgeable in matters of psychology and emotional health. In addition, many of us have become accustomed to hearing the message of the gospel presented in the language of emotional and psychological healing, recovery and human wholeness.

But where do we go when we have no crisis yet find ourselves in a spiritual malaise? There is no problem to solve, yet we know deep in our heart and soul that "something is not right" or "something is missing." Where can we go that will help us not get well but get better? To whom can we go for help in dealing with questions of meaning rather than functioning, of discernment rather than decision? While contemporary pastoral counseling has its place, perhaps these matters of the spirit can best be addressed in the context of the older practice of spiritual direction.

Interest in spiritual direction has increased in the past few decades among pastoral counselors. This ancient practice is being recognized, and in some religious traditions is being reclaimed, as a legitimate approach to caring for the needs of the spirit.

REVIVAL OF INTEREST IN SPIRITUAL DIRECTION

Tilden Edwards (1980) identifies two reasons for the upsurge in interest in spiritual direction. First, he claims many people feel a need for personal growth in a

Christian way of life. Forming a uniquely Christian worldview is an increasingly critical issue for believers who live in a world that is increasingly relativistic. It is difficult for Christians to form and maintain a unified worldview in an complex society with multiple voices that compete for attention. Lacking a holistic and authentically religious framework leaves people without the ability to interpret the meaning of their experiences, whether sublime or painful. Many are unable to distinguish one experience from another. When discernment is lacking, an unhealthy experience is just as acceptable as an healthy one. For many, it makes no difference if they feel good as a result of medication or as a result of the peace of mind that comes after having engaged in a spiritual struggle.

Wayne Oates reminds pastoral counselors of the importance of using spiritual language in the therapeutic relationship as a way to maintain a particularly Christian frame of reference. "Historically, our task . . . has been and will continue to be one of translation and interpretation as we help persons . . . grasp and put into effect the intention of God in the long sweeps of persons' life stories" (Oates 1985:57).

The second reason Edwards identifies for the rise of interest in spiritual direction is an increasing awareness of the limitations of the psychological helping relationship when it ignores the spiritual dimension of persons. He notes that "the increasing interest among therapists in transpersonal and Jungian therapies and in Eastern (and to some extent Western) mystical traditions attests to this hunger" (1980:100). Edwards suggests that although the quest often is veiled in psychological language, it reflects a yearning for a transcendently rooted way of life.

PASTORAL COUNSELING IN SEARCH OF AN IDENTITY

On the surface, the care of souls that is provided in pastoral counseling and in spiritual direction seems quite similar. But while practitioners of each may articulate similar goals in their faith-oriented helping stance, neither would claim that they are doing the same thing. In this chapter we will attempt to arrive at a clearer picture of the distinctiveness of spiritual direction by comparing and contrasting it with pastoral care and counseling.

One of the difficulties in addressing the needs of the spirit is the fact that most of the people entrusted with the care of souls today have been given the same kind of training and conceptual assumptions about human development as the secular mental health professional. William A. Barry and William J. Connolly (1982) observe that with the emergence of modern theories of therapy and counseling, pastoral care has too often looked like a carbon copy of those secular models.

Jean LaPlace (1975) issues a caution concerning overdependence on psychology, stating that the focus and technique of spiritual direction lie elsewhere. For the busy parish clergy for whom the pastoral care of congregation members in life crises is the primary helping function, reliance on psychological explanations and techniques is understandable. It is convenient to be able to draw on therapeutic emotional frames of reference, psychological concepts and language, and practical counseling techniques. But those who do so to the neglect of deeper existential and spiritual issues in the life of parishioners neglect the distinctive role and function that clergy are able to provide. The result is that the person seeking help from a religiously oriented counselor will be denied the resources he or she requires to address the needs of the spirit.

However, despite spiritual directors' concern about overdependence on secular models of psychology within pastoral counseling, most would recognize the need to give attention to clinical counseling theories. The majority of writers on spiritual direction stress the need for responsible knowledge of the psychological disciplines. Alan Jones suggests that in many religious circles "we have suffered from a form of spirituality that has repressed the awful knowledge which the psychoanalytic revolution has brought us" (1982:37). An understanding of psychology contributes to an integrated understanding of the normative life span. The psychological disciplines provide frameworks and methods for dealing with all dimensions of the person's life structure, body, psyche and spirit. As Morton Kelsey puts it, "I doubt if either the religious or psychological dimensions of life can be dealt with adequately without a knowledge of the other" (1986:42).

Unless one holds to a rigid dichotomy of spiritual and psychological dimensions of human nature, it must be admitted that psychological healing cannot take place without spiritual healing, and vice versa. According to Wallace B. Clift (1982:41), many of the clinical methods used by Carl Jung were similar to those found and taught in Ignatian spiritual direction. For example, Jung accepted liturgical worship and prayer as key elements in the process of individuation (Clift 1982:65).

Spiritual direction and pastoral counseling offer much to patients and seekers in addressing the needs of the spirit, but there are essential differences. Comparing and contrasting these distinctives will help us better understand what each has to offer in addressing the needs of the spirit and the care of the soul.

SIMILARITIES OF SPIRITUAL DIRECTION AND PASTORAL COUNSELING

Both practices are crisis-centered. Since spiritual direction and pastoral counseling both deal with human experience, there is natural overlap in their practices. Spiritual direction is not indifferent to a person's emotional difficulties or developmental arrests. Like pastoral counseling, spiritual direction at times is crisis-centered. The spiritual director, like the clinical pastoral counselor, understands that developmental life issues are integrally related to the spiritually oriented person's process of integration. Despite a believer's desire to be "in the world but not of it," we are all of the world and a part of it. Christians are not immune to the effects of developmental crisis issues or the toxicity of dysfunctional relationships.

Both practices deal with the person holistically. Despite the particular focus of each discipline, both spiritual direction and pastoral counseling strive to deal with the person in a holistic manner. Both give attention to the interplay between the spiritual and psychological dynamics in the life of the person seeking help. Each (1) addresses the self-discovery necessary for emotional maturity, (2) attends to the physical body in relation to both psychological and spiritual health, and (3) recognizes the need to "travel the way of the unconscious in order to recover the awareness of God" (Leech 1977:28).

Both practices give attention to a person's history. Like pastoral counseling, spiritual direction is interested in the life history, thoughts, hopes and feelings of the person seeking help. Both disciplines give special attention to personal relationships, past and present. In pastoral counseling it is not an uncommon practice to begin with intake procedures that review information about the patient's personal history—including facts about family of origin, past counseling experiences and any history of medication. In spiritual direction life review is also a common beginning point. But in direction the review will focus on the person's relationships with God and others, experiences of faith and belief, and history of religious practices such as prayer and spiritual disciplines. Both counseling and direction are concerned with enabling the person to come to terms with aspects of the past that hinder growth in the present or make engaging in mature relationships problematic.

Both practices teach. Another similarity between direction and counseling is that both contain a didactic dimension. Clarification, simple instruction and correction of misinterpreted facts are important parts of the process in both disciplines. Pastoral counselors do a lot of teaching in their work with patients. They teach coping skills, educate their clients about resources, language and concepts, and provide information. And many who have been recognized as great spiritual directors have been educators. Spiritual directors teach skills in the spiritual disciplines. They educate their directees about resources and the use of language, introduce them to new concepts, and provide information in the course of practicing spiritual direction.

Both practices work with a person's motivation. Both spiritual direction and pastoral counseling depend on the motivation of the person who comes for help. The reasons people seek spiritual direction may parallel those of counseling and therapy: crises of self, a sense of a divided self and a need for integration, ego desperation, feelings of restlessness, a search for meaning, a need for self-awareness. In fact, Kenneth Leech (1977:120) accepts psychological illness as a legitimate motivation for seeking spiritual direction. On the other hand, not all pastoral counseling relationships are initiated by or center on a crisis.

Both practices help people make decisions. Training in decision-making is another helping stance common to both pastoral counseling and spiritual direction. Both disciplines strive to make the individual more aware of his or her unconscious self, bringing it to conscious awareness, in order to facilitate rational life choices. In spiritual direction, this process is traditionally called discernment. "Like the psychotherapeutic techniques, discernment results in a better knowledge of the self and the various influences which affect the self" (Studzinski 1985:8). Similarly, one important helping function of pastoral counseling is to help people get "unstuck" when they are unable to make a decision or to see options for themselves beyond either-or stances.

When asked what he does for a living, one pastoral counselor I know at times playfully responds, "I'm a window washer." He explains that that is his metaphor for how he helps people who are unable to see beyond the confines of their walls. When people feel trapped, this counselor's job is to wash the dirty windows so that they can see the horizons beyond the walls.

Both practices have helping goals. Carolyn Gratton points out that the shift in psychotherapeutic goals, giving a more holistic dialogical attention to the meaning of the person's problem, has resulted in a blurring of the lines that traditionally divided "therapy from spiritual guidance, psychological practice from sacred tradition" (1980:83). This trend seems to continue on a more popular level, most notably in areas like the so-called men's movements, the New Age movement and the new metaphysics, which tend to integrate (often uncritically) psychology, research, spirituality, and appreciation for myths and legends in their desire to offer meaning, healing and hope. Some of the emerging goals of psychotherapy that parallel those of spiritual direction include cultivating a meditative presence, a more intentional reflective living, transcendence of the more mundane experiences of daily living, a search for meaning and authenticity of being (Gratton 1980:83-90).

Both practices are centered in love for the person. Jones articulated well this similarity, and it has been echoed by others: "For both therapist and director, insofar as each is participating in a double process of healing and of growth, love is the supreme requirement" (1982:41). Psychoanalyst Erich Fromm wrote that therapy "is essentially an attempt to help the patient gain or regain his capacity for love. If this aim is not fulfilled nothing but surface changes can be accomplished" (1950:87).

So then, the helping disciplines of pastoral counseling and spiritual direction have much in common. Arguably, it may appear that pastoral counseling is in effect a contemporary form of spiritual direction. In fact, Edwards has suggested that one reason for the neglect of spiritual direction was the rise of humanistic and developmental psychologies in the twentieth century (1980:29). But practitioners and writers in the discipline of spiritual direction caution that psychology and counseling have real limitations in addressing the needs of the spirit. According to Jones, for example, modern therapy at its best can only help prepare the person for a deeper and a more wonderful engagement with life by removing internal obstacles (1982:20). Often even in pastoral counseling the tendency is to do this by emphasizing the client's consciousness and seeking an intellectual, cognitive mastery over the subconscious and emotions. But the ancient literature of spiritual direction demonstrated the primacy of "firsthand spiritual awareness and humble, purifying loving in the spiritual life, for which no intellectual mastery can substitute" (Edwards 1980:53).

The loss of attention to spiritual direction, the lack of a tradition of spiritual direction among pastoral counselors, and the rise of psychology to prominence in seminaries have taken a toll, according to Edwards:

> The price has been a tragic Western categorization of the truth into bits and pieces that never seem to weave a single cloth. In the mainline churches, for example, theologians offer broad scale analysis. Helping a person with the integral appropriation of the truth to which theology points, however, is left to "practical" people, especially pastoral clergy. Unable adequately to translate their theological training into the nitty-gritty of the personal crises and developmental help asked of them by people and goaded by the lack of perceived spiritual concern on the part of many people coming for help, . . . they usually turn to the empirical sciences for assistance. In terms of practical human guidance, this has bred clinical pastoral education and the pastoral counselor. (1980:53)

Gratton agrees, arguing that typical pastoral counselors lack a holistic, unified foundational orientation in their practice. Schooled in theology and usually coming from a particular religious background and worldview, they have had a formal clinical training that tends not to be very profound "and may well consist of a fairly eclectic amalgam of Freudian, Jungian, transactional, gestalt and a variety of other theories" (1980:78).

Overreliance on the psychological disciplines results in a tendency to become either too abstract and remote in the helping situation or too quickly pragmatic in attempting to help the other to "solve the problem." This is done, for example, in the application of psychological language to the person's situation or identified problem ("affective underdevelopment," "identity crisis," "inability to achieve psychic intimacy" or the result of living in a "dysfunctional family system"). Though these terms may accurately describe the person's predicament, they do not adequately represent what may be the most important dimension of all: the spiritual, concrete relationship the person has with God. Practitioners of spiritual direction are of the conviction that in order to address the needs of the spirit, the kind of guidance needed is more than just psychological.

Both counselors and spiritual directors fall too easily into the false assumption that to *understand* something is the answer. People are too complex, the soul is too deep, the spirit is too transcendent, and emotions are too inexplicable to naively assume that we can understand them. Much less will the person under stress or existential angst be able to understand them. The fact is that a lack of comprehension is rarely at the heart of people's pain. People *know* that certain things are bad for them and that certain relationships are not healthy. They *know* when they engage in destructive practices and habits. The issue is not a lack of knowledge, or even a lack of awareness that they are engaging in behaviors that are unhealthy.

Helping people get unstuck spiritually lies in a domain other than the cognitive—the solution lies in the person's faith. But faith is not merely a mental assent to the propositions of a religion or the confession of a creed. The reasons (if that is the right word to use here) people commit themselves to a religion are not primarily rational. Few people are moved to join the church through a rational analysis of theological propositions or responsible interpretation of the biblical texts. The needs that motivate most people to embrace a faith orientation lie primarily in their affective domain. Those emotional needs are satisfied through symbols of meaning, ritual and the communal relationships found in a worshiping community of faith.

And faith is not only the religious experiences people have, no matter how intense, euphoric or meaningful. Faith is, at heart, the central relationship that gives meaning to our life; we are able to interpret our experiences in light of that relationship. Or as Katherine Dyckman and L. Patrick Carroll put it, "To 'faith' is to hand over the direction of one's journey to another, to yield up . . . 'the illusion of control' to someone who is essentially beyond our control, over whom we have no power" (1981:8-9).

DIFFERENCES BETWEEN SPIRITUAL DIRECTION AND PASTORAL COUNSELING

Clearly, spiritual direction has much in common with pastoral counseling. And admittedly, spiritual direction has benefited from the insights and techniques of psychology and psychotherapy. But there are unique dimensions in the practice of spiritual direction that make it qualitatively distinct from pastoral counseling.

The helping relationship in direction goes beyond crises. Though a crisis situation may have been the trigger for the person's seeking direction, the relationship between spiritual director and directee ideally continues after the immediate problem is solved. This is because in spiritual direction there is a concern with larger issues of continued growth and development in the context of personal relationships. The director relates to the directee in terms of a life continuum of spiritual and human growth. On this continuum crises are not so much issues to be solved as opportunities for insight into one's faith, discernment of one's relationships with God and others, and achieving self-understanding. Raymond Studzinski argues, "This life, if it is to be fully understood, calls for a sensitivity to the dynamics of belief and the challenges to faith development" (1985:6).

The temporal focus in spiritual direction is broader. While spiritual direction does give attention to the past and present of the individual, the temporal perspective is more transcendent in that it looks from the present to the future—even beyond death. In spiritual direction there is an attempt to discover a unique plan in the individual's life structure "whose source is God and which leads to full religious and human development through deliberate choices in the here and now" (Studzinski 1985:6). There is in spiritual direction a deliberate attempt to unapologetically and intentionally interpret the person's life experiences in the context of faith. This being the case, the language of spiritual direction is drastically different from that of pastoral counseling—which relies heavily on clinical language, metaphors and schemas. Spiritual language is needed when addressing the needs of the spirit, because the soul listens for its own language.

Attention to the operation of grace is central to spiritual direction. Because most people who seek pastoral counseling are experiencing anxiety due to a crisis of some sort, the helping relationship often is tense, sometimes conflictual; at times the person seeking help is even suspicious of the helper. In the process of spiritual direction, however, the atmosphere tends to be more relaxed, and the focus is on the way grace is operating in the life of the directee. Both the spiritual director and the directee attempt to discover how grace is accepted, resisted and being responded to in prayer and action (Edwards 1980:98). In this context, the person undergoing spiritual direction, unlike the client in pastoral counseling or therapy, participates actively in a mutually accepted approach to reality, the Christian faith.

Spiritual direction requires a shared confessional stance. Unlike what happens in pastoral counseling, the spiritual director does not attempt to offer a different clinical reality to the subject to help him or her "see things differently" or "understand the world more accurately." Both the spiritual director and the directee have the same basic view of reality—the view found in their mutually confessed faith. For example, the belief that God is active and present in the life of the world and in the life of the directee is assumed. The spiritual director has no need to convince the directee that this is true. The problem, more often than not, is that the directee holds to the belief that God is real and present but does not "experience it." Another common frustration is that the person is clear about what he or she believes but does not see the working out of that belief in daily life.

This salient feature of faith is what is unique to spiritual direction. The chief difference between spiritual direction and traditional pastoral counseling thus lies not so much in the practice or technique but in the faith orientation of both the director and the directee (Jones 1982:41, 47-48). Dyckman and Carroll refer to this shared faith dimension as fidelity to the gospel—by which they mean, in effect, belief in Christ (1981:24-25). This shared faith affects the whole helping relationship and centers it on Christ. With this shared faith context, the aims of the spiritual direction experience take on a distinctive dimension. Dyckman and Carroll explain, "As a director we are not just enabling people to reflect on and integrate life, as any good counselor would do, but to do so in the light of 'who they are called to become in fidelity to the Gospel.' This meeting with Jesus in faith is the decided and distinct difference between counseling and spiritual direction" (1981:27).

With faith as the central domain of the spiritual life, the capacity of the individual for religious experiences—whether mystical or mundane—becomes a secondary concern. In other words, spiritual direction is less about "experiencing" faith and more about being faithful to what one confesses.

Faith in God is central in the spiritual direction process. The element of faith provides the distinctiveness of spiritual direction. Gordon E. Jackson claims that "the most critical problem in contemporary pastoral care and counseling [is] the missing element of God" (1981:45). Spiritual direction, in contrast, is concerned with helping the person see his or her total world in light of God's plan of redemption. In this perspective every part of one's life includes God and the Spirit who prompts and calls persons into relationship with God. Regardless of what helping techniques are offered to the directee and what therapeutic methods the director uses, it all comes down to helping the person in his or her relationship with God.

Issues of surrender and conversion are overt in spiritual direction. Spiritual direction is attentive to one of the central concerns of Christianity: the dynamic of change through conversion, the radical transformation of the person in Christ. Conversion or *metanoia* is never an exclusively cognitive activity, a changing from one belief system to another. Rather, it is a personal surrender to a personal, living God.

This movement toward surrendering will and self to the divine is a particularly significant difference between spiritual direction and models of pastoral counseling that have secular conceptual foundations. The embrace of conversion in spiritual direction turns on its head secular therapeutic notions of "taking control" or of "being in charge" of one's life. For the Christian believer the normative stance is to give control over to God, willingly and completely. But this is not done irrationally. This is clear enough from the apostle Paul's admonition to be "transformed by the renewing of your mind" (Rom 12:2 NIV), and what he meant by the statement "But we have the mind of Christ" (1 Cor 2:16 NIV). The ability to give self and control over to God is based on a confessional belief about the kind of personal and gracious God we worship.

The biblical metaphor of becoming childlike in one's faith and relationship with God illustrates the attitude of surrender. While such a posture of surrender is a metaphor the spiritual director can readily embrace, Edward E. Thornton observes how challenging this could be for the pastoral counselor: "What could be less to the liking of theologically sophisticated pastors and clinically competent counselors than 'childlike awareness of spiritual reality'?" (1985:17).

There is a distinct communal focus in spiritual direction. The issue of Christian conversion provides another point of contrast between pastoral counseling, where conversion rarely is addressed, and spiritual direction. In spiritual direction, metanoia is understood as affecting the person's whole life. The effects of conversion are not restricted to a perceived exclusive "spiritual" realm.

Metanoia also gives rise to another distinction between spiritual direction and pastoral counseling in regard to evaluation. The reference point for evaluating the results and benefits of counseling and therapy traditionally lies in the individual's needs and desires concerning personal issues: security, anxiety, depression, dependence, anger and so on. Struggles in all these areas can interfere with functioning in the person's social arena of work, community and family, yet therapy's impetus and focus remains chiefly personal. Ruth Tiffany Barnhouse points out that in spiritual direction, in contrast, the reference points for evaluation are the directee's relationship to God and his or her participation in the Christian community, the church (1979:152-53).

Healing is redefined in spiritual direction. While pastoral counseling and spiritual direction are both healing disciplines, each has a distinct understanding of what healing constitutes. Pilch's anthropological study of healing in the New Testament offers important insights regarding the corporate nature of healing (Pilch 2000). Some models of pastoral counseling adopt the clinical diagnostic focus on symptom and cure that is inherent in modern Western medicine. The goal is to isolate the problem and remove it. This includes the assumption that whatever "the problem" is, it is apart from or extraneous to the person; if we remove the problem, we cure the patient. In contrast, Pilch argues, a biblical perspective on illness involves not simply identifying the symptoms but *finding their meaning*—to "discover how to integrate these symptoms into a meaningful life. That is what healing an illness entails" (2000:76).

The biblical approach to healing has a more corporate frame of reference than the clinical approach to "curing" the individual allows. Healing is less about diagnosing a problem and then excising it from the individual and more about the restoration of the individual to the community. "For this reason, it is erroneous to consider the healer as the central element in any healing system. The entire system heals, not just the healer" (Pilch 2000:77). The epistemological difference here is that in the Western mentality the individual is autonomous and unique, while a more biblical understanding defines the person in relation to others in his or her family and community. "Healing is the restoration of meaning to life" says Pilch (2000:141). For the Christian believer, then, restoration means reclaiming appropriate ways of relating to the body of Christ. The restoration of the person to the discipline of community life begins with the confession that "we need the presence of others to be fully human, for it is through life in a community that sees the image of God in us that we are unable to see in ourselves" (Westerhoff 1985:48).

There is a place for community in spiritual direction. In contrast to this corporate perspective, therapy and pastoral counseling traditionally do not provide an ongoing community of faith to sustain a client through the periods of personal upheaval that are the usual impetus for seeking counseling. The experiences of heightened awareness that come as a result of personal crises and interiority, and are part of the process of integration and individuation (though these often are unrecognized as such), may leave the person feeling perplexed and alienated. Jones asserts that a breakthrough in insight into the soul may not make much sense to the person unless "there is an interpreter or companion and unless it happens within the broadening context of a worshipping community" (1982:64). Spiritual direction more often attempts to bring the resources of the church into the life of the person than does pastoral counseling, which more and more seems to be separated from the common life of the local church. As Leech observes, "The counseling movement has been clinic-based or office-based rather than church-based or community-based" (1977:101). In contrast, the spiritual director maintains the perspective that both he or she and the directee are confessing members of the body of Christ. The work of spiritual direction does not happen in isolation from the full participation in the body of Christ on the part of both.

Spiritual direction has a narrower helping scope. Another major difference between spiritual direction and pastoral counseling is that the former deals primarily with the healthy individual. Deep emotional and psychiatric problems lie outside the boundaries of the practice of spiritual direction. Spiritual direction is the province of persons who "seek *coherence* and *communion,* a renewed meaning in their lives, and a deepening relationship with the Source of their being" (Fairchild 1985:31). The emphasis in the spiritual direction relationship is on growth motivation rather than deficiency motivation. The challenge within direction goes beyond functional living to optimal Christian living.

Jones argues that therapy and counseling cannot answer the spirit's longing for meaning and purpose (1982:65). It can be argued that pastoral counseling, which itself embraces a spiritual orientation, does address issues of meaning and purpose when dealing with the individual. But ultimately, spiritual direction, in the context of relationship, a faith community, conversion and faith, can better and more appropriately help persons explore the profound dimensions of meaning and purpose in their spiritual journey.

Spiritual direction requires maturity. Unlike the helping situations of pastoral counseling and therapy, there is a prerequisite need for maturity and self-knowledge on the part of the individual in spiritual direction. Pastoral counselors work with a broader range of persons needing help—including some who may not have the personal resources to take responsibility for inner change and growth. One limiting reality of spiritual direction is that the person seeking direction must possess certain emotional and psychic resources in order for the helping relationship to work. The sobering reality is that spiritual direction is not suitable for everyone. Some persons, because of immaturity, will not be able to take full advantage of the dynamics of spiritual direction. Spiritual direction will be of only minimal help to those who are incapable or unwilling to engage in an honest, critical and perhaps painful introspective journey into their spiritual life.

Entering spiritual direction in response to a personal crisis is not inappropriate. But the real work of direction begins after the crisis is resolved—in contrast to the pastoral counseling relationship, which ends with the resolution of the crisis. Spiritual direction will help best those persons who raise questions that arise from the depth of their being—questions that, as Studzinski puts it, spring from a deep concern that religious fidelity is not getting them anywhere or that the way they have practiced faith has not brought a sense of peace and integration (1985:5). That level of questioning rarely is attained by a person who does not have a faith orientation or who lacks the maturity to be able to recognize, even in the midst of a crisis, that the problem lies within him- or herself.

CONCLUSION

In addressing the needs of the spirit, both spiritual direction and pastoral counseling have much to offer. With the increased interest in spiritual direction, it becomes necessary to clarify its difference from traditional pastoral counseling. In the best of all possible worlds, not just anybody will be allowed to hang up a shingle on the door and claim to be a "pastoral counselor." Similarly, not everyone with clinical training should be allowed to engage in direction. A clear understanding of the distinctive dynamics of the spiritual direction relationship is needed. Kelsey urges that additional training be offered to pastoral counselors and clergy so that they can provide the kind of care of the soul that spiritual direction calls for:

> Although many ministers are given some training in pastoral care, very few are given any background or experience in [the] kind of spiritual direction that we have described. If the Christian Church, Catholic or Protestant, is to meet the challenge of agnostic secularism, militant atheism (which has captured much of the earth), or other quite different religious approaches to life, it needs to provide this kind of experiential grounding. (1986:173)

Barnhouse (1979) provides a good example of the kind of training a director must experience in her description of the Ignatian exercises. Grounded in a scriptural interpretation of the life of Christ, the Ignatian exercises point toward the orientation of spiritual direction: overtly religious imagery and language, an emphasis on experiencing one's relationship with God, and a deeply personal and dependent relationship to one's spiritual director. The need for formal training in spiritual direction as a requisite for its practice cannot be overemphasized.

Pastoral counselors wishing to explore spiritual direction as a means of more intentionally addressing the spiritual issues of their clients need to pay attention to the unique dynamics of spiritual direction. Having compared and contrasted pastoral counseling and spiritual direction, we can conclude that there are four distinct dynamics that will not allow spiritual direction to become just another technique in the pastoral counselor's repertoire: (1) mutual accountability of directee and director, (2) the role of the faith community in the life of the directee, (3) the importance of faith orientation and the legitimacy of conversion experiences, and (4) the work of the Spirit in the life of the directee.

Of these four dynamics, the latter two are the most significant. Spiritual direction flows out of an epistemology that often is at odds with models of psychotherapy used in pastoral counseling. Religious affections, conversion experiences and messages from God more often than not are dismissed—even regarded as deviant or neurotic—in some paradigms of clinical pastoral care. In contrast, within the epistemological framework of spiritual direction, these overt and highly personal religious experiences, when appropriate, often are accepted as normative, can be integral to the healing or discernment process, and can even be treated as desired goals.

Pastoral counselors must be willing to acknowledge and accept these four distinct dynamics in addressing the needs of the spirit in the care of the soul. Further, counselors need to be responsible enough to submit themselves to the experience of being under direction as part of their training. If not, then persons seeking help with issues of the soul are perhaps best served by spiritual directors—those who are trained and willing to entertain the realm and role of the Spirit in caring for the needs of the soul.

References

Barnhouse, Ruth Tiffany. 1979. Spiritual direction and psychotherapy. *Journal of Pastoral Care* 33:149-63.

Barry, William A., and William J. Connolly. 1982. *The practice of spiritual direction.* New York: Seabury.

Clift, Wallace B. 1983. *Jung and Christianity: The challenge of reconciliation.* New York: Crossroad.

Dyckman, Katherine M., and L. Patrick Carroll. 1981. *Inviting the mystic, supporting the prophet: An introduction to spiritual direction.* New York: Paulist.

Edwards, Tilden. 1980. *Spiritual friend: Reclaiming the gift of spiritual direction.* New York: Paulist.

Fairchild, Roy W. 1985. The pastor as spiritual director. *Quarterly Review* 5 (Summer):25-35.

Fromm, Erich. 1950. *Psychoanalysis and religion.* New Haven, Conn.: Yale University Press.

Gratton, Carolyn. 1980. *Guidelines for spiritual direction.* Studies in Formative Spirituality 3. Denville, N.J.: Dimension.

Jackson, Gordon E. 1981. *Pastoral care and process theology.* Lanham, Md.: University Press of America.

Jones, Alan. 1982. *Exploring spiritual direction: An essay on Christian friendship.* Minneapolis: Seabury/Winston.

Kelsey, Morton T. 1986. *Companions on the inner way: The art of spiritual guidance.* New York: Crossroad.

LaPlace, Jean. 1975. *Preparing for spiritual direction.* Trans. J. C. Guiness. Chicago: Franciscan Herald.

Leech, Kenneth. 1977. *Soul friend: The practice of Christian spirituality.* San Francisco: Harper & Row.

Oates, Wayne. 1985. The power of spiritual language in self-understanding. In *Spiritual dimensions of pastoral care,* ed. Gerald L. Borchert and Andrew D. Lester, pp. 56-71. Philadelphia: Westminster Press.

Pilch, John J. 2000. *Healing in the New Testament: Insights from medical and Mediterranean anthropology.* Minneapolis: Fortress.

Studzinski, Raymond. 1985. *Spiritual direction and mid-life spirituality.* San Francisco: Harper & Row.

Thornton, Edward E. 1985. Finding center in pastoral care. In *Spiritual dimensions of pastoral care,* ed. Gerald L. Borchert and Andrew D. Lester, pp. 11-26. Philadelphia: Westminster Press.

Westerhoff, John H. 1985. The pastor as spiritual educator. *Quarterly Review* 5 (Summer): 44-53.

THREE VOICES, ONE SONG

Perspectives on the Care of Persons
from a Psychologist, Spiritual Director
and Pastoral Counselor

Theresa Clement Tisdale, Carrie E. Doehring
and Veneta Lorraine-Poirier

True soul care does not make distinctions between dimensions of persons; body, soul, and spirit are seen as aspects of one totality with mutual and reciprocal influence, as David Benner (1998) has eloquently stated. Although persons exist as a totality, there is currently no well-articulated applied or clinical model that effectively captures what care with a multifaceted focus would look like in practice.

Benner (1998) asserts that practitioners need to view all issues as psychospiritual in nature and view persons as somatopsychospiritual beings. This concept highlights the need for more sophisticated approaches and models of care based on the interconnectedness of issues across dimensions of being. Such models would act as important safeguards against reductionism and artificial compartmentalization.

However, until we are blessed with working models that provide guidance on how to operate in this way, practitioners are constrained to work from within the frameworks they know. This reality calls to mind the age-old story of the blind men and the elephant, each of them thinking the part he touched represented the whole. The risk of such error gives us occasion for both humility and curiosity. Humility, because within our discipline we see only one aspect (and then often only "through a glass darkly"), and curiosity, so that we might forge ahead in articulating models that reflect true soul care.

Here we present the perspectives on care of a psychologist, a spiritual director and a pastoral counselor, reflecting on how crossdisciplinary dialogue will enhance the development of holistic applied models of care. Because no two practitioners within a discipline are alike, we include a brief narrative introduction that highlights how each author approaches her work and ministry. Our hope and prayer is that as we "lift up our voices," both harmony and melody will arise in the song of soul care.

THE AUTHORS AND THEIR DISCIPLINES

Psychology: Theresa Tisdale. I identify myself as a Christian psychologist. Currently I teach both integration and clinical courses in the doctoral and master's programs at Azusa Pacific University.[1] Prior to that I was a staff psychologist at the Danielsen Institute at Boston University, a pastoral counseling center and licensed mental health and training clinic. Before that I directed a pastoral care and counseling center in New Beford, Massachusetts.

I pursued a vocation in the care of souls in response to what I would term a calling that focused on the ministry of Jesus (providing comfort, vision and freedom) foretold in Isaiah 61. I intentionally sought training in an APA-accredited Christian program that was psychodynamic in nature (Rosemead), because that orientation resonated with my understanding of persons, health and change.

Theologically, I would describe myself as a hybrid conservative evangelical and charismatic, but my roots are in the Roman Catholic Church. Two aspects of my theology that relate to clinical practice are transformation and what I would term *essential relatedness.* This latter term refers to humans as created in the image of God. Part of that image is the intimate connection between Father, Son and Spirit. In a similar way, humans are created to relate intimately with self (dimensions of body, soul and spirit), others, God and creation.

Developmentally and clinically, this understanding leads me to the British Middle School of Object Relations (Fairbairn 1952; Guntrip 1949, 1953, 1956; Winnicott 1958, 1971) as articulated by Althea Horner (1984, 1990, 1991). In practice I use a psychodynamic framework informed by my theology. Therefore I am interested in the spiritual life of my patients in whatever way that might be expressed. At its best, psychotherapy is a metaphor for the incarnation (Benner 1983), as the therapist participates in the transformation of the patient. What psychodynamic theory terms insight and repair (working through), in a theologically informed paradigm are revelation and redemption. The method looks similar in some ways, but the outcome is healing and transformation, not simply change.

Spiritual direction: Veneta Lorraine-Poirier. I am a spiritual director and have been

---

[1]Some portions of this article written by Theresa Clement Tisdale were presented at a conference held at Azusa Pacific University in May 2002: "Bringing Together Values, Beliefs and Clinical Practice: Faculty Perspectives on Intradisciplinary Integration."

involved in the ministry and in the training of spiritual directors for the past twelve years. I practice in the Ignatian tradition (Fleming 1978), developed by Inigo (his family name before conversion) of Loyola in the 15th century.

Faith and my denominational connection (I am Catholic) were integral parts of my formative years, as was my biological placement as the oldest in a very large family. In my early twenties I remember wanting to be in some sort of ministry, "working for God," I might have said then. I explored as many opportunities as my role of wife and mother would allow. Actual involvement in ministry emerged after much personal growth, education and gained wisdom.

I define spiritual direction as the interaction between one person, trained to listen for the movement of God, and another who desires to develop and cultivate an intimate, personal relationship with God. This process requires commitment to openness and honesty. The discipline of spiritual direction uses various entryways for insight and understanding, including the imagination, dreams, gospel or other faith stories, memories, life crises, and especially prayer, meditation and theological reflection. The focus of spiritual direction is on the sensate, affective experiences that these avenues facilitate in a directee's life and their effect on the directee's sense of who they are, who God is and how they relate with others.

My personal approach in spiritual direction is to help a person become conscious of his or her "operative images" (my term) of God. The basic premise is that how persons perceive God is integrally connected with their perceptions of themselves, their value as a human being and their valuing of others. Every aspect of life is the context for transformation when it is seen in light of who God is, as described in the Hebrew and Christian Scriptures, and when we have faith that God desires for us what we cannot accomplish ourselves.

Pastoral counseling: Carrie Doehring. I am a psychologist and an assistant professor in pastoral care and counseling at Iliff School of Theology, Denver. Although I was raised Catholic, I am currently a Presbyterian minister. In my ministry, teaching and research I have specialized in the relationship between religion/spirituality and sexual and family violence.

In my work in psychological and religious and theological studies, I have used a particular crossdisciplinary method that is narrative and contextual. It is experientially grounded in the stories of people, families, communities and cultures in crisis or transition. Pastoral counselors using this method reflect on whether their own stories are resources or roadblocks in their clinical work. Of particular interest are the similarities and differences between the counselor's and client's social identities (for example, having to do with religion/spirituality, gender, sexual orientation, social class and race).

This method is also correlational. Psychological and religious studies are brought into a dialogue that values both the consonances and the dissonances between disciplinary voices. The correlational method has been used by pastoral theologians historically identified with liberal Protestant religious traditions (Browning 1991; Hiltner 1958; Poling and Miller 1985; Poling 1996; Doehring 1999). These correlational dialogues often become arguments for reconstructing religious doctrines and practices that are controversial, like the ordination of women or gay and lesbian persons. In contrast, the integration method seeks "unity of truths" and is used by Christian psychologists and mental health practitioners who are often committed to conserving religious doctrines and practices under question (Eck 1996:102).

In my postmodern use of this method, the goal of correlational dialogue is to arrive at provisional truth claims that become the basis for strategies seeking healing and justice for individuals, families, communities and cultures. These truth claims are not intended to be universal or transhistorical; nor are they relativistic, since they must be meaningful within a critical correlation of crosscultural and crossdisciplinary research and practice.

THE CASE OF A CONFUSED PASTOR

The person described in the following vignette is actual and real. Certain components have been altered to disguise his identity. This information is used with permission.

Mark (not his real name) is a fifty-year-old Caucasian male who presents with symptoms of depression and sexual dysfunction. This is his first time seeking any form of treatment. He is of average height and weight. Mark is very attractive and engaging in his manner. He is a pastor of a local church and has been married for over twenty years. He has two grown daughters.

Mark has been a very successful pastor for the last twenty years and recently transitioned from a very large church to pastor a much smaller church in a poor community. His support base has changed significantly due to the geographic distance between his former and current church. Recently he assumed a leadership role in a local council of churches.

Mark began experiencing sexual difficulty (impotence) in his marriage approximately six months ago. He states that he has been feeling sad and somewhat confused about his choice of career as a pastor. He no longer knows what he believes about God or about what he describes as a call from God to this work. He reports that his wife is unhappy with their recent move and misses her friends. His daughters have both recently left home to attend college, and one is scheduled to be married in the coming months.

In the course of treatment he reveals that he recently ended an affair he was having with a parishioner at his previous church. His wife had been confronting him about this possibility, but he was denying it until the revelation within the last two weeks. He does not want to leave his wife but is thinking of leaving his current church and possibly the pastorate.

CONCEPTUALIZATION AND APPROACH FROM EACH PERSPECTIVE

Psychology

Approach to assessment of the case. In my response to this case, I will be offering comments on my approach to both process and content elements of my work with Mark. I will be reflecting on what I would actually do if Mark were my client, what I hypothesize to be the nature and source of Mark's difficulties as described, and how I would approach treatment.

Initial process. Before I meet Mark, I have begun praying for him. I am wondering what purpose God might have in our meeting, how I might be an instrument of healing in his life and where he is in his journey with God. I am wondering how our work together will fit into God's overall purposes for his life. I pray for discernment and wisdom in my initial meeting with him.

Intake process. I want to create a sacred space for our work. I am intentional in communicating warmth and compassion for him. I want him to feel safe, heard and understood. I listen attentively to his story. I pray for God's presence to be in the room and for the Holy Spirit to guide me in how and what I say.

Intake content. During intake, I will set about the task of conducting a thorough evaluation. My immediate concern is with Mark's level of depression and possible suicidality. If a risk assessment yields no cause for immediate intervention regarding suicidality, I would assess Mark's level of depression using DSM-IV (1994) criteria as a guide. Depending on the severity of his symptoms, I would discuss with him the possibility of a referral for psychiatric evaluation for medication. I will also ask the date of his last physical examination and recommend that he see a physician to rule out an organic cause of his depression. It would seem that the etiology of his depression (and concomitant impotence) is situational, but I would not want to assume that and inadvertently miss a possible biological component or source.

Once we have progressed through Mark's presenting concerns and the history of these, we will begin to explore various aspects of his background. Areas I plan to explore include family of origin and current family constellation (possibly including a genogram); social history, including the type and nature of his significant relationships, ethnic background, educational background, developmental history (significant childhood maturational milestones), employment history, religious history (his affiliation both past and present), spiritual history (his personal spiritual life and formation), moral development (such as how he learned right and

wrong and what his understanding of social responsibility is), legal history
(whether he has had any difficulty with the law) and medical history (whether he
is taking medication; whether he has had any significant illnesses or operations).

As we explore these areas of Mark's history, we will begin to piece together the
narrative of his life. Some questions we might consider as we talk are the following: Who were the significant people in his life? Where were the crossroads and
decision points at which crucial life decisions were made? What or who influenced
those decisions? What has been Mark's experience of significant others? Was his
family of origin a place where he could freely express and explore who he was, or
was he forced (explicitly or implicitly) to adopt a certain persona in order to be
loved and accepted?

Because of his current crises, we will particularly explore his family-of-origin
relationships and his early spiritual history, all of which somehow contributed to
his feeling called to the pastorate. In terms of Mark's spiritual history, I will ask
when he first became consciously aware of God in his life and the circumstances
surrounding his calling. I will also explore how his spiritual life has evolved over
time and determine how he nurtures his spiritual growth. If things in his life seem
cloudy or obscure now, when were they last clear? What changed, and when?

With regard to his family of origin, I particularly wonder about his relationship
with his father, from whom he would have gotten his sense of masculinity and
purpose in life. Did his father encourage Mark to develop his unique personality
and gifts, or was Mark given messages about needing to behave in a particular way
in order to be accepted? Are Mark's image and experience of God more like his
mother, or father, or both?

We will also explore the nature of his relationships and whether he has had
meaningful connections with others. This can be a particular challenge for a pastor, who is very aware of the image he or she holds within a congregation. We will
also explore the nature and extent of his self-cohesion. Is the person he knows
himself to be internally the same person he is able to be externally? If not, why not?

I am also interested in understanding his representation of God (cf. Rizzuto
1979). Who is God *to* him and *for* him? How does he feel God *feels* and *thinks*
about him? Where is God for him now?

I will want to weave these and other questions into our dialogue as we endeavor
to understand as much as we can about what has brought Mark to this crisis point
in his life. Through articulating Mark's narrative we will begin to see the connections between his relationships with God, himself, others and the world.

Not all of these questions or areas of interest will be fully explored at intake.
They will be touched on and then elaborated in treatment. In addition, during intake I will explore referrals for couples therapy for Mark and his wife, as well as

some type of clergy support group that can be a venue in which to explore his feelings of confusion and disillusionment about his ministry and calling.

Conceptualization of the case. In terms of Mark's presentation and history, the following details stand out to me: his age (fifty); he has two grown daughters, one of whom is getting married; he is impotent; he is sad and confused about his role as a pastor; he questions both his understanding of God and his calling to ministry; and he had an affair sometime within the last few years.

Based on this information, I would hypothesize that Mark suffered an early interruption in the development of his self-esteem and self-cohesion. This faulty development may have produced a dichotomy in Mark that Winnicott (1965) describes as the true and false self.[2] I would wonder whether Mark was a "golden boy" in his family who received praise from his parents for being a particular way and doing particular things. Having grown up in the 1960s, it is likely that Mark entered the pastorate somewhat idealistically. Because of his charismatic nature, he was likely very well received and admired. His underlying fragility, however, would potentially compromise his ability to remain true to his convictions. It may have been the case that if others praised him, he felt good about himself; if others criticized him, he felt terrible. Because he did so well at the pastorate, his underlying wound was hidden from others, although acutely felt by both him and (I would imagine) his wife.

Some connections between these hypotheses and Mark's narrative are as follows.

His age: Mark is fifty years old, which places him in Erikson's (1963) stage of "generativity versus stagnation." Successful negotiation of this stage results in feeling that one is leaving behind a worthwhile legacy. Mark may be in crisis because he has reached fifty and realized that his life has not turned out the way he wanted. He may be tired of feeling responsible to and for everyone else and not receiving what he feels he needs.

He has two grown daughters, one getting married: This reality also potentially relates to his crisis. His role is changing, even with his daughters. This may be a cause for sadness, for relief or both. Mark may not be sure of who he is now to his daughters and his family, or he may feel that now that his daughters are moving on, he can enjoy life.

He is impotent: Barring any medical reason for this, the fact that Mark is impo-

---

[2]D. W. Winnicott suggests that prolonged impingement by the mother of her child results in fragmentation of the infant's experience. This fragmentation is a split between the true self, which is the source of spontaneous needs, images and gestures, and the false self, which provides an illusion of existence created out of maternal expectations. The child becomes what the mother expects. The false self protects the integrity of the true self, which remains in hiding for fear of psychic annihilation due to disregard.

tent potentially has profound symbolism. Does Mark feel impotent about his life? Does he feel impotent regarding achieving the things he wants in life? Does he feel unable to obtain or achieve the things he wants and needs to feel fulfilled? Is he impotent with his wife and his mistress or just his wife? Might this be because of guilt?

He is sad and confused about his role as a pastor: Mark has likely operated with a certain understanding and model for being a "good pastor." Because he craves admiration and praise, it is likely he has been invested in being "all things to all people," not realizing how this might leave him feeling depleted and empty. He may believe he "followed all the rules" and still didn't feel fulfilled; he may have felt angry and resentful about this, so he decided to get his needs met some other way (the affair).

He questions both his understanding of God and his calling to ministry: Exploring how Mark developed his understanding of God may shed some light on this aspect of his crisis. He may have been serving a God he believed would reward him for good behavior; he may have felt himself to be in a contractual relationship in which he did certain things and God did certain things. When this understanding faltered, Mark became confused and angry.

He had an affair in the last few years: This breach of morals and clear abuse of power suggests the strong possibility that unconscious forces are at work in Mark. Because of his history of being the "perfect pastor" who is loved and admired by others, making such a blatant flight from the sacred vows he made to his wife and to God would likely come as a result of a build-up of intense pain, anger and rage. I would wonder if Mark felt "used" by God in some way, which thereby entitled him to "use" the parishioner God entrusted to his care.

Approach to treatment of the case: Treatment process. In light of these hypothesized realities, I will be attentive to the possibility that Mark will be keenly aware of and interested in my perception of him. He will likely feel that he needs to please me, which may result in his making a "flight into health" that may lack corresponding deeper changes. I will explore this if and when I sense Mark's anxiety about our relationship. Given his recent malfeasance, I will also be aware of gender issues in treatment and explore them when needed.

I will continue to pray for Mark before, during and after sessions. I will continue to invite God into the process, believing that God cares more for Mark than I ever could and that God is intimately concerned with Mark's healing. I will hold the belief that the therapy process is providing Mark with an invitation and opportunity for transformation.

Treatment content. As sessions commence and progress, I will be listening for how Mark talks about his psychological, moral and spiritual life (cf. Doherty 1999). I will encourage and allow Mark to bring into the room whatever is most salient for him; if needed, I will wait in silence until he begins the session. I anticipate that this might be difficult for Mark, because he may wonder what I am thinking and feeling about him during the silence, but this waiting is very important given the need for his true self to emerge. I anticipate that in time he may feel relief that he has found a place where he can discover and reveal his inmost being, in a context where he does not have to take care of the other person involved (although out of habit he may try to do so).

During treatment I will be keeping in mind all the questions and areas we touched on during the intake phase and weave them back into the dialogue as it unfolds. The connections between his early life experiences and his current way of being in the world are of central concern. Somewhere in his internal economy his actions make sense, and we are on a quest together to discover those connections. We are seeking revelation concerning his life and history and how it relates to today.

I will be listening for the metaphors that express his way of being in the world and how that was formed. I will be asking him to remember his dreams and fantasies and encourage open expression of these. When appropriate, I will make connections between, and interpretations about, his dreams, his past and our relationship in an effort to bring his experience more fully into the room for processing. Whatever is brought into the light is available for healing and transformation.

I will also be listening for the connection between his experience of his mother and father and his experience of God, others (particularly his wife and his congregation) and myself. If Mark did not have a secure relationship with his parents in which he was encouraged to become himself, that will likely be his experience with others. He may also wonder whether God really wants him to grow and thrive. He may see others as drains on his existence rather than as life-giving sources of support. Alternatively or concurrently, if he was taught to be overly responsible for the needs and feelings of others, this has likely become a burden that has left him bereft and empty. He may feel it is "his turn." He may be tired of performing for God and feel he deserves a break.

The work may progress slowly. I would hope Mark would be willing to come to therapy twice a week if possible, so that we can fully and consistently access his inner life. This frequency will enable him to stay in touch with his deepest feelings and needs in a way that may protect him (and others) from his acting out in inappropriate ways.

Our work would also include an exploration of his moral breach. What led up to his involvement with this parishioner? What did he think would be the impact of this involvement on her, on his wife, on his ministry, on his relationship with God? I would endeavor to explore this in an open way that would facilitate understanding and revelation. His deepest needs are in some way driving his behavior, and to the extent that he is unaware of these motivations, they will continue to rule him. The goal of our exploration is his freedom to fully be who he was created to be.

I will continue to work with Mark to unravel the truth about his life, believing that the truth he discovers in facing his life as it was, as well as how it is and how it can be, will set him free. Mark's ability to see and embrace the truth will result from his capacity for confession, repentance, forgiveness, grace and mercy. His transformation through the process will hopefully result in his ability to live authentically, to make a conscious choice about his ministry, to seek and receive forgiveness from those he has wronged, and to deepen his relationships with God, himself, others and the world around him.

Spiritual Direction

Approach to assessment of the case. When Mark presents himself for spiritual direction, the first assessment to make is his appropriateness for spiritual direction. Spiritual direction requires a significant level of awareness and honesty about God, self and relationship to others, and it is important to know Mark's level of openness. To discern this, first I will ask how he understands God and how he has experienced God in the past, going back to early childhood. Looking at his early life and determining something about his relational faith development is important. The relationship with God being our primary focus, it is necessary for Mark to have, or at least to want or desire, as Ignatius would say, an integration between his belief systems and an encounter with God (Fleming 1978). As I listen to his faith story and the components of his early experiences of God, his family history and perceptions of himself, I am paying attention to the language he uses to describe God, his physical reactions and his desire for something new. I may suggest to Mark that we begin by meeting every two to three weeks in order to build trust and continuity in the process.

Talking to Mark about his adult development, considering his age and the potential of a midlife invitation to growth in authenticity and self-development, I will be assessing whether this is a prime moment in his spiritual life. What he wants to emerge from this spiritual direction relationship needs to be clearly stated, including how he views the outcome, where he wants to move in relationship to God and his beliefs about God. Noticing those places where he is conflicted and where he has questions about relationship to his church, his marriage, himself and God is part of the assessment process.

Another important question for determining readiness for spiritual direction is whether Mark prays. How capable is he to reflect on the content of his prayer and his life? Does he look to God as a source for healing? It is in this reflective, prayerful context that he begins to know his personal value in the sight of God. Prayer of this sort begins the healing process in spiritual direction. Without prayer and a capacity to reflect on life, there is little fodder for the conversations that take place in spiritual direction. In addition, it will be necessary to consider if he has sufficient ego strength to pursue authenticity, especially in light of his current identity issues. If not, he would benefit from therapy prior to or possibly in conjunction with entering a spiritual direction relationship.

Spiritual direction does not address psychological issues directly; when these issues are predominant, attention to them must take precedence. To be in spiritual direction requires the capacity to look at what one really wants. This is possible only when personal identity is sufficiently intact and the ego has sufficient strength to name these desires and to embrace failures and limitations. If Mark's ego is too inflated or fractured, or if his superego is too punitive, he will not easily sustain critique without his ego collapsing. Although both super and fractured egos can be spiritual issues, the insights of psychology are more helpful at this point of development. It is possible that Mark could engage with a spiritual director while he is concurrently in therapy, though this can cause conflicting feelings until ego strength is gained.

Conceptualization of the case. Several issues affecting Mark's sense of self-worth are significant in his spiritual journey. These issues undoubtedly are both spiritual and psychological in nature. It is in the focus of spiritual direction that the distinctions between spiritual and psychological issues arise most clearly. I will first list the issues that seem evident to me and then identify ones that seem most significant to his spiritual journey. From these issues I would pursue with him ones that are pressing—either most inviting or creating the most tension—at that particular time, with the belief that we are a triad in this process of transformation that God directs; therefore what is pressing may in fact be God's invitation for healing.

The first issue in the vignette seems to be Mark's loss of identity in his calling. He is in transition from ministry in a place that was familiar, supportive and prestigious; he moved from a very large church to a smaller, poor, unfamiliar and distant place. His support base no longer exists and must be built again if possible. There is a loss of identity as well a loss of the rewards of his prior pastorate. Moving has separated him from his support system, and he finds himself having to face his reality in a more honest way, as there are no structures with which to mask his inner reality.

The issue of his marriage comes to the surface here, and it is highlighted by his unfaithfulness and feelings of responsibility for his wife's unhappiness. Now he must face the reality of isolating his wife in two areas, his uprooting of her and his unfaithfulness. Added to these issues is the loss of identity and role as a father.

His daughters are adults, leaving home for college and marriage. Now he has only his wife.

His personal identity as a pastor comes into question as he begins to address questions of his own integrity. He has been dishonest with his wife and indirectly with his parishioners. He is guilty of sexual misconduct. He now recognizes the contradiction between his outer role and his inner life, and the incongruity is exceedingly difficult. He feels he has lost intimacy with God because of his sin, intimacy with his wife because of his unfaithfulness and intimacy with his church because this is a new parish. He left a ministry where a support system existed and moved to a place where he has not yet identified himself fully as leader and pastor, a place where there is not as yet any substantive personal connection.

There is a modicum of openness and honesty in Mark, evidenced by the revelation to his wife of the affair. However, the revelation of his sexual misconduct to his community remains, the lack of which affects his decision-making process. The path of least resistance guides him toward leaving the church rather than leaving his wife. He holds on to that which makes him feel more grounded, which at this time is his marriage, and struggles with relinquishing that which might expose him publicly, which is his ministry.

Approach to treatment of the case. Mark is in a wonderful moment of the spiritual journey. He is at a critical junction where a choice and an opportunity for transformation, integration, authenticity and maturity are available to him. The "revelation," a moment of insight, clarity and truth, is fresh and is a significant invitation to decide for something new, something more aligned with who he most deeply desires to be, someone more whole and holy, someone more relational and integrated. Does he in fact want to be a leader, but a leader from a place of inner strength and authenticity? Can he be an authentic leader? It will all rest on his capacity to internalize and accept his failure as a pastor, a husband and a child of God, and then to grow from it.

Helping Mark to see himself as God, who is unconditional Love, sees him is the goal of direction. Traditional Christian spirituality says that there is a basic foundational desire in every human person to be accepted, known, heard and loved by God, however that is articulated in one's experience. It is a goal of direction to encourage Mark to pursue contexts where he might experience this love. Prayer, moments of connection with God where intimacy, goodness, honesty, truth, compassion or wisdom are encountered, helps to facilitate a reprogramming of Mark's memories of past experiences.

As Mark begins to experience God differently and to recognize God's unconditional love for him personally, this recognition will conflict with internal opposing images of himself in relationship to God that are also emerging. Perhaps learned early in his life, in his faith tradition or from his own perceptions of life experiences, these internal conflicting images will cause Mark to make choices. Either he will commit himself to the process of inner work and transformation, or he will flee and be faced with these images at another time.

Helping Mark to notice these encounters, to identify them as originating from the One who is Love, to see them as an invitation and then to be willing to hold the tension of the internal conflict, is the beginning of Mark's transformation. Mark does not need to make changes within himself, but he must be willing for change to happen in him.

What is discovered at this phase of spiritual direction is Mark's operative image of God. Who is the god that lives in Mark's body-held memories (feelings and reactions that live on in the body but not in consciousness or belief systems)? An approach to caring for Mark is to help him consider what images of God are functioning in his inner life versus what he most deeply desires in his relationship with God.

As this process of discovery proceeds, Mark comes to recognize distinctions between what he believes about God, which is a thinking function, and what the voice of his operative image of God, a feeling function, is saying. Because spiritual direction is not necessarily concerned with resolving issues, including internal struggles of authenticity, the emphasis will begin with what God is like in Mark's inner reality.

As these images reveal themselves, Mark is invited to dialogue with God about them, holding the tension of opposites and listening for the insights that move him closer to a truer image of God and to the authentic person he wants to be. Staying with the tension in a contemplative way of holding, waiting, brooding and listening can produce the context that changes Mark's experience and moves him closer to an awareness of his true identity in Christ—he is the beloved of God.

According to Thomas Merton's notion of the "true self" (Finley 1994), Mark's identity as the beloved is illuminated by the reality of his failures as a pastor and a husband and by the acknowledgment of his limited ability to provide for himself what he most wants—to be known. Mark then has the potential to discover deep intimacy with himself and true acceptance and intimacy with God that translate into his relationships with his wife and community. In addition, he becomes internally free so that he can say yes to the values that sustain his authenticity no matter what the cost.

This brings us to my final point. At some time in his healing process, Mark needs to take responsibility for his unethical and immoral conduct within his pastorate. Deepening integrity will demand that he does. This requires great faith and trust in a God who loves unconditionally, along with a deep desire for wholeness. It is a very delicate issue, but a crucial one in the ongoing integration of his authenticity and his freedom to say yes to God's true call on his life: holiness.

God's will for Mark is his well-being, which will increase as Mark becomes more authentic and filled with integrity. But the difficulty of revealing his affair cannot be understated. There is much at stake. When the thought or desire for this depth of integrity is present, the genius of Ignatius of Loyola and the whole Christian mystical tradition can be very helpful. Ignatius suggests that we ask for the grace to attain the transformation that we truly desire—meaning we ask God to accomplish in us what we are incapable of accomplishing for ourselves (Fleming 1978). At present Mark may find it too difficult to reveal the fact of his affair, but by God's grace there will come a time when he chooses to do so.

Relying on God to help him accomplish what he is not fully capable of doing offers Mark an avenue for completion of healing in this dimension of his moral life. This highlights one aspect of spiritual direction that makes it truly different from other healing modalities: the belief that only by grace—God's intervention—are we able to be truly free.

Pastoral Counseling

Approach to assessment of the case. In doing a bio-psycho-social-spiritual assessment of Mark, I will first evaluate his physical and mental health. My mental health diagnosis will use DSM-IV categories of depression and sexual dysfunction. I will use psychodynamic and family systems perspectives to describe his formative relationships. I will be particularly interested in the intense power struggles that are part of family systems and psychological development. Did such struggles result in abuse or neglect, or did they lead to a deepening of Mark's capacity for empathy and sense of self-agency? Answers to these questions will help me better understand the intense internal conflicts Mark was experiencing when he crossed professional boundaries and used a sexual relationship to overpower a woman who came to him for pastoral care (Doehring 1995).

In doing a spiritual assessment of Mark, I will ask Mark first about his faith journey (especially his calling to ministry) and his relationship with God. I will listen for how formative dynamics in early childhood and his early experience of religion have shaped his relationship with God. In asking about his spiritual and faith practices, I will be interested in how he relates to God under stress. Is God sometimes like a disengaged, harsh parent whom he has to obey? Does he sometimes relate to God in superficial ways, as if God were a friend who should be always available to rescue him when he's in trouble? When is God experienced as an empathic and empowering presence to whom Mark can reveal his vulnerabilities, needs and gifts? Helpful references for understanding how people use religion to cope with stress can be found in Pargament 1997. Another resource is the work I have done (Doehring 1993, 1995) on understanding the power dynamics in people's relationships with God.

In my spiritual and theological assessment I will seek to understand the theological language Mark uses to describe his crisis, so that I can become fluent in this language. Does he understand his crisis in terms of sin, particularly his individual sinfulness and the collective sinfulness of communities and cultures? Does he see the need for repentance? In this conversation I will listen for the extent to which Mark has developed his beliefs during crises and transitions that may have forced him to reformulate them. Helpful resources for assessing Mark's faith system and how well it helps him make sense of life crisis are James Fowler's (1996) theory on faith development and Robert Neville's (1996) discussion of how people's religious symbols break as God is revealed in new ways in the midst of suffering.

A related area of assessment has to do with Mark's support systems, especially those related to his spiritual and religious identity. Does Mark have opportunities for theological conversations with others? In these conversations is he able to reflect honestly on how he lives out his belief system? For example, is there spiritual intimacy in his marriage, such that he and his wife together can use their belief systems to understand their relationship and their lives? Does he experience this sort of spiritual intimacy with friends or colleagues? Is he part of a support group with peers in which he explores his religious beliefs and how he acts on them?

To understand Mark in terms of his cultural system, I will assess how aspects of his social identity, like his gender, age, ethnicity, social class, sexual orientation and religious faith shaped the crisis he is in. When he crossed boundaries with the woman seeking care, was he feeling overpowered in other arenas of his life? While Mark seems to be someone who would experience social privilege because of his gender, race and professional identity, were there dynamics in the family, community or cultural system that were causing him to feel overpowered, such that he acted out by overpowering someone in his care?

Another set of questions having to do with his social identity concern the present moment. Is his age a liability in seeking new kinds of ministry, or even a new profession? If the misconduct becomes public, will he be labeled as a sexual predator, with all the meanings that label has in our present context? It seems likely that such a label would cause many people to become disengaged from his full humanity and to see him as a monster of some kind. The bio-psycho-social-spiritual assessment that unfolds as his psychological, familial, community and cultural dynamics are explored will build a foundation for pastoral counseling.

Conceptualization of the case. In the assessment and ongoing pastoral counseling with Mark, I will draw primarily on the following theories. I will use psycho-dynamic perspectives on Mark's intrapsychic and family systems, especially the power struggles that occur in such systems. Such perspectives will also be helpful in processing the ongoing power dynamics Mark experiences with me and the extent to which therapy can be an empathic, empowering experience for him.

I hope that Mark and I can construct new theological ways of understanding where and who God is, ways that respect Mark's belief system and also allow me to draw on my theological perspectives. For example, I will use my own theological perspectives on sinfulness and evil to understand Mark's crisis. Process theologian Marjorie Suchocki (1994) reexamines traditional Christian understandings of sin as individual pride and proposes that original sin be understood, both individually and collectively, as a fall to violence. Collective sinfulness, in the form of systems that abuse and neglect people, can be understood as evil (Poling 1996).

I will use psychological perspectives on Mark's social identity, looking at how social advantages or disadvantages may ameliorate or exacerbate his crisis. We will especially pay attention to how his experiences of social disadvantages and advantages can deepen his sense of empathy. Finally, I will use theological and psychological perspectives on clergy sexual misconduct, as Mark and I together seek to understand his betrayal of the trust of a congregational member.

I will use a correlational method to relate these theoretical perspectives by listening for the consonances and dissonances among them, particularly in the areas of healthy, abusive or neglectful ways of coping with intense power dynamics. There will likely be similarities in how these power dynamics shape his experience of his body, his marriage, his professional relationships, his social identity and his relationship with God. Out of this correlational dialogue I will formulate some truth claims.

I see such faith claims as provisional (Graham 1996) and pragmatically necessary for doing contextual theological assessments and providing a theological basis for treatment plans. I also acknowledge the danger of making faith claims based solely on solitary reflections and particular contexts. I work as a pastoral theologian and counselor within circles of accountability, which include colleagues in clinical, ecclesial and academic settings. Within these circles I am accountable for how I use psychological and theological sources and norms of authority to make faith claims that form the theological basis for assessment and treatment of clients.

One provisional faith claim is that God abhors the abuse of power by those entrusted with responsibility over others, and that such abuse of power arises out of the interaction of individual and collective sinfulness. Another claim is that redemption involves naming individual and collective sinfulness, seeking repentance by resisting and fighting violence, and establishing the safety and trust that are essential to life-giving relationships and systems. These provisional truth claims can become the basis for a plan of care, outlined in the next section.

Approach to treatment of the case. My first goal is to establish a sense of safety and containment for Mark by addressing his symptoms of depression and also his faith and vocational crisis. I will develop an alliance based on a shared psychological and religious understanding of his crisis and also on a shared sense of God's role in the therapeutic process. I will also help Mark to find healthy ways to cope psychologically and spiritually with his symptoms of depression and sexual dysfunction and his marital and vocational crises. The spiritual strategies he uses to cope with stress will help Mark connect with God in ways that are a resource to him.

The next goal of therapy will be for Mark to experience the depths of his losses, especially unmourned losses. He may need to return to any traumatic events in which he felt overwhelmed, abused or neglected. The challenge at this stage in therapy will be to sustain an empathic, empowering process rooted in Mark's connection with me as his counselor, with God and with those who can form a support system during this time. When empathy is maintained, Mark will become more deeply connected with himself, his counselor and others.

Such empathy will allow him to acknowledge the ways he has been hurt and has hurt others. It will be important for him to acknowledge whether his abuse of power happened in only one professional relationship or whether there has been a pattern of abusing power. If possible, Mark and I will together assess whether he will experience continual difficulty in maintaining the professional boundaries necessary for the often intense dynamics of pastoral care. These and broader discussions about his vocation may help Mark fully participate in making sound decisions about his vocation and what to do with the rest of his working life.

Therapy will move, in a termination phase, toward reconnecting with the ordinary goodness of life. The more Mark is able to maintain an empathic connection that helps him work with power struggles in ways that deepen his connection to himself, others and God, the more he will be able to function without therapy.

This treatment approach focuses on Mark and will likely need to be supplemented with marital counseling in which Mark and his wife can address the crisis involving the disclosure of his infidelity, his wife's unhappiness with their recent move, and the shift in their family system that occurred when both of their daughters left home. In such counseling they may be able to mourn losses together, be accountable for the dynamics of their marital system and reach mutual decisions about the future of their relationship. Referrals may also be made for psychopharmacological treatment of depression, spiritual direction and group therapy with men who have had difficulties maintaining appropriate sexual boundaries.

The description of pastoral counseling I have provided is based on a narrative, contextual, correlational, postmodern method. This method is used by pastoral theologians and counselors primarily involved in reconstructing aspects of religious doctrines currently under debate. Pastoral theologians using theological norms that conserve aspects of the tradition, such as the patriarchal ordering of creation, would describe their pastoral counseling of Mark quite differently.

For example, Thomas Oden (1984) might describe pastoral counseling in terms of the supportive care clergy could offer. He would likely base such care on norms gleaned from the writings of the early church fathers. The conserving of what is seen as the historical roots of pastoral care would have particular value for him. By emphasizing the need for care rather than counseling, he would not draw on the therapeutic and, more recently, contextual traditions of pastoral counseling (Patton 1993) associated in the twentieth century with liberal Protestant theological traditions. In a cultural climate in which a chasm exists between pastoral counselors who use reconstructing theological norms and those who use conserving theological norms, it is important for me to identify the reconstructing norms that I use and to acknowledge respectfully the existence of alternate approaches to pastoral counseling.

REFLECTIONS AND RESPONSES ACROSS DISCIPLINES

Psychology to spiritual direction and pastoral counseling. In reading the work of my coauthors, I (Theresa Tisdale) am struck by what was referred to earlier as the harmonies and melodies created by our dialogue. While our voices are distinct, they create a song I found very deep and rich.

Reading the opening sections, I found myself recalling Richard Foster's book *Streams of Living Water* (1998), in which he traces the history of the major Christian traditions. In general, Veneta represents the Contemplative tradition, Carrie the Social Justice tradition, and I a hybrid of the Evangelical and Charismatic traditions. These perspectives shape how we view life, circumstances and healing. As Foster notes, each stream represents a significant part of the Christian faith. In this article the respective streams have a voice with their distinct and important perspectives on care.

In our approaches to the care of Mark, it seemed we all had a common goal: the psychological and spiritual well-being of Mark. Although we shared this goal, the path to get there was in some ways quite different and highlighted distinct and important aspects of his life that need attention and focus.

Spiritual direction is marked by a central focus on faith and relationship with God. Faith is the central meaning-making principle or framework. The goal is transformation. As I read Veneta's work, I was reminded of the words of Pierre Teilhard de Chardin (as quoted in Walsh 1999:3): "We are not human beings having a spiritual experience; we are spiritual beings having a human experience." Spiritual direction values and reflects the centrality of spirituality to all persons.

Table 12.1. **Highlights of Perspectives on Care**

Dimension	Psychotherapy	Spiritual Direction	Pastoral Counseling
Presenting Problem	Depression; impotence; alienation from self, others, God; negation of moral values	Loss of identity in his calling, his marriage and his role as a father; loss of former pastorate; sexual misconduct	Depression; impotence; emotional and spiritual disengagement from self, others and God; abuse of power
Goals	Insight/revelation; restitution/repentance; working through/redemption; change/transformation; psychological and spiritual well-being	Transformation; increase in authenticity; integrity between outer role and inner life; restitution for sexual misconduct	Healing where possible, including healing of relationship with self, God and others, and as part of healing, seeking justice, at least in terms of his abuse of power
Procedure	Comprehensive spiritual, psychological and physical assessment; once or twice weekly sessions; insight-oriented narrative approach; illuminate where fractures exist in relationships with self, others, God and environment; use therapy relationship to surface and heal internal and external fractures	Assess level of awareness and openness; assess need for therapy; meet every two or three weeks; primary focus is relationship with God; attend to nature and content of prayer life; use images, dreams, memories, reflections to reveal inner life and operative image of God	Narrative, contextual, correlational crossdisciplinary method that moves from (1) doing a bio-psycho-social and theological assessment to (2) a plan of care that seeks healing and justice through establishing safety and trust, mourning losses, acknowledging trauma and abuse of power, and reconstruction of identity as person of faith
Resources	Medication; couples therapy; clergy support group; spiritual direction; pastoral care	Prayer; meditation; theological reflection; therapy; experiences where God's love would be most felt	Medication, couples therapy; clergy support group; spiritual direction; pastoral care; denominational resources; vocational counseling

Veneta's approach to the case reflected an intentional focus on Mark's relationship with God as the organizing principle of care. I especially appreciate her statement that crises or circumstances present us with opportunities for transformation, but we have a choice about yielding to the process.

One point of note is that it seems spiritual direction presupposes a level of psychological health and a capacity for honesty and authenticity. Perhaps these implicit prerequisites would result in a natural self-selection for care, such that those ill-suited or ill-equipped for direction would not pursue it. However, it would seem that opportunities for collaboration between spiritual directors and psychologists or pastoral counselors are potentially both ripe and rich.

In most of the theoretical and empirical psychological literature, the emphasis has been on how human relationships reflect, shape or transform God's image (Birky and Ball 1988; Brokaw 1992; Brokaw and Edwards 1994; Corzo 1981; Day 1980; Hall, Brokaw, Edwards and Pike 1998; Spear 1996; Tisdale 1998; Tisdale et al. 1997; Wootton 1991). However, as Moshe Spero (1992, 1996) has noted, one's relationship with God may also be transformative of human relationships. Collaboration across disciplines in order to better understand and articulate this reality might serve to inform applied models of soul care and enhance the healing process in potentially profound ways.

I found Carrie's approach to pastoral counseling compelling for several reasons. Her work reflects an insightful, extensive and intricate weaving of theology, psychology and pastoral care. She has obviously walked the road she describes.

Her background as a clergyperson and her location within the social justice tradition provide a distinctive perspective regarding power dynamics and occasions of abuse. In her conceptualization of Mark, Carrie remarks on how a family systems analysis of abuse of power suggests that such violations result from disengagement from the humanity of the other. This conceptualization posits that in the family system of the church, Mark's moral turpitude potentially reflected a disengagement from the humanity of his parishioner. Psychologically and spiritually speaking, one might also wonder if this infraction followed a progression of disengagement from himself, God and others (especially his wife).

I found Carrie's explicit theological conceptualization both inspiring and challenging. She is clear and systematic in articulating theological and psychological factors. I realized as I read her careful delineation that in my model some of these considerations are only implicit, which challenges me to be more explicit to others and myself about my theological conceptualization of pathology, health and healing. Although my theology differs from Carrie's, I am impressed with her masterful method of clarifying theological and psychological aspects of care, then applying them to the case of Mark by highlighting consonance and dissonance between the disciplines.

Spiritual direction to psychology and pastoral counseling. The writing of this article was truly a clarifying exercise. Although I (Veneta Lorraine-Poirier) have known the distinction between modalities to be primarily a different focus on issues and problem resolutions, this writing has brought an expansive clarity to that awareness. It is increasingly noticeable how minimal is the attention given to resolution of problems by spiritual directors, myself in particular. Instead it is intentionally and primarily focused on developing the relationship with God, despite individual behaviors. Yet the similarities among the disciplines are extensive as well. The historical context of the client, the faith development, the understanding of God by the client—each is present in all disciplines. Each modality uses a particular wisdom, and each source of wisdom enables the client to heal.

I now believe that psychology and pastoral counseling function from a more holistic approach than does spiritual direction. In many ways spiritual direction is quite limited. I say this while stipulating that there are benefits unique to spiritual direction in the consideration of care of a person like Mark. It provides a different lens that sees an inherited identity of every human person as the beloved of God, just as Jesus knew himself to be in the Synoptic Gospels.

As I read Theresa's psychological excerpts, I recognize the strong emphasis placed on early childhood development and the effect of Mark's early experiences on his current behaviors. Carrie's pastoral counseling emphasis is located in an awareness of present behaviors and the theological/moral implications that are innately involved. Spiritual direction pays closest attention to the ability to know and receive unconditional Love and a client's desire to live out of that reality.

As I read and reread each of our approaches to care, I began to sense an underlying trend that might be a helpful image for understanding distinctions and each modality's unique wisdom. The discipline of psychology has a primary orientation that *connects the past to present,* while pastoral counseling primarily attends to the *present* state of a client's life and spiritual direction is more focused on creating the *future context* for a client's reality.

Supporting this insight is the value and importance of the intake process in each discipline. For psychology, the historical context is highlighted and later systematically processed. For pastoral counseling, the historical and the theological contexts are surveyed and woven into ensuing conversations. In spiritual direction there is a much more informal practice for intake. Spiritual direction asks for important basic information but often does not use a detailed intake structure.

There is a basic premise in the spiritual direction process that is an acceptance of the person as she or he presents her- or himself. It is accepted that a person comes to spiritual direction with a basic faith orientation and honest desire to deepen spiritual awareness. This acceptance is not so naive that it takes everything at face value; resistance, denial, transference and countertransference are deeply embedded in the lexicon of spiritual direction. Yet spiritual direction moves within the context of the client's expressed desires for relationship with God and for God's initiative within her or his experience, always trying to discern that initiative's potential for growth. It is God, working in and through the psyche, the environment, other individuals, symbols, rituals, stories and so on, who reveals to the client what is important. The agenda is clearly set by the client's initiative and is then held by the director. The client brings material into the conversation, and the director looks for the manifestation of God in that revelation. On the spiritual director's part, there is a presumption of basic psychological health. Therefore she or he is not looking to determine from life details what issues are presenting, but rather what growth, virtue or value God is inviting this individual to bring forth. This seems significantly different from the psychological focus of creating a safe environment for transference to be projected on to the therapist.

A significant insight this project has resurfaced in me is the importance of recognizing and validating all types of knowledge and knowing: the learned, intuited or "gut," and faith knowledge of our clients as well as our own. Each has a place in healing, and each is necessary and valuable. Wisdom, coming to us in many forms, has veracity, a sense of the whole and the potential for healing. Each modality is embedded with this wisdom that is learned but is also a gift, originating from the God who leads us into wholeness. How grateful I am for all that Theresa and Carrie bring to the ministry and work they represent.

Pastoral counseling to psychology and spiritual direction. I (Carrie Doehring) believe the image captured in the title, of three voices singing one song, describes the commonalities of our perspectives. We are indeed singing one song, a song that (as Theresa notes) is focused on the psychological and spiritual well-being of someone entrusted to our care.

Another way our voices harmonize as we sing the same basic song is that we are all women of faith whose care of others is grounded in the relationship we have with God. We sing a song of faith. The particular psychological and theological perspectives we use share a common assumption: that relationship with God is understood to be a core feature of people's psychological and spiritual lives and also a core feature of how the world is created.

Each of us brings two voices to the song, our psychological voice and our theological voice, such that *six* voices sing one song. We have each received a theological education and have learned to sing the songs of theology. We are caregivers who share Mark's religious tradition and can sing from within that tradition. We are insiders, as James Griffith and Melissa Griffith note (2002:19), who can use theological sources and norms of authority (like Christian Scriptures and the biblical-critical methods used to interpret them). While I have been more explicit about the theological ways I assess a client's relationship with God, clinical psychologists and spiritual directors who are theologically trained, such as my colleagues, have the background to assess theologically a client's images of God. More explicit theological assessments would, I believe, enhance the work of clinical psychologists who are "insiders," spiritual directors and pastoral counselors.

Even though we each took a different path toward a fulfilling vocation involving psychospiritual care, we have much in common and can enhance each other's perspectives and practices. We live in a time when conserving approaches to religion often seem at odds and even at war with reconstructive approaches, and theological differences can seem to be insurmountable. When we are open to engaging in dialogue across theological differences, we may become more aware of the deep consonance between our stories of faith. We may be surprised to find that we sing one song.

CLOSING THOUGHTS

The purpose of this article was for a psychologist, a spiritual director and a pastoral counselor to share perspectives on providing care. While the chapter began with a focus on psychotherapy and spiritual direction, the discipline of pastoral counseling is an important voice in the conversation on soul care, and the first and third authors thank the editors for their suggestion to add this valuable voice to the article. A brief summary highlighting the perspectives on care in the case of Mark may be found in table 12.1. These perspectives reflect both harmony and melody.

Some cautionary notes or commentaries are offered here regarding aspects of practice within respective disciplines. For instance, there is a need for standardization in the training and certification of spiritual directors, which illuminates the importance of inquiring about these factors when practitioners of other disciplines are making referrals to, or collaborating with, spiritual directors. In a similar vein, directors or pastoral counselors making referrals to psychologists are advised to make inquiries about the level of training or experience they have for working with spiritual issues in therapy. Religion is an area of diversity that does not often receive adequate attention in graduate psychology training programs (cf. Yarhouse and Fisher, 2002). In this particular case, experience was crucial. However, depending on one's view of persons and soul care, some level of training in the spiritual life of persons may be needed by practitioners of any discipline for use in work with all clients.

Harmonious notes within the article were evident. As it happened, all three authors operate with a psychological paradigm that is basically insight-oriented. This created a certain consonance across perspectives. Additionally, all the authors are Caucasian women and all were raised Catholic, although two currently have other affiliations. The article and conversation would likely have flowed quite differently if, for example, the psychologist operated from a cognitive-behavioral rather than a psychodynamic paradigm or if the pastoral counselor had operated from a short-term solution-focused model of care. A different mix of gender, race, ethnicity or religious tradition would also likely have affected the piece in particular ways.

These factors illuminate what may be one of the most important messages of this article: the approach one takes to care is profoundly affected by one's biography or history, which influences one's theoretical and theological orientation. This may be an important distinction between theoretical and applied models of care. While theoretical models are focused on the content of disciplines and how ideas may be integrated (see Eck 1996), applied models of care naturally require emphasis on the person offering the care and how he or she approaches this endeavor. As this article has suggested, one's history, theoretical orientation and theological tradition all have considerable impact and influence on one's approach to care. As Doehring's work has enumerated, history includes considerations of race, class, gender, ethnicity and other factors. The complexity of these factors may create questions regarding whether it is possible to fully articulate more broadly defined applied models of care. Clearly this represents a frontier as yet to be fully explored, but it is a rich area to pursue.

A possible component of this exploration might be to develop interdisciplinary working groups that foster and encourage dialogue about approaches to care. As we have noted, we learned much from one another in the context of this project alone. There is clearly considerable potential to advance the field by initiating collaboration across disciplines, across perspectives and streams within disciplines. With this type of cooperative effort, the song of soul care may yet reach a full and resounding crescendo.

REFERENCES

American Psychiatric Association. 1994. *Diagnostic and statistical manual of mental disorders.* 4th ed. Washington, D.C.: American Psychiatric Association.

Benner, David G. 1983. The incarnation as a metaphor for psychotherapy. *Journal of Psychology and Theology* 11:287-94.

———. 1998. *Care of souls: Revisioning Christian nurture and counsel.* Grand Rapids, Mich.: Baker.

Birky, Ian T., and Samuel Ball. 1988. Parental trait influence on God as an object representation. *Journal of Psychology* 122:133-37.

Brokaw, Beth F. 1992. The relationship of God image to level of object relations development. Ph.D. diss., Rosemead School of Psychology, Biola University. *Dissertation Abstracts International* 52:6077.

Brokaw, Beth F., and Keith J. Edwards. 1994. The relationship of God image to level of object relations development. *Journal of Psychology and Theology* 22:352-71.

Browning, Donald S. 1991. *A fundamental pactical theology: Descriptive and strategic proposals.* Minneapolis: Fortress.

Corzo, Diana M. 1981. Perceptions of God, parents and self as a function of depression and Christian faith. Ph.D. diss., Rosemead School of Psychology, Biola University. *Dissertation*

Abstracts International 42:1164-65.

Day, David N. 1980. Religious orientation, God concept, religious experience, social interest and self-concept. Ph.D. diss., Rosemead School of Psychology, Biola University, La Mirada, Calif.

Doehring, Carrie. 1993. The absent God: When neglect follows sexual violence. *Journal of Pastoral Care* 47:3-12.

———. 1995. *Taking care: Monitoring power dynamics and relational boundaries in pastoral care and counseling.* Nashville: Abingdon.

———. 1999. A method of feminist pastoral theology. In *Feminist and womanist pastoral theology,* ed. Brita Gill-Austern and Bonnie Miller-McLemore, pp. 95-111. Nashville: Abingdon.

Doherty, William J. 1999. Morality and spirituality in therapy. In *Spiritual resources in family therapy,* ed. F. M. Walsh, pp. 179-92. New York: Guilford.

Eck, Brian E. 1996. Integrating the integrators: An organizing framework for a multifaceted process of integration. *Journal of Psychology and Christianity* 15:101-15.

Erikson, Erik H. 1963. *Childhood and society.* 2nd ed. New York: W. W. Norton.

Fairbairn, W. Ronald D. 1952. *Psychoanalytic studies of the personality.* London: Tavistock.

Finley, James. 1994. *Merton's palace of nowhere: A search for God through awareness of the true self.* Notre Dame, Ind.: Ave Maria.

Fleming, David L. 1978. *Spiritual exercises of St. Ignatius: A literal translation and contemporary reading.* St. Louis: Institute of Jesuit Sources.

Foster, Richard J. 1998. *Streams of living water.* New York: HarperCollins.

Fowler, James W. 1996. *Faithful change: The personal and public challenges of postmodern life.* Nashville: Abingdon.

Graham, Elaine. 1996. *Transforming practice: Pastoral theology in an age of uncertainty.* London: Mowbray.

Griffith, James L., and Melissa E. Griffith. 2002. *Encountering the sacred in psychotherapy: How to talk with people about their spiritual lives.* New York: Guilford.

Guntrip, Harry. 1949. *Psychology for ministers and social workers.* London: Independent.

———. 1953. The therapeutic factor in psychotherapy. *British Journal of Medical Psychology* 26:115-32.

———. 1956. *Psychotherapy and religion.* New York: Harper & Brothers.

Hall, Todd W., Beth F. Brokaw, Keith J. Edwards and Patricia L. Pike. 1998. An empirical exploration of psychoanalysis and religion: Spiritual maturity and object relations development. *Journal for the Scientific Study of Religion* 37:303-13.

Hiltner, Seward. 1958. *Preface to pastoral theology.* Nashville: Abingdon.

Horner, Althea J. 1984. *Object relations and the developing ego in therapy.* Northvale, N.J.: Jason Aronson.

———. 1990. *The primacy of structure: Psychotherapy of underlying character pathology.* Northvale, N.J.: Jason Aronson.

———. 1991. *Psycho-analytic object relations therapy.* Northvale, N.J.: Jason Aronson.

Neville, Robert C. 1996. *The truth of broken symbols.* New York: State University of New York

Press.

Oden, Thomas. 1984. *Care of souls in the classic tradition.* Philadelphia: Fortress.

Pargament, Kenneth I. 1997. *The psychology of religion and coping: Theory, research, practice.* New York: Guilford.

Patton, John. 1993. *Pastoral care in context: An introduction to pastoral care.* Louisville, Ky.: Westminster John Knox.

Poling, James N. 1996. *Deliver us from evil.* Nashville: Abingdon.

Poling, James N., and Donald E. Miller. 1985. *Foundations for a practical theology of ministry.* Nashville: Abingdon.

Rizzuto, Ann Marie. 1979. *The birth of the living God.* Chicago: University of Chicago Press.

Spear, Kathy. 1996. Conscious and preconscious God representations: An object relations perspective. Ph.D. diss., Fuller Theological Seminary, School of Psychology. *Dissertation Abstracts International* 56:4609.

Spero, Moshe H. 1992. *Religious objects as psychological structures: A critical integration of object relations theory, psychotherap, and Judaism.* Northvale, N.J.: Jason Aronson.

———. 1996. *Psychotherapy of the religious patient.* Northvale, N.J.: Jason Aronson.

Suchocki, Marjorie H. 1994. *The fall to violence: Original sin in relational theology.* New York: Continuum.

Tisdale, Theresa C. 1998. A comparison of Jewish, Muslim, and Protestant faith groups on the relationship between level of object relations development and experience of God and self. Ph.D. diss., Rosemead School of Psychology, Biola University. *Dissertation Abstracts International* 58:5144.

Tisdale, Theresa C., Teresa L. Key, Keith J. Edwards, Beth F. Brokaw, Steve R. Kemperman, Henry Cloud, John Townsend and T. Okamoto. 1997. Impact of treatment on God image and personal adjustment, and correlations of God image to personal adjustment and object relations development. *Journal of Psychology and Theology* 25:227-39.

Walsh, Froma M., ed. 1999. *Spiritual resources in family therapy.* New York: Guilford.

Winnicott, Donald W. 1958. *Collected papers: Through paediatrics to psycho-analysis.* London: Tavistock.

———. 1965. *The maturational process and the facilitating environment.* London: Hogarth.

———. 1971. *Playing and reality.* London: Tavistock.

Wootton, Raymond J. 1991. God-representation and its relation to object relations and defensive functioning. Ph.D. diss., Boston University. *Dissertation Abstracts International* 51:5600.

Yarhouse, Mark A., and Wyatt Fisher. 2002. Levels of training to address religion in clinical practice. *Psychotherapy* 39:171-76.

AFTERWORD

It is still too early to determine the significance of the recent rise of interest in spirituality—not only in society or the church, but also in such soul care professions as psychotherapy and pastoral counseling. We would like to believe that it represents a fresh breath of the Spirit of God, a revival of hunger for deep personal engagement and transforming surrender to the divine. And we are hopeful that the attention it is receiving from pastoral counselors and psychotherapists represents more than a short-lived curiosity.

But it is also clear that these developments contain faddish elements. How easily the church—some sectors of it being notably more vulnerable than others—becomes caught up with current fashion. Pastoral counseling and psychotherapy have often been guilty of the same. How sad it will be if it turns out that they have all done so once again. How sad if sectors of the church that are beginning to be interested in spiritual direction simply fit it into the programmatic approaches to spiritual formation that they have excelled in developing.

This makes it essential that those of us who seek to nurture spiritual growth in others ground our practice in an understanding of our extraordinarily rich tradition of Christian spiritual formation and direction. It also makes it essential that we offer our ministrations in ways that respect the boundaries and distinctives of each of the major soul care professions. This has been the purpose of this book.

The rediscovery of spiritual direction by Christian traditions that had lost touch with this rich aspect of our shared heritage represents, to our mind, the recovery of the lost jewel in the crown of Christian soul care. For too long soul care has been dominated by mental health professionals. Consequently, the church lost its place of preeminence in the care and cure of the inner self. The recent rise of interest in spiritual direction holds the possibility of redressing this anomaly. It also holds the possibility of helping both pastoral counseling and psychotherapy discover the unique ways appropriate to each to attend to the spiritual dimensions of personal experience. All share a concern with the inner world of persons—a world that cannot be artificially divided into psychological and spiritual parts. But each also has important distinctives, and each has a unique and essential part to play in full-spectrum Christian soul care.

Spiritual direction offers twenty-first-century Christians an ancient and time-honored relationship of accountability and accompaniment for walking the Christian path. It provides us a place within which we can know ourselves as we are truly known. It gives us a place to meet God. And it also allows both psychotherapy and pastoral counseling to do what each does best while attending to the inner life of persons and learning from their sister soul care profession.

LIST OF CONTRIBUTORS

Father Gene Barrette is a Missionary of La Salette priest, ordained in 1967. He has an M.A. in English from Boston College and an M.A. in spirituality from the Gregorian University in Rome, Italy. He has taught in the seminary, worked fifteen years on the La Salette General Administration in Rome, Italy—six of those as superior general of the international La Salette Congregation—and has been in parish work since 1989. He is especially involved in spiritual direction, retreat work and adult faith formation. Presently he is serving as parochial vicar in St. Thomas the Apostle parish in Smyrna, Georgia. Correspondence regarding his chapter should be addressed to Father Gene Barrette, M.S., St. Thomas the Apostle Parish, 4300 King Springs Rd., Smyrna, GA, 30082. E-mail: EGBarrette@aol.com.

David G. Benner, Ph.D., C.Psych., is an author, lecturer and retreat director. For the past thirty years his work has focused on the development and practice of a spiritually sensitive depth psychology and the nurture of a psychologically grounded Christian spirituality. Dr. Benner currently serves as Distinguished Professor of Psychology and Spirituality at the Psychological Studies Institute (Atlanta, Georgia) and as the founding director of the Institute for Psychospiritual Health (http://psy.edu/iph).

Carrie E. Doehring earned a B.Mus. and an M.Div. from McGill University, an M.Th. from Wilfrid Laurier University, and a Ph.D. from Boston University. She is currently assistant professor of pastoral care and counseling in the Iliff School of Theology, Denver. Her areas of special interest are pastoral care, models of religiously based care, feminist pastoral theology, clergy sexual misconduct, counseling psychology and religion. She may be reached at Iliff School of Theology, 2201 S. University Blvd., Denver, CO 80210-4798.

Israel Galindo is professor of Christian education at the Baptist Theological Seminary at Richmond. He is the author of several books and serves on the faculty of Leadership in Ministry Workshops (www.leadershipinministry.com), a clergy leadership training program informed by Bowen systems theory. Dr. Galindo is executive director of Educational Consultants (www.galindoconsultants.com).

Jerry A. Gladson (Ph.D., Vanderbilt University) is senior minister at First Christian Church (Disciples of Christ) in Marietta, Georgia. He holds ordained standing in both the Christian Church (Disciples of Christ) and the United Church of Christ. In addition to his pastoral duties, he serves as adjunct professor of religion at the Psychological Studies Institute, Atlanta, and adjunct professor of Old Testament at Columbia Theological Seminary, Decatur,

Georgia. Correspondence regarding his chapter should be addressed to Jerry A. Gladson, First Christian Church, 569 Fraiser St., Marietta, GA 30060. E-mail: jagladson@prodigy.net.

Ben Campbell Johnson is professor emeritus of Christian spirituality at Columbia Theological Seminary in Decatur, Georgia. He is the author of more than thirty books that focus on Christian spirituality, church renewal and evangelism. His theological training includes degrees from Asbury, Southern Baptist, San Francisco Theological and Emory University, where he received the Ph.D. At Columbia he developed the doctorate of ministry in Christian spirituality and the certificate in spiritual formation. He and his wife, Nan, have five children and seven grandchildren. E-mail: bjohn1923@aol.com.

Veneta Lorraine-Poirier has an M.A. in pastoral theology from the Episcopal Divinity School. Her work's focus is spirituality, spiritual direction and women's spirituality. She is program director, spiritual director and retreat leader at Our Lady of Peace Spiritual Life Center (PO Box 507, Narragansett, RI 02882).

Oliver McMahan serves as associate dean and professor of pastoral care and counseling at the Church of God Theological Seminary in Cleveland, Tennessee. He holds M.Div. and D.Min. degrees from Brite Divinity School and a Ph.D. from Georgia State University. He has more than twenty-five years' experience as a pastor, associate pastor and evangelist. He is the author of several books, including *The Caring Church* (2002, Pathway). Correspondence regarding his chapter should be addressed to Oliver McMahan, Church of God Theological Seminary, PO Box 3330, Cleveland, TN 37320. E-mail: omcmahan@cogts.edu.

Gary W. Moon, M.Div., Ph.D., is a psychologist and author who serves as vice president for spiritual development and professor of psychology and spirituality at the Psychological Studies Institute (Atlanta). He also serves as a writer and editor of Christian formation resources through LifeSprings Resources.

Father F. Gregory Rogers serves as priest at St. Catherine Antiochian Orthodox Church in Aiken, South Carolina, and at St. Barnabas Antiochian Orthodox Church in Lexington, South Carolina. He is also instructor of comparative religion and sociology at Aiken Technical College. He earned his B.A. in Christian Ministries from Lincoln Christian College, his M.A.L.S. at Valparaiso University and an M.A. in Divinity at the University of Chicago. His dissertation on the history of Christianity at the University of Chicago remains in progress. Correspondence regarding his chapter should be addressed to F. Gregory Rogers, St. Catherine Orthodox Church, 1085 Brookhaven Dr., Aiken, SC 29803. E-mail: fgrogers@aol.com.

Len Sperry earned his B.A. from St. Mary's University, his M.A. from Loyola University, a D.Min. from Barry University and a Ph.D. from Northwestern University. Currently he serves as clinical professor of psychiatry at the Medical College of Wisconsin and as professor and coordinator of the doctoral program in counseling at Florida Atlantic University. His specializations include personality disorders and integrating spirituality and psychotherapy. He can be reached at Bldg. 47, Rm. 270, Florida Atlantic University, 777 Glades Rd., Boca Raton, FL 33431-0991.

Siang-Yang Tan earned B.A. and Ph.D. degrees from McGill University. He is professor of psychology in the Graduate School of Psychology, Fuller Theological Seminary, specializing in cognitive-behavior therapy, religious psychotherapy, intrapersonal integration and spirituality, lay counseling, pain, epilepsy, and crosscultural counseling, especially with Asian Americans. He is also senior pastor of First Evangelical Church Glendale in Glendale, California. Correspondence may be sent to Dr. Siang-Yang Tan, Graduate School of Psychology, Fuller Theological Seminary, 180 N. Oakland Ave., Pasadena, CA 91101.

The Reverend Canon Gray Temple Jr. has been rector of St. Patrick's, Atlanta, since 1975. He holds an M.Div. degree from Episcopal Theological Seminary in Virginia and has completed additional graduate work at Göttingen and Oxford universities. He is the author of *52 Ways to Help Homeless People* (1990) and *Molten Soul* (2001). Correspondence regarding his chapter should be addressed to Gray Temple, St. Patrick's Episcopal Church, 4755 N. Peachtree Rd., Atlanta, GA 30338. E-mail: grayt1@mindspring.com.

Theresa Clement Tisdale has a B.A. from Radford College and earned the M.A. and Ph.D. from Rosemead School of Psychology, Biola University. She serves as associate professor in Azusa Pacific University's Department of Graduate Psychology. Her specializations include contemporary psychoanalysis and religious experience, and the clinical integration of psychology and religion. Correspondence regarding the chapter she contributed with Carrie Doehring and Veneta Lorraine-Porrier should be sent to her at Theresa Clement Tisdale, Department of Graduate Psychology, Azusa Pacific University, 701 E. Foothill Blvd., PO Box 7000, Azusa, CA 91702-5015. E-mail: tctisdale@apu.edu.

Wesley D. Tracy, D.Min., S.T.D., is an ordained minister in the Church of the Nazarene. He has served as pastor in Kansas, Indiana and Pennsylvania. The eight Christian periodicals of which he was the editor include two Nazarene journals: the *Preacher's Magazine* and the *Herald of Holiness*. Tracy has taught at MidAmerica Nazarene University, at Nazarene Theological Seminary and in adult education projects in ten countries. He has authored or coauthored some twenty-five books and has published a thousand articles in popular and scholarly publications. Tracy, now retired, has held several positions in the Wesleyan Theological Society, including the office of president. He may be contacted at 12603 W. Keystone Dr., Sun City West, AZ 85375. E-mail: drwdt@cox.net.

Index

OK